W9-ACG-193

LIGHT & SPICY

OTHER BOOKS BY BARBARA GIBBONS
The Slim Gourmet Cookbook
The Diet Watcher's Cookbook
The International Slim Gourmet Cookbook
Lean Cuisine
The 35+ Diet for Women
The Light and Easy Cookbook
Salads for All Seasons
The Year-Round Turkey Cookbook
Creative Low-Calorie Cooking
Slim Gourmet Sweets and Treats
The Diet Cookbook
The Calorie Watcher's Cookbook
Calories Don't Count

LIGHT & SPICY

BARBARA GIBBONS

A Roundtable Press Book

PERENNIAL LIBRARY

Harper & Row, Publishers, New York
Grand Rapids, Philadelphia, St. Louis, San Francisco
London, Singapore, Sydney, Tokyo

A Roundtable Press Book

Directors: Susan E. Meyer, Marsha Melnick
Project Editor: Sue Heinemann
Text Editor: Mel Minter
Cover and Interior Design: Michaelis/Carpelis Design Assoc. Inc.
Illustrations: Ray Skibinski

Grateful acknowledgment is made to the following for their assistance: *Alaska Seafood Marketing Institute*, for recipe for Szechuan-Style Snow Crab (p. 88); *American Spice Trade Association*, for photos of French Apple Charlotte (p. 39), Tandoori-Style Spiced Chicken (p. 72), and Moroccan-Style Chicken Kebabs (p. 113); *California Table Grape Commission*, for recipe for Grape Pork Burritos (p. 64); *California Tree Fruit Agreement*, for photos of Healthy Fresh Peach Ice Cream and Peach-Raspberry Ice Cream (p. 48), Warm Plum and Smoked Chicken Salad (p. 120), Indonesian Chicken and Pear Salad (p. 121), and Nectarine Mousse (p. 127); *Campbell Soup Company*, for photos of Quickie Garden Chicken Salad (p. 38), Greek-Style Puffy Pancake (p. 45), and Turkey Lasagna Swirls (p. 126); *Evans Food Group, Pacific Kitchens Division*, for photos of Grape Pork Burritos (p. 47), Szechuan-Style Snow Crab (p. 124), and Provençal-Style Tuna and Pear Salad (p. 125); *Jerry Gallagher*, for photo of Barbara Gibbons on back cover; *Jennie-O Foods, Inc.*, for photos of Turkey Cacciatore (p. 33) and Turkey and Fresh Fruit Salad (p. 46); *Keebler Company*, for photo of Spinach Puff (p. 36); *Mueller's Pasta* (distributed by Best Foods, CPC International, Inc.), for photos of Quick Broccoli Pasta (p. 115) and Petaluma Pepper Pasta (p. 123); *National Broiler Council*, for photo (p. 118) and recipe (p. 70) for Lemon Chicken; *National Fisheries Institute, Inc.*, for photos of Seafood Risotto, Microwaved Fillet of Sole Mediterranean, and Italian-Style Seafood Stew (p. 34), Sautéed Catfish with Red Pepper Cream (p. 35), Baked Cod Fillets with Basil (p. 37), Tuna Chowder, Spicy Crab Soup, and Cajun Shrimp and Oyster Gumbo (p. 43); Spicy Cajun Shrimp (p. 114), Crab Imperial–Stuffed Shrimp, Crab Imperial–Stuffed Flounder, and Louisiana Hot Sauce (p. 117), Microwaved Oriental Swordfish Steaks and Italian-Style Microwaved Halibut Steaks (p. 119), and Mussels au Gratin (p. 122); *National Livestock and Meat Board*, for photos of Beef and Pepper Chili (p. 40), Mexican Beef Stir-Fry (p. 41), and Microwaved Spicy Beef in Tortillas (p. 116); *NutraSweet Consumer Products, Inc.*, for photo of Strawberry Vanilla Bavarian (p. 128); *Oregon Washington California Pear Bureau*, for recipe for Provençal-Style Tuna and Pear Salad (p. 25); *Washington Apple Commission*, for photo of Light and Spicy Borscht and Golden Vegetable Piroshki (p. 42) and recipe for Golden Vegetable Piroshki (p. 142).

LIGHT & SPICY. Copyright © 1989 by Barbara Gibbons, Inc. All rights reserved. Printed in the United States of America. No part of this book may be used or reproduced in any manner whatsoever without written permission except in the case of brief quotations embodied in critical articles and reviews. For information address Harper & Row, Publishers, Inc., 10 East 53rd Street, New York, N.Y. 10022.

Library of Congress Cataloging-in-Publication Data

Gibbons, Barbara.
    Light & spicy / Barbara Gibbons.—1st ed.
        p.   cm.
    "A Roundtable Press book."
    Includes index.
    ISBN 0-06-055153-4 : $22.95.—ISBN 0-06-096361-1 (pbk.) : $10.95
    1. Cookery, International.   2. Spices.   3. Low-calorie diet—
Recipes.   I. Title.   II. Title: Light and spicy.
TX725.A1G373   1989
641.5'635—dc20
                                                                89-45091
                                                                    CIP

89 90 91 92 93   10 9 8 7 6 5 4 3 2 1

CONTENTS

A World of Answers to Weighty Eating Problems

SPICY, savory, not necessarily hot . . . well-seasoned cuisine for busy Americans . . . low in fat, salt, sugar, calories, and cholesterol! *Light & Spicy* is for you if you . . .

- love to eat and hate to diet
- want or need to watch your weight . . . without giving up the joy of cooking or the pleasure of eating
- want to help yourself or those at your table cut down on calories, cholesterol, salt, fat, and saturated fat . . . without feeling deprived
- like to eat at home but have a little time to cook very complex recipes
- enjoy exploring new foods or trying old favorites in exciting new ways

While many of the world's most flavorful foods are high in fat and calories, it's generally not the fat and calories that make these beloved ethnic dishes so delicious. Rather, it is the unique combination of strongly flavored ingredients.

Each culinary culture's unique seasoning gives the food its regional or national identity— the flavor that makes the taster exclaim, "That's Italian!" Or Mexican. Or Tex-Mex. What makes a dish flavorful can be borrowed, without the unwanted calories, and reapplied to another dish made with lean, low-calorie ingredients.

Forgettable food is an insidious inducement to overeating. Unable to fulfill the psyche's desire for flavor satisfaction, it feeds the search.

Because we travel more, we've become far more adventurous in our search for flavorful food. We've grown bored with the haute-calo-ried blandness of hotel "Continental," and we're worried about the effect of meat and potatoes (and hamburgers and french fries) on our arteries and waistlines. We've been told to eat more fish, chicken, beans, grains, fresh fruits and vegetables—the very foods that spicy cuisine is all about. So an around-the-world tour—in our kitchens, at least—is just what the doctor ordered!

The most flavorful food of other countries was born in home kitchens rather than city restaurants, created not by chefs but by moms, who had to deal more often with scarcity of food than with abundance. Lack of enough meat challenged native cooks to create combinations that were at once appealing and nourishing. The spices and herbs that grew wild added to their allure, along with the sting of hot peppers and the natural sweetness of fruits.

Light & Spicy addresses the convergence of two hot culinary trends: the interest in spicy, highly seasoned food and the desire for healthier, lighter foods. It is not about "hot stuff" exclusively but about spicy food that invokes your attention with assertive seasoning . . . food that won't be ignored or forgotten.

Rather than literal translations, the recipes in *Light & Spicy* are adaptations, interpreted for American kitchens and health concerns. Most use ingredients widely available in U.S. supermarkets or suggest easily found alternatives. Regardless of the original cooking method, all have been tested using commonly available American appliances and work savers.

The ABCs and XYZs of Herbs, Spices, and Seasonings

REMEMBER the days when a "spice rack" could be installed on the inside of a 10-inch kitchen cabinet door? Department stores still persist in selling these silly 10- or 12-bottle contraptions in their kitchenware section. But a gadget properly designed for today's taste for highly seasoned foods would probably require the entire backside of the kitchen door . . . with an annex in the garden for fresh herbs and freezer space to store them off-season. No doubt about it, herbs and spices are the important ingredients of the era!

The new, adventurous love for spicy ethnic foods shares the culinary spotlight with the "light" revolution: the search for food that is nutritious and nonfattening.

"Light" and "spicy" aren't disparate trends that just happen to coexist. Without help from the spice rack and the herb garden, "light" food is merely dietetic. Unless they are also delicious, dishes that are lower in fat, sugar, and salt would never find popular favor. In this cookbook, we show you how to borrow flavor from spicy and exotic ethnic cuisines—without the unwanted extra calories, the unneeded excess salt, sugar, and fat.

HERBS AND SPICES

ajma seed   a cousin of celery seed, with a bitter-spicy taste, used in Indian cooking.

allspice (whole berry or ground powder) called the "all" spice because its scent suggests a blend of cinnamon, cloves, and nutmeg. Used in Jamaica (where it is known as "pimento"), Mexico, the Caribbean, and Central America. Use whole allspice in soups, on steak, with seafood and poultry, in fruit salads, and for pickling.

anise seed   native to Asia Minor, with a sweet, licoricelike taste (similar to fennel). Used in the Middle East, China, Italy, Spain, and southern Europe to flavor pickles, pork and veal dishes, vegetable and fruit salads, cakes, cookies, candies, soups, stews, and liqueurs. Use it as a substitute for star anise, if necessary, for tasty oriental combinations.

anise, star   a dark brown, flower-shaped seed from China with a more intense licoricelike taste than anise seed; used in Chinese cooking.

annatto seed   used in Latin countries as a yellow coloring agent. Cooks sear the seeds in hot oil, then use the strained oil in cooking to color soups, stews, rice dishes, and gravies.

basil (leaves)   sweet and pungent with a faintly licoricelike flavor. Used in Italy, France, southern Europe. Try with tomatoes, blended into cottage or pot cheese, in "pesto" dressings, with oregano and garlic in Italian combinations.

bay leaf (also called laurel leaf)   pleasant but strong flavor and fragrance. Used in France, Spain, Portugal, Italy, Greece, and Turkey. (Used in wreaths by ancient Greeks to crown heroes, athletes, and poets.) Use sparingly in vegetable, minestrone, and tomato soups, chowders, and pot roasts; with corned beef, poultry, and fish; in dressings and marinades, sauces and stews. When preparing kebabs, add a few leaves to the skewer, alternating them with the beef or lamb cubes.

caraway seed mild but tangy flavor similar to dill seed (gives rye bread its characteristic taste). Favored by Dutch, Polish, and other middle and northern European cuisines. Good in cheese spreads, dips, and dressings, in breads, rolls, and biscuits, with ham, roast pork, and pork chops, in marinades for beef, in salads (especially in coleslaw and potato salad) as well as sauerkraut, and also in potato, noodle, or rice dishes.

caraway seed (black) similar to the lighter caraway seed in flavor; used in Russian dark breads and in Middle Eastern cookery.

cardamom seed (whole and ground) sharp, pungent, cinnamonlike, and more sweet than sharp. Native to India, also used in South American, Turkish, and Middle Eastern cooking; combine with other sweet spices (cinnamon, cloves, nutmeg). A necessary ingredient in Danish pastry (brought to Scandinavia by the Vikings); also used in apple and pumpkin pies, Swedish meatballs, spareribs, roast pork and ham, marinades, pickles, and spicy oriental combinations. Essential to most curries.

cayenne pepper a very hot, tongue-burning red pepper from the Cayenne region of South America. Used sparingly, it will add an exclamation point to other seasonings; use it more generously to give a delicious "bite." Widely used in hot cuisines, such as Mexican, Indian, Polynesian, Caribbean, South American, Tex-Mex, Chinese (Szechuan), African, and Creole. Add just a pinch to liven mild and creamy foods, sauces, or salad dressings.

celery seed (salt and powder) celerylike flavor. Used in France, other Western countries, India, the Middle East, and the Orient. Add it to potato and macaroni salads, tuna and other seafood salads, coleslaw, pickles, and salad dressings.

chervil (seed and ground) unusual spicy taste. Used in middle European cuisines. Use with fish, with macaroni, potato, and Caesar salads, coleslaw, and pickles; also try adding it to mayonnaise.

chervil leaf a delicate herb similar to parsley but more aromatic, with a hint of tarragon (often called French parsley or gourmet's parsley). Popular in French and other European cuisines. Try it with fish, in macaroni salad, Caesar salad, and coleslaw, and add it to pickles and mayonnaise.

chives the mildest member of the onion family; may be used generously in salads, cheese dishes, omelettes, pancakes, soups, herb butters, and many other dishes.

cilantro (leaf) a distinctively pungent herb with parsleylike leaves from the coriander plant (also known as Chinese or Mexican parsley).

MORE MAXIMIZING IDEAS

Here are a few pointers to help you get the most from your herbs and spices.

- Enhance the flavor of seeds like poppy and sesame by toasting.
- Keep spices in a cool, clean, dry place to prevent evaporation of oils and flavor.
- Keep containers tightly closed after each use.
- Herbs tend to lose flavor a little faster than spices.
- Ground spices should be used up within a year for maximum flavor.
- Whole spices keep their flavor almost indefinitely and may be purchased in larger amounts.

Use it in Mexican and Tex-Mex, as well as oriental combinations.

cinnamon (stick and powder) a sweet, fragrant spice from the dried inner tree bark of the *Laurus Cinnamonum*. Used in Mexican and South American foods, and in desserts, fruit dishes, and spiced beverages. Adds an interesting dash to meat and poultry dishes. Combine with nutmeg and lemon to season lamb the Greek way. Also good in Mexican and Greek salads, spicy tomato marinades for meat, poultry, or seafood, chili combinations, chutneys, sweet pickles, relishes, and curries.

cloves unopened buds of the clove tree (a type of evergreen), used in spiced drinks, pickled fruits and vegetables, marinades, meat glazes, cakes, cookies, and breads. Adds spicy flavor to Cajun and Creole cookery. Its fragrance makes clove popular in potpourri and pomander balls.

coriander (seed and ground) spicy and citruslike. Used in the Middle East, Orient, and South America. One of the basic ingredients in curry powder and Indian cooking. Can be used in place of cilantro (coriander leaves) in Spanish recipes. Good in pickling mixtures and marinades, chili combinations, spicy oriental salads and stir-fry mixtures, and coleslaw.

cumin (seed and ground) predominant flavor in most commercial chili and curry powders. Widely used in Mexican, Latin American, Indian, and Middle Eastern cooking (called "*comino*" by Spanish-speaking cooks). Especially good in yogurt dishes, salads, and dips; with tomatoes and in tomato-based sauces, marinades, dressings, and bastes; in chick-pea dips and on marinated eggplant. Sprinkle cumin on spicy meat mixtures for pita or pocket sandwiches. Similar to caraway in appearance.

dandelion leaf old English recipes call for dandelion leaves as a seasoning for lentils. Fresh early-spring dandelion leaves, available on some produce stands, add a chicorylike bitterness to tossed green salads. If you pick your own, be sure they're free of insecticides and road salt.

dill leaf (dill weed) the feathery leaf of the dill plant, with a pungent flavor and distinctive fragrance. In the Middle Ages a bit of this herb put into wine was believed to enhance passion. Widely used in Scandinavian and Middle Eastern cooking. Delicious in seafood and fish sauces, in potato and macaroni salads, and with pickled or marinated vegetables—especially cucumbers. Fine in sour cream sauces, dips, and spreads, in yogurt, sprinkled on cold soups, and added to cottage cheese. Use dill leaf in cold, uncooked dishes; dill flavor is released more quickly from the leaf than from the seed.

dill seed similar in taste to dill weed, but sharper and more pungent, with a distinctive carawaylike flavor and fragrance—slightly bitter. Widely used in middle European cuisines and often used with mint in Middle Eastern dishes. Adds zest to rice dishes, lamb stew, and fish dishes and is used in making dill pickles. Sprinkle it on potato and macaroni salads, use in coleslaw, on pork and ham, and in savory cottage cheese dishes. Use dill seed in hot dishes (heat will bring out the flavor) or when the texture of seed is desired.

fennel seed licoricelike, sweet, and fragrant seeds similar to anise but milder. Used in the Middle East and Europe in Italian sausages, fish stews, and cioppino, for example. Use with oily fish to cut the "fishy" taste. Sprinkle on pork, poultry, or seafood salads. Use with tomatoes, sweet peppers, and other raw vegetables, and with fruit salads. Add fennel to stir-fried oriental combinations and to spaghetti sauce.

fenugreek leaf (also called methi) used as a dried vegetable in Indian cooking; also makes a tasty tea either by itself or with alfalfa or mint.

fenugreek seed spicy, slightly bitter maplelike flavor characteristic of curry mixtures. Common in Asia, Morocco, North Africa, and the Middle East. Use in pickles, marinated vegetables, cold meats, poultry, and seafood.

galangal   a root from Laos, closely related to ginger. Used in Indonesian cookery. Try flavoring teas or vinegar with just a touch of root.

garlic (fresh, powdered, dried minced, and juice)   distinct, pungent flavor and fragrance. Widely used, especially in southern Europe. Add to any savory salad or dressing combination. Use with meats, poultry, seafood, vegetables, dips, sauces, and marinades.

ginger (fresh—whole root)   a sharp, spicy taste and sweet fragrance suitable to many main-course foods, not just desserts and baked goods. Used in Chinese and Indian cooking, as well as in preserves. Available in oriental markets and increasingly found on produce stands. Chinese cooks usually grate a little fresh ginger root onto fish before steaming it. Keep fresh ginger root in the refrigerator. For longer storage, grate or chop fresh ginger and freeze it.

ginger (dried)   chopped, dehydrated pieces of ginger can substitute for fresh ginger in soups, stews, and other slow-cooked dishes.

ginger (ground)   can be used in place of fresh. Adds zest to many dishes such as pickles, chutneys, soups, gingerbreads, pies, cakes, cookies, preserved and stewed fruits, cheese dishes, stews, oriental stir-fry combinations, and soy-based marinades and sauces. Combine with tomato and lime juice for Caribbean baste for poultry or seafood.

ginger (crystallized)   mainly sugar; high in calories.

green peppercorns   see *pepper*.

gumbo filé   dried, powdered young sassafras leaves, used for both aroma and thickening power in Creole dishes. Add 1 tablespoon of filé powder per 6 portions of shrimp or chicken gumbo after dish is finished cooking. Do not cook further.

horseradish   a white root with a hot and spicy bite and earthy flavor, usually sold in its pre-pared form: grated or shredded and preserved in vinegar. Use prepared horseradish as a condiment with meat courses, or add to cream sauces, seafood cocktail sauces, or gravies.

juniper berries   the dried fruit of an evergreen shrub, slightly larger than a blueberry, and the predominant flavor in gin. Use sparingly in marinades and sauces for game (venison, rabbit, duck, etc.; even lamb). Delicious in sauerkraut dishes. Also made into a tea.

lemongrass   a fragrant herb common in Indonesian cooking. Use it also in salads, soups, and potpourris, or to make a pleasant and soothing tea that's popular in the Caribbean Islands, Mexico, and Central America. A natural source of vitamin A.

lemon peel (grated)   used in cakes, breads, cookies, and sauces.

mace   the ground outer covering of the nutmeg, with a similar flavor but more pungent fragrance. Widely used in many regions. Often used in cakes, cookies, pies, pickles, and preserves. A pinch greatly enhances cherry and chocolate dishes. Add a pinch also to dressings and sauces, to the poaching liquid for seafood, and to the cooking liquid for vegetables, especially spinach. Mace and nutmeg may be interchanged in recipes.

marjoram (leaf)   a milder cousin of oregano; often blended into bouquet garni and mixed herb seasonings. Popular throughout Europe, especially in France and Italy, and the Middle East. Used in veal and poultry stuffings, with lamb and other meats, in salads, in dips and sauces, and with fish and vegetable dishes.

mint (leaf)   fragrant and flavorful, fresh or dried. Often used in a soothing brew, either by itself or, as the Arabs drink it, with green tea. Used as an herb in British, Greek, Adriatic, Middle Eastern, and Southeast Asian cooking. The British make it into a mint sauce to serve with lamb. The French like to flavor cooked vegetables with mint. Good with lamb and red meats, cheese, fresh fruit, creamy cold soups, tossed green salads, and iced drinks. Peppermint is more biting than other mints. Spearmint is milder.

mustard (seed, ground, or prepared) hot and spicy; the degree of heat varies with the liquid it is mixed with. For hot mustard, use vinegar and a little salt. If you prefer milder mustard, use water. For hot Chinese-style mustard, mix with an equal amount of warm water and wait 10 minutes. For interesting mustards, blend the powder with wine, beer, or even milk, or you can flavor it with marjoram, tarragon, chervil, chives, or numerous other herbs. Use the powder by itself in salad dressings, mild and creamy sauces, cheese dips, seafood sauces, omelettes, soufflés, and vegetable dishes. Use the seeds in pickle mixtures.

nutmeg (ground) distinctive in fragrance and flavor (interchangeable with mace in recipes). Widely used, particularly in French and Caribbean cuisines and in northern Italian cuisine (often with grated lemon peel); combined with cinnamon and other spices in Middle Eastern and Adriatic dishes. Add a pinch of nutmeg to mild cheese or cream sauces, to chicken dishes, salad dressings, stuffings, mild cheese dips, fruits, fruit salads, fruit sauces, sweet cottage cheese combinations, milk drinks, and creamed soups. Good with cabbage, cauliflower, and spinach.

oregano (leaf, ground, and crumbled) most familiar as the predominant herb in pizza or spaghetti sauce. There are many types, traditionally used throughout Mediterranean and Latin countries. Similar to its milder cousin marjoram, oregano is of the same genus and is sometimes known as "sweet marjoram" or "wild marjoram." Oregano is essential in Italian, Greek, Mexican, and Puerto Rican cooking. Use with tomatoes, peppers, zucchini, eggplant, all meats, poultry, seafood; with mild cheese, sauces, salad dressings, and dips.

paprika a mild ground spice of the *Capsicum* family, native to the Western Hemisphere. *Hun-*garian paprika, more pungent than Spanish, is a must in Hungarian goulash and chicken paprikash. Also delicious in salad dressings, dips and spreads, omelettes, and poultry, meat, and seafood dishes. *Spanish* paprika, the most common type in the U.S., is used mainly as a garnish on a variety of dishes.

parsley the ubiquitous garnish, with a distinctive flavor that makes a noteworthy contribution to soups, stews, sauces, salads, and salad dressings. Widely used all over the world. There are many kinds of parsley; the two main types are curly and flat leaf. The latter is more flavorful and is preferred in Italian dishes. Fresh parsley is a natural breath freshener thanks to its chlorophyll content; eat it after garlic or onions.

pepper, black, green, and white (whole peppercorns, coarsely ground, finely ground) a spicy berry that grows on a vine in the tropics of Asia. All three varieties are from the same family. *Black* pepper is the most familiar form: the berries are picked green, before maturity, and allowed to shrivel, dry, and blacken to become the whole black peppercorns we use to fill our pepper mills. They have a distinctively hot and biting flavor. Ground black pepper, the kind we put in our pepper shakers, is commercially available in three forms: fine, coarse, and cracked. Black pepper is widely used as a table seasoning on all types of food. *Green peppercorns* are whole pepper berries that are picked before they ripen, then bottled in a brining liquid. The whole green peppercorn berries are used as an attractive garnish that's salty and piquant as well as peppery. Restaurant chefs are particularly fond of them for the "gourmet touch" they add to French and Continental cooking. Use in steak au poivre and in duck and poultry dishes. *White pepper* comes from the same berry as black pepper, but the berry is allowed to ripen and turn bright red. Then the outer skin is removed, leaving the white kernel. White pepper has less flavor and fragrance than black, and it costs more. It's favored by professional chefs for white, light, and creamy foods, primarily for an esthetic effect: the avoidance of black specks in a white sauce.

pepper, cayenne   see *cayenne pepper.*

pine nut (pignoli)   soft pine-cone seed with a rich texture and mild nutty taste; used in Middle Eastern and Italian cuisine. Especially good in rice dishes, stuffed grape leaves, and cookies.

poppy seed (navy)   a tiny seed with a distinctively pleasant taste and texture, widely used in many European cuisines. Add to macaroni and potato salads, crunchy vegetable dips, cheese spreads; sprinkle on cottage cheese; serve on hot noodles; add to yogurt or sour cream toppings.

poppy seed (white)   a variety often used in Indian cooking.

rosemary (leaf; dried, whole or crumbled) fragrant, strongly flavored, spiky leaf that resembles a pine needle. Most popular in France, Spain, Italy, and around the Mediterranean. Pleasant, slightly mintlike flavor. Use rosemary on roast chicken, with poultry, pork, lamb, and shellfish, in meat marinades, in breads, with vegetables, stuffings, and cheeses, and in fruit (especially citrus) salads.

safflower (Mexican saffron)   often used as a substitute for Spanish saffron to impart yellow coloring (does not have saffron's delicate flavor).

saffron (Spanish)   the most expensive of spices, from the stigma of a crocus flower. Saffron is the spice that gives authentic Spanish paella rice its sunny yellow color. Saffron is also traditional in bouillabaisse, saffron buns, risotto, couscous, and many other dishes from the Mediterranean region.

sage (leaf; dried, whole or crumbled)   a strong but pleasant, sweet herbal fragrance and flavor; the most common seasoning ingredient in sausage and poultry stuffings. The symbol of wisdom. Popular in many European cuisines. Italians use it with veal and pork; Germans use it to season eel; the French add it to bean dishes. Use it also in sauces, soups, stews, garden salads, herbed cheese spreads; to flavor rice or pasta; with poultry, mushrooms, fillings and stuffings, tomatoes, mixed green salads, dressings, bastes and sauces, soups and stews.

savory   a pleasant thymelike taste. Used in France, Italy, and Spain. A great complement to bean dishes (the French combine it with sage). Adds special fragrance to meat loaf and pâté. Use with game, roast turkey, and baked fish.

sesame oil (toasted)   a delicious toasted flavor (derived from the seed). Use just a *few* drops to give added taste to your regular salad oil, or use in Chinese cooking.

sesame seed   mild, nutlike flavor. Very prevalent in Middle Eastern and oriental cookery, particularly Korean. Toasted sesame seeds are

---

FOREIGN FLAVOR FROM THE GARDEN

❧❧

Here are some combinations to consider:

- Italian: basil, oregano, rosemary, sage, flat-leaf parsley
- French: thyme, savory, tarragon, rosemary, chives
- Mexican: cilantro, oregano (with chili pepper, garlic, lime juice)
- Greek: oregano, mint, dill, parsley (with nutmeg, cinnamon, lemon, yogurt)
- Middle European: dill, parsley, caraway (with garlic, onion)
- Middle Eastern: mint, parsley (with garlic, lemon juice, cumin, and other spices)
- Indian: mint, cilantro leaves (with yogurt, curry, cumin, and other spices)
- Oriental: cilantro leaves (with soy, ginger, garlic)

These are simple guidelines; each country's cuisine has many regional variations.

sprinkled on top of Italian breads and are also good in vegetable, fish, chicken, and meat dishes, cheese dips and spreads, and especially in salads. To make sesame salt, combine 5 parts natural sesame seeds to 1 part coarse salt. Toast them, crush together, and store in an airtight container. It is a delicious substitute for plain salt, especially for those who wish to cut down on their salt intake.

sesame seed (black)   delicious nutty fragrance and flavor; sometimes toasted. Widely used in European, Middle Eastern, and oriental (particularly Japanese) cuisines. Sprinkle on salads for flavorful crunch. Use in stir-fry dishes.

sesame tahini   a paste of crushed sesame seeds with the texture of peanut butter (it can be used as a grown-up alternative!). Used in Israeli and Middle Eastern recipes, and as a main ingredient in such spreads as hummus (chick-pea spread) and baba ganoush (garlicky, mashed eggplant spread). Use tahini in salad dressings to replace part of the oil.

shallots   a mild member of the onion family, essential in French *haute cuisine*. Delicious in salads, on steaks; a must in béarnaise sauce.

sour salt (citric acid)   used in sweet-and-sour dishes, pickles, and preserves. Sour salt is a main ingredient in commercial lemon pepper.

tamarind   the fruit of a tropical tree, used as a condiment in Thai, Middle Eastern, Indian, and Spanish cookery. Substitute lemon juice.

tarragon leaf   sweet flavor and fragrance slightly reminiscent of anise, but unique and quintessentially French. Also used in other Continental cuisines. Dried tarragon has a dried tea flavor, so tarragon is best used fresh or frozen. Be sure to buy French tarragon rather than Russian tarragon, which has little flavor. Crush a few leaves, and if the scent is weak or absent, pass it by. Good with chicken, seafoods (particularly shellfish), meats, tomato and egg dishes, mild cheeses, mushrooms, wine-based foods, soups, and creamy dairy dishes.

thyme (leaf; dried, whole or crumbled) distinctive, pleasant herbal flavor and fragrance that is widely used. Good with most meats, poultry, and seafood, with tomatoes or tomato-based sauces, in salad dressings, marinades, and bastes.

turmeric   a brilliant yellow ground spice with a peppery aroma and a gingerlike flavor. Adds saffronlike natural coloring in curry powder; a common ingredient in commercially prepared mustards. Used also in Caribbean and Middle Eastern cuisines. Use as a substitute for saffron in rice dishes, curries, pickles and relishes, sauces, dressings, marinades, and soups.

vanilla bean   fruit of the orchid plant; native to Mexico and brought to Europe by the Spanish Conquistadors. Used for flavoring ice cream, puddings, cakes, custards, fruit sauces, etc.

vanilla extract   made commercially by combining crushed vanilla pods with alcohol.

HOT STUFF . . . THE LATEST DIET AID?

Chili peppers have been used for centuries to ward off evils. West Indian natives trailed them behind their boats to keep sharks away. Smoke from burning chilies repelled invading Spaniards from South American Indian villages. In the Caribbean it was believed that spirits were scared off by chili pepper amulets.

But now research indicates that chili peppers may help ward off a health "evil"—fat. Not only are chili peppers low in calories themselves (averaging 40 calories apiece for jalapeños), but when you eat them, your body starts to burn calories faster, at least for a short time. One study showed that eating chili peppers as part of a 700-calorie meal used up an additional 45 calories, on average. In other words, those peppers "erased" 45 calories of eaten food!

This may be especially true if you're new to eating peppers. The increase in calorie burn, or metabolic rate, seems to be highest if you're not used to hot food. That's why you sweat: it means your body is kicking up its effort to use up food. The sweating response diminishes as people get used to hotter foods; research hasn't looked into whether that means that the calorie burn slows down, too. But hot peppers come in so many degrees of "heat" that it's a real challenge to become used to all of them!

Mildest of the peppers, of course, is the bell pepper, which registers 0 on the heat scale. In contrast, the jalapeño scores 4,000, and cayenne, 20,000. But when you're ready for searing heat, try the habanero, registering at 200,000 to 300,000! (You'll have a hard time finding it fresh; try it dried.)

But peppers offer more than just that extra calorie burn. Here are some more benefits of pepper eating:

- They contain important nutrients—vitamins A and C, iron, magnesium, thiamin, riboflavin, and niacin—and can be an ideal substitute for calorie-laden toppings like ketchup, guacamole, and sour cream.
- They loosen the congestion of the common cold.
- They can reduce the chance of heart disease and help circulation by increasing the production of fibrinolysin (a blood clot dissolver) in the blood. This keeps blood flowing smoothly—and the increase in fibrinolysin can follow within 30 minutes of pepper eating.
- They're "feel good" food, because when the body senses pain—its first reaction to spicy food—it produces a natural morphine, which makes us feel good all over.
- And contrary to what you might think, pepper eating won't hurt your ulcer. The stomach protects itself by secreting a protective mucus that coats the stomach. Peppers actually improve digestion by producing saliva and gastric juices.

Whether "hot stuff" is a cure for the common cold, obesity, or heart disease remains to be seen. In the meantime, the judicious addition of hot spices is a sure cure for one common ailment . . . bland and boring food!

MUSTARD

Mustard is available in three forms: mustard seeds, mustard powder, and prepared mustard (of which there are over 400 brands in the United States).

Mustard seeds come in two basic types: the white or yellow kind used to make the bright yellow stuff, and the dark brown seeds known as oriental mustard. (The Chinese have been using mustard, which originated in Asia, for thousands of years.) Seeds can be stored at room temperature in your kitchen cabinet for a year or more.

Mustard powder is nothing more than finely ground seeds. It too can be stored in the kitchen cabinet but keeps for only 6 months or so.

To make mustard at home, mix 1 tablespoon powdered mustard or finely ground mustard seeds and 2 teaspoons of water. Wait 10 minutes for the "fire" to develop . . . and gangway!

The pungency of freshly made mustard lasts only for about an hour; then it begins to lose its heat. (It's the result of an enzymatic reaction triggered by the liquid.) If you use very cold water, you'll have a hotter mustard than if you use warmer water. You can make a more mellow mustard by substituting an acid liquid for the water—say, wine or vinegar.

Commercially prepared mustard can range in hotness from the bland and creamy kid stuff used on hot dogs to the brain-blowing English varieties known for clearing the sinuses. Prepared mustard should be refrigerated after opening to preserve its bite. Some commonly available types include:

- *Dijon*—The imported French mustard from the Dijon region. It's mellow because it is made from white wine, in a manner strictly controlled by the French government. (The word *mustard* comes from the French word for must, or unfermented wine.)
- *English*—A very hot mustard with a bright yellow color that looks disarmingly like ballpark mustard, despite its very pungent taste.
- *Grainy*—Made with a combination of ground and partially ground seeds. The heat can vary according to its other ingredients. Grainy

mustards frequently come packed in crocks.

- *German*—Dark, pungent, and very fragrant. Some are grainy. Bavarian-style mustards are usually very sweet, due to the addition of sugar, and are higher in calories.
- *Chinese*—Should be made fresh from cold water and ground mustard. Prepared varieties are rarely as pungent.

HORSERADISH

Prepared horseradish is made from the white horseradish root, shredded or ground and mixed with vinegar to create the hot and spicy condiment so prized as an accompaniment to beef and other meats. The plant is a perennial, originating in Eastern Europe, and is common in German, Russian, Scandinavian, and other middle and northern European cuisines. Red horseradish is prepared by adding grated beets to the mixture, resulting in a condiment that's sweeter and less hot.

Fresh horseradish root is sometimes available; it can be washed, peeled, and coarsely grated as a garnish for cold meats. Dried grated horseradish is also available for reconstituting with water.

Japanese wasabi horseradish is a green horseradish grated from the root of the *Eutrema wasabi*. It is extremely hot! Fresh wasabi is hard to find and very expensive. Green horseradish powder is more readily available, in gourmet shops and oriental food stores. It too is very hot. It should be mixed to a paste with a little cold water—and used with care!

HERB AND SPICE BLENDS

apple pie spice predominantly cinnamon but also including cloves, nutmeg, and other sweet spices. Use in any food in which cinnamon or nutmeg might be used effectively.

barbeque spice (or seasoning) paprika plus chili powder, garlic, and cloves, usually with salt and sugar added. Use as a basic seasoning in marinades and basting sauces, also in meat casseroles, egg and cheese dishes, and dressings. (Make your own, sugar and/or salt free, by combining equal parts paprika and chili, seasoned with garlic powder and clove; vary the proportions to suit your taste.)

chili powder ground chilies, oregano, cumin seed, garlic, and salt. Use in chili con carne and Mexican-style dishes; also to add savor to cocktail sauces, egg dishes, stews, meatballs, and meat loaves. (For a salt-free alternative, use 3 parts red pepper to 1 part ground cumin, with fresh or instant garlic and oregano added to taste.)

curry powder a mixture of as many as 15 to 20 ground spices, including ginger, turmeric, fenugreek seed, cloves, cinnamon, red pepper, and cumin seed. Use in curries of all kinds and Indian cooking. Delicious too in meat, poultry, seafoods, potato salad, pea soup, and corn or clam chowder. (For a less fiery curry that's spicy but not hot, use less curry powder and add a pinch of apple pie spice and ground cumin.)

fines herbes blend predominantly tarragon, marjoram, thyme, and rosemary. Use in soups, stews, and on roasts—especially in French cookery.

5-spice powder (Chinese) a sweet and pungent mixture of spices, predominantly star anise, with a strong licoricelike taste. Especially good in pork, chicken, and duck dishes (use sparingly). A dash of pumpkin pie spice and some anise seeds can substitute.

guaram masala a mixture of spices used in Indian cooking. Black pepper, cumin, and a pinch of pumpkin pie spice can substitute.

herb seasoning milder herbs—such as parsley, chervil, marjoram, and savory—blended with some salt. Especially convenient to add to cooked vegetables and salads.

Italian seasoning an herb and red pepper blend that gives characteristic Italian flavor to pizza, spaghetti sauces, and salads. Oregano, basil, and thyme predominate.

lemon pepper a nippy blend of coarse black pepper, salt, and sour salt (citric acid crystals), flavored with lemon oil, garlic, and other seasonings. Gives a distinctive lemony bite to seafood, lamb, chicken, vegetables, and tossed salads. Add it to salad dressings and marinades. (To make your own salt-free lemon pepper grind dried lemon peels and combine with cracked pepper in a covered container.)

mixed pickling spice a mixture of whole spices, usually including mustard seed, bay leaves, red pepper, cinnamon, allspice, and ginger. Use in pickling and preserving meats and to season marinades for meats, and vegetables.

poultry seasoning ground blend of sage, thyme, marjoram, and occasionally savory. Not only good for stuffings, but an ideal seasoning for hamburgers, meat loaves, chowders, and homemade low-fat sausage. Add poultry seasoning to lean ground pork or turkey and it will taste like sausage!

pumpkin pie spice ground blend of cinnamon, nutmeg, ginger, and cloves. Perfect aroma for pumpkin pie, but use it also for fruit desserts, apple pies, and sweet yellow vegetables. Use as an emergency replacement for Chinese 5-spice powder, with a pinch of anise or fennel seeds to provide the fifth spice.

seafood seasoning a ground blend of savory and pungent spices especially handy when seasoning seafood sauces and chowders. Paprika, ground red pepper, and celery powder predominate.

seasoned pepper black pepper and other spices, flavorful and convenient for seasoning meats, poultry, fish, salads, and sauces. Formulas vary. Use as an alternative to seasoned salt if you're cutting down on salt.

seasoned salt mixed spices and herbs with salt. Formulas vary with the manufacturer, so different brands aren't interchangeable in recipes. It's easy to make your own herb-seasoned salt by mixing well-dried, chopped fresh herbs with salt in a covered container. Use about 4 times as much salt as herbs.

shrimp spice or **crab boil** a mixture of whole spices—with the emphasis on red peppers, bay leaves, whole peppercorns, and mustard seed—to be added to the cooking water for seafood.

Szechuan pepper Chinese anise pepper. Pepper and star anise (or a pinch of anise or fennel seeds) can substitute.

CALORIC INFORMATION ON SPICES AND SEASONINGS

Most spices and seasonings are between 3 and 10 calories a level teaspoon according to the new data.* Since most recipes specify only pinches and dashes—½ teaspoon at most—divided among 6 or 8 portions, spices contribute only a fraction of a calorie per person. The same holds true for the fat, protein, and carbohydrate content of spices.

Since most herbs and spices are equally low in sodium and potassium as well, spices can save the day for most "special" dieters, too. Those on the restricted regimens (particularly low-sodium diets) and allergy sufferers should follow their physician's advice about herbs, spices, and other seasonings.

Spices at *5 calories a teaspoon or less* include basil, bay leaf, garlic powder, marjoram, parsley flakes, rosemary, sage, savory, tarragon, and thyme.

Seasonings with *6 to 10 calories a teaspoon* are allspice, caraway, cardamom, cinnamon, clove, coriander, cumin, dill, fennel, ginger, mace, mustard (dry), onion powder, oregano, paprika, pepper, sesame seeds, and turmeric.

*This fact is verified by the American Spice Trade Association, which publishes comprehensive information on the nutritional makeup of spices.

Celery seeds and nutmeg have *11 calories a teaspoon*. At *13 calories a teaspoon*, poppy seeds are the highest on the list.

When you combine lean meat, poultry, and seafood, healthy high-fiber vegetables, beans, and grains with no-cal (practically) seasonings, you are creating pure gold—kitchen "alchemy" at its best.

SPICY CUISINE AND THE LOW-SODIUM DIET

The spiciest cuisines are often the saltiest, revealing their origins: warm weather areas where people work hard and sweat a lot. Hot climate cuisines from all over the world—whether Spanish or Szechuan, Cuban or Cajun, Turkish or Tex-Mex—share three features: saltiness, spiciness, and heat. None of these are necessarily fattening, and only the last two are needed for flavor.

With an emphasis on herbs, spices, hot chilies, and strongly flavored ingredients like garlic and tomatoes, spicy dishes are the easiest to desalt—and to defat, desugar, and decalorize as well.

If you're on a low-sodium diet, you needn't be denied the pleasures of good dining. While it's true that you can't use salt in your food—or any condiment that contains salt or sodium—you can use onion, garlic, pepper, mustard, sage, or savory. In fact, any spice or herb. For all practical purposes, you can disregard the sodium content of spices, considering the small amount used per portion of food, except for celery seed, celery flakes, and parsley flakes. Once you know that, you can make up your own recipes and season them to suit yourself.

If you're trying to cut down on salt use, it's better to cook without salt and add it at the table (unless it's against your doctor's orders). Researchers have found that when food is cooked without salt and people are free to add as much as they want at the table, they use less salt. Despite liberal shaking, people generally never add as much as they would have used in cooking the same dish . . . and they seem satisfied. They are more responsive to salt on the surface of food than diluted throughout. (The same, incidentally, is true of sugar.)

MAKE YOUR OWN EASY-TO-USE SEASONING COMBINATIONS

You can vary the proportions to suit your taste!

Mexican 5-spice powder: This shake-on Mexican seasoner adds quick Mex taste to lots of light dishes. It's a combination of cayenne pepper or chili powder, cumin, oregano, cinnamon . . . and a touch of cocoa. Mix together equal parts of the last four ingredients, then stir in an amount of red cayenne pepper or chili powder equal to the mixture. Example: 1 tablespoon each of ground cumin, dried oregano, ground cinnamon, and plain unsweetened cocoa powder plus 4 tablespoons of either red cayenne pepper or chili powder. Put the mixture in a covered shaker and use it as a quick south-of-the-border, salt-free seasoning.

Homemade curry powder: In a covered jar, combine 2 tablespoons each ground coriander, black pepper, cumin, red cayenne pepper, and turmeric and 1¼ teaspoons ground ginger. Makes slightly over ½ cup.

Creole spice mix: Blend together ¼ cup ground red pepper, 2 teaspoons each ground cumin and ground cloves, 1 tablespoon each paprika, ground coriander, and black pepper, and 1½ teaspoons garlic powder. Store tightly covered in a cool place. Makes slightly more than ½ cup.

Homemade guaram masala: This is a spice blend called for in various Indian recipes. Use whole spices and grind to a powder: ½ teaspoon black peppercorns, ⅓ teaspoon cumin seeds, ¼ teaspoon coriander seeds, ¼-inch cinnamon stick, 1 clove, and seeds of one cardamom pod.

Salads and Salad Dressings

IF you could "live on salad," this chapter's for you! Our light and spicy culinary collection goes beyond mere side-dish salads. Many are meal-size creations that can serve as the main course at lunch or supper, at any time of year.

Even when salad is part of the meal, we believe in elevating it to up-front status rather than relegating it to a puny-proportioned, end-of-the-meal afterthought. A great big salad for openers makes it easier to keep portion sizes under control when you get to the meat of the matter!

SHEDDING LIGHT ON SALAD OIL CLAIMS

Salad oil is the world's most fattening ingredient: 120 calories per tablespoon. It's pure fat, and there's nothing more fattening than that!

Oil accounts for nearly all the calories in conventional salad dressings. In vinaigrette dressings, salad oil contributes 120 calories a tablespoon, while vinegar is only 2 calories. Bottled, regular mayonnaise is 101 calories a tablespoon: 100 calories in oil and 1 calorie's worth of everything else!

Because oil makes such a significant calorie contribution to salads and dressings, it's important to choose oil wisely and use it sparingly. Some food for thought:

- *No calorie difference:* There's no significant difference among brands, despite manufacturers' efforts to suggest otherwise. Corn, sunflower, safflower, sesame, soybean, and cot-tonseed oil are all 120 calories per tablespoon. Olive oil and peanut oil contain marginally more solids (and flavor), so their calorie count is 119 per tablespoon.

- *Cholesterol:* Salad oil doesn't contain cholesterol; cholesterol is found only in animal foods and products.

- *"Light" salad oils:* A salad oil that's touted as light may trick you into thinking that it's lighter in calories—when, in fact, it's light only in color and flavor. Keep in mind that when an oil is promoted as light, what the word really means is tasteless.

- *Low in saturated fat:* All salad oils are low in saturated fat, some more than others. But while this fact is of interest to cholesterol watchers, it does not affect the calorie count. Some would-be weight watchers misread claims of "low saturated fat"; thinking safflower or corn oil low in fat, they drench their salads in them. These two oils are lowest in saturated fat, but their calorie count is the same as other oils.

- *Low-fat salad oil?* There's no such thing as a low-fat or nonfattening salad oil. (The only "nonfattening" oil you can buy is medicinal mineral oil, sold in drugstores to alleviate constipation. It has no calories because it's not absorbed, which makes it a useful internal lubricant. It does, however, interfere with the absorption of needed vitamins and nutrients, so its regular use as a diet aid is nutritionally unsound—despite recommendations for it in outdated diet books.)

- *Low-cal fat of the future:* There's another non-absorbed fat, not yet on the market: sucrose polyester. This synthetic fat helps lower cholesterol levels in the blood; someday it may be available in commercial, diet salad dressings. Another kind of fat substitute may eventually be available; it mimics the texture and creamy rich feel of fat even though it's not a fat and doesn't have fat's calorie count.

Oil makers have turned the lack of taste in their highly processed products into a perceived advantage: "No oily taste" or "Won't interfere with the flavor of food." To my mind, there's little point in using an ingredient that costs 120 calories a tablespoon and can't be tasted. When you do use salad oil, look for the most strongly flavored oils you can find.

- Spanish, Greek, Sicilian, and Portuguese olive oils have a pronounced, full-bodied fruity flavor that tastes like olives.
- Walnut, sesame, and peanut oils all have a pleasant nutty flavor.
- For flavor with less fat, use mashed olives, olive liquid, ground nuts, or a scant teaspoon of ground peanuts (peanut butter) or sesame tahini in homemade low-fat, low-calorie salad dressings.
- The salad oils with no taste are corn, safflower, and sunflower oil.

CHOOSE VINEGAR FOR FLAVOR

Vinegar can add its own unique flavor note to salads and other food, along with its sour-power sharpness. You can choose the taste you want from several varieties:

- *White vinegar* is water clear, with the sharpest, purest flavor; best when you want to add pure, one-dimensional sourness with no other color or flavor notes. Because white vinegar is pure sour power—sharper than other vinegars—use it sparingly.
- *Apple cider vinegar* has a long tradition as the salad favorite. It has a fragrant, ciderlike flavor and a tawny color. It can be made milder by diluting it with cider or apple juice.
- *Red wine vinegar* has a deep wine flavor and color. Once popular primarily in wine-grow-

SALAD NIBBLES FOR STARTERS

Having friends over for a casual dinner? Instead of the usual high-calorie cocktail nibbles, greet your guests with crunchy crudités: raw veggie sticks and dippers surrounding a tangy yogurt dressing. Having served raw veggies, you can dispense with the tossed salad course.

ing regions, it's become a favorite in the U.S. Its sharpness can be cut by diluting it with a little red wine.
- *White wine vinegar* is the white wine version of wine vinegar; it has a fruity wine flavor but no red color to tint foods.
- *Oriental rice wine vinegar*, like white wine vinegar, is clear and colorless. It's much milder than other vinegars, so you can dress your salad with more of it . . . and use proportionally less oil!
- *Balsamic vinegar*, imported from the same Italian region that gives us Chianti wine, is a dark, mellow, richly flavored vinegar that's not too sharp. It accents the flavor of meats, poultry, and seafood as well as vegetables. Use it in barbecue bastes as well as salad dressings.

Flavored vinegars are made by adding herbs, seasonings, or other highly flavored ingredients to any favorite vinegar. Commercially bottled varieties are usually expensive, but seasoned vinegars are easy to make at home with either fresh or dried herbs. *Caution:* vinegars seasoned with fresh ingredients should be stored in the refrigerator.

- *Herb vinegar:* Wash and dry freshly gathered young herb leaves (mint, oregano, basil, tarragon, thyme, or any favorite). Bruise the leaves slightly to speed up the release of flavor. Loosely fill a small bottle or jar halfway with the leaves, then fill it to the top with any favorite vinegar. Store it in the refrigerator. Or add 1 or 2 tablespoons of dried herbs to a pint of any favorite vinegar. Dilute with additional

GAZPACHO

4 large tomatoes, chopped
1 cucumber, chopped
1 onion, minced
1 green bell pepper, seeded and diced
6 pitted ripe olives, sliced
1 clove garlic, minced
1 cup tomato juice
1 tablespoon red wine vinegar
2 tablespoons extra virgin olive oil
   Salt and pepper to taste
   Lettuce leaves for garnish

1. Mix all ingredients except lettuce. Chill for several hours; mixture will thicken. Spoon into lettuce-lined bowls.

MAKES 8 APPETIZER SERVINGS, 85 CALORIES EACH.

✦

CANARY ISLANDS GAZPACHO

4 large vine-ripe tomatoes, chopped
1 cucumber, chopped
1 green bell pepper, seeded and diced
½ cup chopped sweet Spanish onion
6 pitted ripe olives, sliced
2 cloves garlic, minced
3 tablespoons chopped fresh cilantro or parsley
1 cup tomato juice
¼ cup olive brine (from jar of olives)
2 tablespoons red wine vinegar
1 tablespoon olive oil
2 teaspoons each paprika and cumin seeds
   Sea salt and black pepper to taste
   Lettuce leaves for garnish

1. Mix all ingredients except lettuce. Chill several hours, allowing mixture to thicken. Spoon into lettuce-lined bowls to serve.

MAKES 8 SERVINGS, 70 CALORIES EACH.

SALADE ENCORE GAZPACHO

If you've made too much tossed salad, there's no need to toss it away. Toss it, instead, into the blender or food processor with enough tomato juice or spicy-seasoned tomato juice to turn it into a spiffy soup. Here's how:

1. Transfer leftover salad mixture to a plastic bag or covered bowl and store in refrigerator. Next day, combine chilled mixture with an equal amount of cold tomato juice in blender; process smooth.
2. Taste for seasonings; add additional herbs or lemon juice, if desired. Spoon into bowls and garnish with thin slices of lemon or cucumber.

EACH CUP HAS APPROXIMATELY 150 CALORIES, DEPENDING ON AMOUNT OF OIL IN ORIGINAL SALAD DRESSING.

✦

COLD CUCUMBER SOUP

1 cucumber, skinned
1 cup plain low-fat yogurt
1 teaspoon lemon or lime juice
1 tablespoon snipped chives or chopped onion
1 tablespoon chopped fresh mint or parsley
   Salt and pepper to taste
   Cucumber slices, with skin, for garnish (optional)

1. Cut cucumber in quarters lengthwise. Remove and discard seeds, and cut cucumber into chunks. In an electric blender, blend cucumber, yogurt, and juice until smooth. Stir in herbs and seasonings. Serve in chilled bowls set in larger bowls of crushed ice. If desired, garnish with slices of cucumber.

MAKES 2 SERVINGS, 90 CALORIES EACH.

KALE OR SPINACH SOUP

1 teaspoon salad oil
1 clove garlic, minced
½ cup chopped onion
2 tablespoons water
3 cups chicken broth, skimmed of fat
½ pound kale or spinach, chopped
   Red pepper sauce or flakes to taste
   Salt and coarse pepper to taste (optional)
1 cup cooked shredded crabmeat or whitefish flakes

1. In a nonstick pot, heat the oil over moderate heat. Add garlic, and cook for 1 minute. Add onion and water; cook until water evaporates and onion starts to brown.
2. Add broth and kale. Simmer for 10 minutes, then season to taste. Add crabmeat and then reheat.

MAKES 2 SERVINGS, 185 CALORIES EACH.

✦

VEGETARIAN MINESTRONE

2 cups tomato juice
1 cup tomato-vegetable juice
1 cup water
8 ounces shredded cabbage
1 can (8 ounces) tomatoes, chopped
1 onion, chopped
2 ribs celery, minced
2 tablespoons chopped olives
1 clove garlic, minced
1½ teaspoons oregano or Italian seasoning
   Pinch dried thyme
   Dash Tabasco sauce (optional)

1. Combine all ingredients in a covered saucepan. Simmer for 10 minutes. Serve immediately.

MAKES 4 SERVINGS, 80 CALORIES EACH.

CAJUN SHRIMP AND OYSTER GUMBO

¼   cup no-fat browned flour (see box)
1   tablespoon olive oil
½   cup chopped onion
1   small clove garlic, minced
¾   cup chopped green bell pepper
¼   cup chopped parsley
½   teaspoon dried thyme
¼   teaspoon salt, or to taste
¼   teaspoon cayenne pepper
¼   teaspoon hot red pepper sauce
2   cups stock (recipe follows)
1   can (16 ounces) tomatoes, with liquid
½   cup cold water
1   package (10 ounces) frozen okra, thawed
1   pound medium shrimp, peeled and deveined, shells reserved
1½   cups shucked oysters, drained, liquor reserved
3   cups hot cooked rice

1. Prepare no-fat browned flour as described and set aside. (If browned flour is unavailable, substitute regular flour.)

2. Prepare a large nonstick skillet with cooking spray and add the olive oil. Stir in the onion; cook until soft and translucent. Add the garlic, green pepper, parsley, thyme, salt, cayenne pepper, and pepper sauce; cook, stirring, 5 minutes more. Add the stock and tomatoes and heat to simmering.

3. Mix no-fat browned flour with cold water to form a smooth paste. Whisk this mixture into the pan. Simmer for 20 minutes, stirring occasionally. If mixture becomes too thick, add a little water.

4. Slice each okra pod crosswise into 5 pieces. Add okra and simmer just until okra is tender—about 5 minutes. Add shrimp and oysters. Simmer just until edges of oysters curl and shrimp is pink and opaque—5 to 8 minutes. Do not overcook seafood. Remove from heat. To serve, mound hot rice in soup plates and then ladle gumbo over the top.

MAKES 6 SERVINGS, 310 CALORIES EACH.

❖❖❖

STOCK

2   quarts water
2   dried hot red chilies
2   slices lemon
1   bay leaf
½   teaspoon dried thyme
¼   teaspoon salt, or to taste
    Shrimp shells (reserved from shrimp)
    Oyster liquor (reserved from oysters)

1. Combine all ingredients in large stockpot. Bring to a boil. Simmer until mixture is reduced to approximately 3 cups—25 to 30 minutes. Strain and discard seasonings.

MAKES 3 CUPS STOCK.

NO-FAT BROWNED FLOUR

Roux is a thickening agent favored by Cajun and Creole cooks; it's normally made by mixing fat with flour, then slow-cooking the mixture until it turns brown. The fat-to-flour ratio is usually equal, so roux is fattening as well as time-consuming.

Two New Orleans cooks who were guest chefs on a *Mississippi Queen* steamboat cruise shared a great lower-caloried alternative with me: no-fat browned flour. Chef Joe Cahn of the New Orleans School of Cooking gave these directions: Sprinkle flour on a shallow, nonstick cookie tin or baking pan and slow-bake in the oven at 325 degrees for 1 hour or longer. The longer you bake it, the darker it becomes. Joe Cahn has four jars for 1-hour flour, 2-hour flour, and so on.

Chef Gary Darling prefers 1-hour flour, noting that the darker the flour gets, the less its thickening power. To thicken soups or stews, combine the required amount of flour with a double amount of cold water—never hot—and whisk it smooth (or shake up the mixture in a tightly closed jar). Slowly whisk the combination into the simmering soup or stew. It will thicken once it reaches 180 degrees.

CHICKEN SOPA DE TORTILLA

4   cups chicken broth, skimmed of fat
2   ribs celery, cut in 2-inch pieces
1   carrot, thinly sliced
1   small onion, chopped
½   small red or green bell pepper, diced
2   tablespoons chopped fresh cilantro or parsley
1   clove garlic, chopped
1   tablespoon uncooked rice
2   teaspoons chili powder, or to taste
¼   teaspoon dried oregano
2   cups diced cooked chicken
2   corn tortillas, torn, or 2 ounces tortilla chips, crushed

1. Combine broth with remaining ingredients, except chicken and tortillas, in a soup pot. Cover and simmer until rice is tender—about 25 minutes.

2. Add chicken and heat through. Before serving, sprinkle with tortillas.

M AKES 4 SERVINGS, 250 CALORIES EACH.

❦

MEXICALI BEEF AND BEER SOUP

8   ounces lean beef round, trimmed of fat and ground, or ground turkey
4   cups tomato juice
12   ounces light beer
1   large onion, chopped
1   green bell pepper, seeded and chopped
1   zucchini or summer squash, chopped
1   package (10 ounces) frozen corn kernels
1   tablespoon lime juice
1   tablespoon fresh oregano or 1 teaspoon dried oregano
1   teaspoon cumin seeds or ½ teaspoon ground cumin
    Hot pepper or Tabasco sauce to taste
¼   cup shredded part-skim mozzarella cheese (optional)

1. Prepare a large nonstick pot with cooking spray. Spread meat in bottom of pot and brown over moderate heat, breaking into chunks and turning to brown evenly. Drain fat from pan and discard.

2. Add remaining ingredients, except cheese. Simmer 8 to 10 minutes. Ladle into bowls and then sprinkle with cheese, if desired.

M AKES 4 MEAL-SIZE SERVINGS, 235 CALORIES EACH WITH BEEF; WITH TURKEY, 210 CALORIES PER SERVING. CHEESE ADDS 20 CALORIES PER SERVING.

❦

SPICY INDIAN CHICKEN MULLIGATAWNY

2   cups tomato juice
2   cups chicken broth, skimmed of fat
2   cups water
2   carrots, sliced
2   onions, sliced
2   ribs celery, sliced
¼   cup chopped parsley
¼   cup uncooked brown rice
2   teaspoons curry powder, or to taste
2   cups diced cooked chicken
2   small red apples, cored and diced

1. Combine all ingredients, except chicken and apple, in a soup pot. Cover and simmer for 45 minutes or until rice is tender. Add chicken and apple; simmer only until heated through.

M AKES 4 MAIN-COURSE SERVINGS, 275 CALORIES EACH.

ITALIAN LENTIL MINESTRONE SOUP

2   cups dried lentils
12   cups cold water
1   can (6 ounces) tomato paste
3   ribs celery, minced
1   cup coarsely chopped cabbage
1   cup sliced mushrooms
1   onion, chopped
1   teaspoon Italian herbs or ½ teaspoon each dried oregano and dried basil
1   teaspoon garlic salt
    Pepper to taste
    Pinch hot pepper flakes
6   tablespoons grated Parmesan cheese

1. Soak lentils overnight in 6 cups water; drain, discarding water. Combine lentils with remaining 6 cups water. Heat to boiling.

2. Stir in remaining ingredients, except cheese. Cover and simmer for 45 minutes. Serve sprinkled with Parmesan.

M AKES 10 SERVINGS, 170 CALORIES EACH.

❦

LIGHT AND SPICY BORSCHT

1   pound fresh raw, pared (or canned) beets, chopped
4   cups shredded cabbage
4   cups canned tomatoes, finely chopped
1   large sweet onion, chopped
2½   cups fat-skimmed beef broth (or water)
4   tablespoons minced parsley
1   bay leaf
    Pinch of grated nutmeg
    Coarse black pepper to taste

1. Combine ingredients in soup pot. Cover and simmer for 50 to 60 minutes. Remove bay leaf before serving.

M AKES 6 SERVINGS, 90 CALORIES EACH.

TUNA CHOWDER

1 can (10-3/4 ounces) low-sodium chicken broth, skimmed of fat
1 cup diced raw potatoes
1 pound yellowfin tuna steaks, skinned and cubed
1/2 cup fresh or frozen corn kernels
1/2 cup chopped onion
1/2 cup carrots
1/2 cup celery
1/2 teaspoon dried basil
1/4 teaspoon dried thyme
1/2 cup plain low-fat yogurt
1 tablespoon chopped parsley

1. In a large saucepan, mix broth and 1 can of water. Add potatoes and simmer for 10 to 15 minutes, until tender.

2. Remove potatoes from broth; reserve liquid. Purée potatoes with 1/4 cup broth. Add tuna, vegetables, seasonings, and puréed potatoes to remaining broth in pan. Simmer for 8 to 10 minutes or until fish flakes easily. Stir in yogurt and heat to serve but don't boil. Sprinkle with parsley just before serving.

MAKES 4 SERVINGS, 245 CALORIES EACH.

SPICY CRAB SOUP

1 can (10-3/4 ounces) low-sodium chicken broth, skimmed of fat
2 cups water
2 cans (16 ounces each) tomatoes, chopped, with liquid
3/4 cup chopped celery
3/4 cup diced onion
1 teaspoon Maryland-style seasoning or a dash paprika and celery salt
1 bay leaf
1/4 teaspoon lemon pepper
1 package (10 ounces) frozen corn kernels, thawed
1 package (10 ounces) frozen peas, thawed
1 pound crabmeat, cooked and flaked, cartilage removed

1. In 6-quart soup pot, bring broth, water, tomatoes, celery, onion, and seasonings to a boil. Simmer mixture for 20 to 30 minutes.

2. Add corn and peas; simmer 10 minutes more. Add crabmeat; simmer until heated through. Remove bay leaf and serve.

MAKES 6 SERVINGS, 205 CALORIES EACH.

MISSISSIPPI DELTA CATFISH CHOWDER

1 quart water
3 potatoes, peeled and diced
2 cups diced fresh vine-ripe tomatoes or 1 can (16 ounces) chopped tomatoes
2 ribs celery plus leaves, minced
1 cup chopped onions
1/4 cup minced fresh parsley
2 bay leaves
2 teaspoons salt or celery salt
1/4 teaspoon each dried sage and ground nutmeg
  Pinch ground cloves
2 pounds catfish fillets
  Juice of 1 lemon

1. Combine ingredients, except fish and lemon juice, in a soup pot. Cover and simmer for 20 to 25 minutes or until potatoes are tender. Meanwhile, cut fish fillets into bite-size cubes. Uncover soup and arrange fish on top. Sprinkle with lemon juice (and additional salt, pepper, and fresh parsley, if desired). Cover and simmer 2 more minutes, until just cooked through.

Discard bay leaves before serving. Serve with hot pepper sauce, if desired.

MAKES 8 MEAL-SIZE SERVINGS, 180 CALORIES EACH.

CAJUN BEEF GUMBO

Spicy corned beef is often used in this New Orleans soup. Our version is made with lean meat and little added fat—keeping the flavor without the calories.

2 teaspoons salad oil
12 ounces fresh okra or 1 package (10 ounces) frozen okra, cut in 1/2-inch pieces
1 cup chopped onion
1/2 cup chopped celery
2 cloves garlic, minced
1 can (8 ounces) tomatoes, undrained
3 cups water
2 cups thinly sliced cooked corned beef round

1. In a large nonstick skillet, heat the oil over moderate heat. Add okra, and cook, stirring occasionally, until liquid from okra evaporates. Remove okra from pan and set aside. Add onion, celery, and garlic to pan; cook for 5 minutes, stirring occasionally.

2. Add tomatoes, water, and okra and simmer for 1 hour, stirring occasionally. Stir in sliced corned beef and heat through.

MAKES 4 SERVINGS, 250 CALORIES EACH.

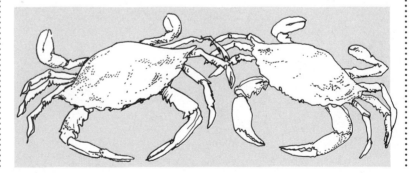

Turkey Cacciatore *(page 77)*

Sautéed Catfish with
Red Pepper Cream *(page 84)*

Microwaved Fillet of Sole
Mediterranean *(page 84),*
Italian-Style Seafood Stew *(page 83)*
Seafood Risotto *(page 132)*

Spinach Puff *(page 143)*

Baked Cod Fillets with Basil *(page 81)*

French Apple
Charlotte *(page 151)*

Quickie Garden
Chicken Salad *(page 24)*

Beef and Pepper Chili *(page 58)*

Mexican Beef Stir-Fry *(page 54)*

Tuna Chowder *(page 32)*,
Spicy Crab Soup *(page 32)*,
Cajun Shrimp and
Oyster Gumbo *(page 30)*

Light and Spicy Borscht *(page 31)*,
Golden Vegetable Piroshki *(page 142)*

Tandoori-Style Spiced Chicken *(page 72)*

Greek-Style Puffy Pancake *(page 144)*

Grape Pork
Burritos *(page 64)*

Turkey and Fresh
Fruit Salad *(page 24)*

Healthy Fresh Peach Ice Cream *(page 155)*,
Peach-Raspberry Ice Cream *(page 155)*

Main Courses... Light Ideas for Meat Lovers

IF you're a minimalist where meat is concerned, "light and spicy" cooking is for you!

The most interesting cuisines hail from the spots on the globe where meat has always been in limited supply. Creative cooks have needed to str-r-retch it with grains, beans, and veggies... and heighten its flavor with strongly flavored ingredients like herbs and spices, onions, garlic, tomatoes, and chili peppers.

In this chapter we show the "light and spicy" cook how to creatively combine minimum amounts of meat with healthy high-fiber ingredients. We use only the leanest cuts of meat, whether beef, veal, lamb, pork, or ham.

The "Red Dread"—the belief that all red meat is bad for you—appears to be abating. Today's nutrition-wise shopper knows that lean beef in moderation is perfectly acceptable.

One reason: lean beef is more readily available than a decade ago. Beef is slimmer now. Those cattle-fattening farms have been remodeled into slim-down spas featuring diet cuisine, and that leads to leaner meat.

Another reason: meat marketers have launched a campaign to let shoppers know that not all cuts of beef are high in fat. (Some beef cuts are leaner than some chicken parts!) Beef grade labels have been redefined so that lean beef is more salable, and thus more available.

A decade ago you couldn't buy lean meat to save your life! Most of it was shipped off to meat-packing plants. The reason? The government meat-grading system damned leanness with faint praise, calling it "Good," while beef that was riddled with fat was labeled "Prime" (the fattest) and "Choice."

"Good" just wasn't good enough to sell meat. On a scale of 1 to 10, it was a 1 in the public perception. The "Good" label was giving lean beef a bum steer!

Beef lower in fat became the goal not only of doctors and dieticians but of cattle ranchers, meat distributors, and supermarketers as well: lean beef is cheaper to produce and sell. So, in 1986, Public Voice for Food and Health Policy, a Washington, DC–based advocacy group for nutrition, petitioned the USDA to change the name of the "Good" grade to "Select" in order to "end discrimination against lean beef and encourage the industry to raise leaner cattle."

The "Select" label is voluntary. Not all supermarket chains participate in the government grading program, but many markets have their own "private label" denoting leanness.

As people became more health conscious, many supermarket chains acted before the government and reworded their grade labels. They responded to public interest in leaner beef by buying ungraded lean beef—the kind of meat the USDA would have labeled "Good"—and applying their own "Light" or "Lean" or "Diet" label. So the first step in beef shopping for the weight wary is: Read the label.

PAPAYA MEAT TENDERIZER

The active ingredient in commercial meat tenderizer is the enzyme papain, which is found in the papaya plant. Primitive cooks were the first ones to use "meat tenderizer." They found that they could soften up any tough hide by wrapping it in papaya leaves. When you sprinkle bargain beefsteak with meat tenderizer, you're doing essentially the same thing. Meat tenderizers are harmless to human tissue; your own digestive enzymes are many times more powerful than the natural enzyme in commercial meat tenderizer.

How can meat tenderizer save you pennies and pounds? Leaner cuts and grades of beef are often significantly less costly than either "Prime" or "Choice" meats. The latter, however, are more tender precisely because of the fat that is marbled through the meat. But thanks to papain, you can enjoy the tenderness of "Prime" at a "Good" price.

Here's my favorite technique for a broiled or barbecued beef round steak:

1. Choose a lean beef round steak at least 2 inches thick. (Anything thinner should be pan-fried.)
2. Allow the steak to reach room temperature wrapped in plastic or waxed paper.
3. Unwrap, then moisten the meat with tepid tap water. Sprinkle liberally with meat tenderizer, about ½ teaspoon per pound. Do not add salt if the tenderizer contains salt. Sprinkle with any other nonsalty seasonings you prefer: onion or garlic powder, for example, or dried herb mixtures.
4. Puncture the meat all over with a fork, angel-food cutter, or deep-penetrating, steel-tipped tenderizing device.
5. Preheat broiler or barbecue. Broil or barbecue about 2 inches from heat source, turning once, until steak is desired doneness. It will be most tender if served medium rare, sliced very thinly against the grain.

Here are a few points to remember about meat tenderizer:

- Tenderizer works best at room temperature, slows down under refrigeration, stops altogether once meat is heated or frozen. If you want to pre-tenderize meat for the freezer,

treat it first, then store in the refrigerator overnight before transferring to the freezer.
- Most meat tenderizers contain salt, so no salt should be added to tenderized meat. Also, avoid soy sauce, onion salt, or other salty seasonings. Those on salt-free diets should avoid using salty meat tenderizers.
- Foods that are naturally tender can become unpleasantly mushy if tenderizer is added. Never add tenderizer to hamburger or any ground meats. There's no point using tenderizer on young chicken or turkey, on fish or seafood.
- Keep in mind that tenderized meat will cook in about 25 percent less time. Adjust your cooking time accordingly or your steak may be overdone.
- Large roasts can be tenderized by combining the powdered tenderizer with warm water. Use a bulb-type baster with an inoculator needle end to "inject" the roast with the tenderizing liquid. (These handy devices are available in kitchen supply stores.)
- For safety's sake, be sure that everything used to tenderize meat is scrupulously clean, including your hands—particularly if the meat is to be served rare. (Remember: meat that is too rare can be a health hazard.)

LIGHT BEEF COOKING GUIDE

Much of the now fashionable "light" cuisine is centered on dressing up poultry and seafood with exotic ingredients and spicy sauces. But if you favor steak over sushi, and roast beef over bouillabaisse, today's new-wave cuisine seems to leave you out in the cold.

If you believe everything you read, you might think that your beef-loving ways will lead to pudgy perdition and cholesterol-stiffened arteries. Not so! Much of today's beef is leaner and slimmer than the fat-marbled steaks and roasts of the past. By shopping wisely and following our Light Beef Cooking Guide, you can still indulge your red-blooded meat passion . . . without a lot of calories!

Light roast beef: For the tenderest of the lean,

moderately priced cuts, choose a fat-trimmed top round roast. Season as you wish: salt, garlic salt or onion salt, pepper, herbs. Place the roast on a rack in an open pan and insert a meat thermometer in the center. Do not cover. Bake at 300 degrees until the thermometer indicates desired doneness—rare or medium, never well done (140 degrees is the United States Department of Agriculture recommendation). Remove the roast from the oven and let sit 10 to 15 minutes before carving.

Light broiled steak: For the leanest of the tender, luxury cuts, choose fat-trimmed tenderloin (filet mignon) cut to desired thickness. Preheat the broiler or fire up the barbecue, and arrange the steaks on the rack, 3 to 4 inches from the heat source. One-inch thick steaks should be broiled about 3 minutes each side for rare, 4 minutes for medium.

Less expensive, but still tender, steaks in the low-calorie category include top round steak and flank steak. To increase tenderness without adding flavor, sprinkle the steak on both sides with unseasoned meat tenderizer, following label directions. Puncture the meat with a fork to allow the tenderizer to penetrate, then broil according to preceding directions. (Tenderizer is salty, so add no salt.)

Light "pan-fried" steaks with no fat added: Pan-fry tenderloin, top round, or flank steak in a nonstick skillet that has been liberally prepared with cooking spray for no-fat frying. Put the steak in the skillet over a moderate flame and fry without turning until juices appear on the surface. Turn with a spatula or tongs and brown the other side. One-inch steaks will require about 3 minutes each side for rare, 4 minutes per side for medium. Make a cut with a sharp knife to determine doneness.

Light hamburgers: Buy only the leanest ground beef, labeled "diet lean." Or for the lowest fat content, have a beef bottom round roast or lean chuck arm roast trimmed of fat and ground to order. Gently shape into 1-inch thick patties, without pressing. Broil or pan-fry, following the same directions for steak. (Never add meat tenderizer to ground meat, because it makes the texture unpleasantly mushy.)

Light meat loaf: Buy only the leanest ground beef (see preceding paragraph on light hamburgers). This is particularly important with meat loaf because the fat will be absorbed by the other ingredients rather than draining away.

For 2 pounds of lean ground beef, add 2 eggs or equivalent no-cholesterol egg substitute, 4 slices dry calorie-reduced bread made into crumbs, and ½ cup fresh skim milk. Optional ingredients include: 1 cup chopped onions, 1 clove garlic, minced, 2 teaspoons salt, ¼ teaspoon pepper. Bake in a loaf pan for 1 hour at 350 degrees. This makes 10 servings, 160 calories each; 10 calories less per serving with egg substitute; optional ingredients add 10 calories per serving.

You can vary the recipe by adding any or all of the following: 1 teaspoon dried herbs, 2 tablespoons ketchup, chili, or Worcestershire sauce, a dash of Tabasco. If you wish, replace the milk with 1 cup undrained tomatoes, mashed. Replace or combine the onion with chopped celery, bell peppers, shredded carrots, or a combination of these fresh raw chopped vegetables.

VEAL IS EXTRA LEAN

Veal is the oft-touted alternative to beef: always tender and lean—and luscious despite its low fat and calorie content. Veal is baby beef and,

---

LEAN BEEF: A BETTER BUY

▰▰▰

The calorie count for boneless beefsteak can range from 600 per pound for fat-trimmed round steak all the way up to 1,800 or more for prime rib. What's worse: the more you pay—in cost as well as calories—the less you get! Because of shrinkage, 1 pound of premium-priced, fat-marbled beef barely serves 2, while 1 pound of the leanest, least-fattening budget beefsteak can serve 4 the same amount of protein.

like all meat from young animals, has relatively little fat. Trouble is, they charge you for the steak it could have been!

While the so-called milk-fed veal cutlets are premium priced, the less expensive, more humanely raised pink veal offers the same low-fat advantages.

For an even better bargain, look for ground veal. Ground turkey can also substitute for veal in any of these recipes.

Vealburger should not contain any added fat. If properly packaged, it will be less than 15 percent fat and under 575 calories a pound, compared with ordinary hamburger, which in many instances can be 30 percent fat and nearly 1,800 calories a pound.

MAKE YOUR OWN "VEALBURGER"

If you can't find vealburger, you can make your own from veal stew meat. It's easy to do in a meat grinder, an electric mixer equipped with a grinder, or in a food processor fitted with the steel blade. Put the lean, fat-trimmed veal cubes into the work bowl, then pulse just until coarsely chopped. Don't overprocess. Processing your own vealburger assures that its fat content is low.

You can also add seasonings as you process: a clove of garlic, a few basil leaves, a squirt of lemon, or a pinch of nutmeg. If you add a few tablespoons of plain low-fat yogurt or part-skim ricotta cheese to a pound of veal stew meat as you process it, the white color will be that of "milk-fed" veal.

LAMB IS POPULAR ALL OVER THE WORLD

Americans are just beginning to discover the pleasures of lamb, a lean and tender meat that's popular all over the world. Like veal, lamb is young. Despite the lack of fatty marbling, even the leanest cuts are reliably tender. Lamb wears most of its fat on the outside where it's easily trimmable. Consequently, the lean meat of roasted leg of lamb is under 850 calories a pound.

Unlike veal, however, lamb is a red meat and has lots of hearty flavor. If you're a red-blooded meat-lover, lamb is your dish. (Contrary to the currently vogue-ish notion, it's *not* necessary to forgo all 4-footed foods in favor of feathers and fins. Not all meat, and not every cut of meat, is fattening.)

LAMB IS BEST SERVED MEDIUM RARE

Many older cookbooks and meat thermometers do lamb a disservice by promoting overcooking. The general agreement today, however, is that lamb is at its luscious best if served medium rare, still slightly pink in the middle. This has the added advantage of ensuring that any meat earmarked for future meals will also be moist and tender.

There is only one accurate way to determine when a roast leg of lamb is done to perfection: a meat thermometer. Insert the thermometer into the lamb so that the tip rests in the very center of the meat.

Keep in mind that lamb is medium rare at 140 to 145 degrees. At 160 degrees it will be medium well, and at 170 degrees lamb is "well done" (which really means "overcooked" by contemporary standards). With only a few degrees of difference between lamb as you like it and undercooked or overcooked lamb, it's easy to see why a meat thermometer to check inner doneness is a must-have investment!

HOW TO ROAST A LEG OF LAMB

1. Thaw in the refrigerator, if frozen, then allow 20 to 25 minutes roasting time per pound. While it's safe to cook lamb from the frozen state, you must increase the cooking time from 30 to 50 percent, and you must delay inserting the meat thermometer.
2. Preheat the oven to 325 degrees. Arrange the roast on a rack in a roasting pan. Insert a meat

thermometer in the meatiest part, not touching bone. Do not cover or add water.

3. Sprinkle with salt, pepper, herbs, garlic, or other seasonings. Our favorite is Middle Eastern: lemon juice, mint, oregano, garlic, cinnamon, and nutmeg.

Other seasoning suggestions:
French: white wine, garlic, tarragon, onion
Italian: red wine, garlic, oregano, basil, onion
Middle European: lemon juice, onion, minced fresh dill
Polynesian: soy sauce, unsweetened pineapple juice, ground ginger
Indian: apple juice, garlic, curry powder, cumin seeds

4. Roast until meat thermometer indicates desired temperature.
5. Remove from oven and let sit about 10 to 15 minutes before carving. (Each serving: 3½ ounces cooked, lean only.)

MICROWAVED LEG OF LAMB ROAST

The American Lamb Council provides these directions for cooking a bone-in leg of lamb in a full-power microwave oven:

1. Brush leg of lamb with desired seasonings. Cover end of small leg bone with aluminum foil. (NOTE: Follow manufacturer's directions for use of aluminum foil; too much foil can damage oven.) Arrange on trivet in glass or ceramic dish. Place in microwave and follow manufacturer's directions, allowing cooking time of 9 to 10 minutes per pound for rare meat.
2. After half of total cooking time, rotate dish half turn and remove foil. Baste lamb with drippings; continue cooking until done. If some parts begin to overbrown, cover at three-quarters of cooking time with bits of aluminum foil where necessary (see note above).
3. At end of cooking time, remove roast from oven, insert thermometer in thickest area of meat; do not allow thermometer to touch any bone. After 2 minutes, read thermometer. At 140 to 145 degrees, lamb will be slightly pink in the middle. For medium-done lamb, roast 11 minutes per pound or to a temperature of 160 degrees. Let roast rest for 15 minutes before carving. (Meat will continue to cook after removal from microwave oven.) Serve on preheated platter.

PORK AND HAM DON'T HAVE TO BE PUDGY

Pork and ham are regularly ignored by calorie-conscious cooks on the assumption that they're high in fat and calories. Just like chickens and cows, however, pigs have been watching what they eat. So today's little piggy comes to market a lot leaner than in the past.

Have you needlessly crossed pork off your menu in the mistaken notion that all pork is fattening? If so, you're a decade behind the times. If you shop wisely, trim fat and cook without adding unneeded calories, there's no reason why pork can't be part of your healthy eating. Of course, there are pork products that still belong on the waistline-watcher's forbidden list: spareribs, sausage, bacon, and high-fat luncheon meats. But then there are other cuts of pork and ham that are so lean that they can be used without qualms. The best of these are center-cut pork chops and ham steaks, both trimmed of fat.

The leanest cut of pork comes from the leg, the pork equivalent of a beef round steak. Trimmed of all fat, it's only 62 calories per ounce. This cut of pork is known by a variety of names: fresh (uncured) ham steak, pork steak, pork leg steak, pork leg slice, and fresh ham slice.

The word *ham* actually refers to pork leg—fresh or cured. When this cut of meat is "cured," it's processed with salt, sugar, and preservatives and smoked, turning a characteristic pink color from its original white. Most cured hams and ham products available in the supermarket are cooked and ready to eat—or heat and eat—and will say so on the label.

BEEF

DEVILED FLANK STEAK AU POIVRE WITH RED WINE

1   flank steak (about 1½ pounds)
2   tablespoons Dijon-style mustard
1   teaspoon garlic paste
2   tablespoons minced onion or 2 teaspoons dried onion flakes
2   tablespoons whole black peppercorns
½   cup dry red wine

1. Score the flank steak diagonally on both sides with a sharp steak knife. Spread one side of the steak liberally with mustard and garlic. Sprinkle with onion and peppercorns.

2. In a large nonstick skillet or electric frying pan prepared with cooking spray, brown steak quickly over high heat, turning to brown evenly. Remove to a cutting board and set aside.

3. In the skillet, bring wine to a boil over high heat, then simmer until slightly reduced. Meanwhile, arrange steak on a chopping board and slice very thinly against the grain. Pour red wine over steak slices and serve immediately. Serve with rice if desired.

MAKES 6 SERVINGS, 185 CALORIES EACH; RICE ADDS 110 CALORIES PER ½-CUP SERVING.

CREOLE-STYLE PEPPER STEAK

1   medium flank steak (about 1¼ pounds)
2   cloves garlic, mashed
5   or 6 bay leaves
½   teaspoon each dried oregano and thyme
2   teaspoons cracked pepper
     Salt to taste

1. Place flank steak on a cutting board. Use a very sharp knife to make shallow, diagonal cuts about 1 inch apart across the steak in a criss-cross diamond design. Don't make the cuts too deep. Repeat on the other side. Sprinkle surface of the steak evenly with seasonings, then roll. Cover and refrigerate for at least 1 hour to allow seasonings to penetrate.

2. Unroll steak and remove garlic cloves and bay leaves. Broil flank steak 3 or 4 inches from heat source to desired doneness. Or pan-fry the steak in a nonstick skillet slick with cooking spray. Slice meat very thinly against grain.

MAKES 4 SERVINGS, 205 CALORIES EACH.

COCONUT STEAK

1   small flank steak (about 1 pound)
2   tablespoons light soy sauce
1   tablespoon lemon or lime juice
1   teaspoon each ground ginger and curry powder
1   cup water
1   large onion, halved and thinly sliced
1   green bell pepper, seeded and sliced
1   clove garlic, minced
2   or 3 bay leaves
4   tablespoons flaked dried coconut

1. On a cutting board, score steak with a sharp knife in diagonal criss-cross pattern on both sides. Combine soy sauce, lemon juice, ginger, curry, and ¼ cup water. Transfer steak to a shallow plate; spoon on soy mixture and roll up steak. Cover and refrigerate 1 hour to allow flavoring to penetrate.

2. In a large nonstick skillet or electric frying pan prepared with cooking spray, brown steak quickly on both sides over high heat. Remove to cutting board. Combine remaining ingredients in skillet, reserving 2 tablespoons shredded coconut. Cover, bring to a boil, and simmer for 2 minutes. Uncover and continue to cook until most liquid evaporates and onion and pepper are crisp-tender.

3. Meanwhile, slice steak against grain into thin slices, which will be very rare inside. Stir steak strips into skillet. Cook and stir to desired doneness. Remove bay leaves. Sprinkle with remaining coconut and serve immediately.

MAKES 4 SERVINGS, 220 CALORIES EACH.

MEXICAN BEEF STIR-FRY

1   tablespoon vegetable oil
1   teaspoon ground cumin
1   teaspoon dried oregano
1   clove garlic, minced
1   red bell pepper, seeded and cut in thin strips
1   medium onion, cut in thin wedges
1   or 2 jalapeño peppers, cut in slivers
1   pound fat-trimmed beef top round steak, cut in ⅛-inch strips
3   cups shredded romaine lettuce

1. Combine oil, cumin, oregano, and garlic; heat half of the mixture in a large nonstick frying pan or skillet over moderate heat. Add bell pepper, onion, and jalapeño (for milder flavor, remove interior ribs and seeds of jalapeño); stir-fry for 2 to 3 minutes or until crisp-tender. Remove from pan and reserve.

2. Add remaining oil mixture to pan. Stir-fry beef strips for 1 to 2 minutes. Return vegetables to pan and heat through. Serve beef mixture over lettuce.

MAKES 4 SERVINGS, 290 CALORIES EACH.

MICROWAVED SPICY BEEF IN TORTILLAS

6   flour tortillas (8-inch diameter)
1   tablespoon vegetable oil
1   pound fat-trimmed beef top round steak, cut in ⅛-inch strips
½   cup chopped onion
½   teaspoon chili powder
¼   teaspoon each dried oregano and ground cumin
½   teaspoon salt, or to taste
1⅓ cups shredded lettuce
½   cup Salsa (recipe follows)
1   ounce Cheddar cheese, shredded
2   tablespoons plain low-fat yogurt

1. Press each tortilla into a 10-ounce glass custard cup. Microwave on high power (100%) for 2 minutes; rotate cups and continue cooking on high power 1 to 2 minutes more (or consult microwave manufacturer's directions). Carefully remove tortillas and cool on wire rack.

2. Spread oil in microwave-safe 11- by 7-inch dish. Layer beef and onion over bottom. Sprinkle with a combination of chili, oregano, and cumin. Cover with wax paper; microwave on medium power for 9 to 11 minutes or until meat is slightly pink, stirring 3 times. Sprinkle with salt; let stand for 2 minutes.

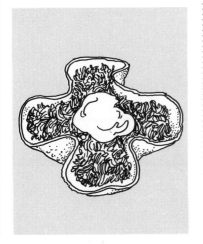

3. Meanwhile, place ⅓ cup lettuce in each tortilla. Divide meat mixture among tortillas and top with equal amounts of salsa, cheese, and yogurt. Serve immediately.

MAKES 6 SERVINGS, 310 CALORIES EACH.

❖❖❖

SALSA

1   jalapeño pepper, minced
1   clove garlic, minced
1   sprig cilantro or parsley, chopped
1   teaspoon vegetable oil
1   large ripe tomato, seeded and chopped
2   tablespoons minced green onion
1½ tablespoons fresh lime juice
1½ teaspoons red wine vinegar
     Salt to taste

1. In small skillet, cook and stir jalapeño, garlic, and cilantro in hot oil for 1 minute; then remove from heat.

2. Combine remaining ingredients; then stir in jalapeño mixture.

MAKES APPROXIMATELY 1 CUP, 115 CALORIES TOTAL.

❖❖❖

SPEEDY SZECHUAN BEEF AND VEGGIES

1   package (10 ounces) frozen oriental vegetables or mixed vegetables, thawed
½   cup thinly sliced onion or celery
¼   cup cold water
¾   cup tomato juice
1   cup leanest roast beef, sliced (about 5 ounces)
1   to 2 tablespoons light soy sauce
⅛   teaspoon ground ginger or pumpkin pie spice

1. Combine vegetables, onion, and water in a nonstick saucepan or skillet and bring to a boil. Cover and simmer for 2 minutes. Stir in remaining ingredients. Cook, stirring, over moderately low heat until liquid evaporates to a thick glaze—3 to 4 minutes.

MAKES 2 SERVINGS, 230 CALORIES EACH.

❖❖❖

HAWAIIAN MEATBALLS WITH PINEAPPLE AND PEPPERS

2   pounds lean beef round, trimmed of fat and ground, or diet-lean hamburger
2   eggs or 4 egg whites or equivalent egg substitute
6   tablespoons light soy sauce
½   teaspoon ground ginger
2   tablespoons cornstarch
2   cans (16 ounces each) unsweetened pineapple chunks, drained, with juice reserved
3   bell peppers (red, green, yellow, or 1 of each), seeded and diced
3   tablespoons honey

1. Combine meat, eggs, 3 tablespoons soy sauce, and ginger. Shape into 36 small meatballs. Broil in a single layer, turning, until lightly browned on all sides; set aside.

2. In a saucepan, combine cornstarch with juice from the pineapple; cook, stirring, over moderately low heat until simmering and thickened. Add pineapple chunks, bell peppers, and honey; cover and simmer for 10 minutes. Add meatballs and heat through. Pour into chafing dish and keep warm.

MAKES 36 MEATBALLS, 60 CALORIES EACH.

Variation

Hot and spicy style: Substitute 1 or 2 finely chopped fresh jalapeño peppers for 1 of the bell peppers.

SPANISH BEEF STEW WITH GAZPACHO-STYLE VEGETABLES

1 pound lean beef bottom round steak, trimmed of fat and cut in 1½-inch cubes
3 tablespoons light Italian salad dressing
1 can (16 ounces) stewed tomatoes
1 onion, chopped
1 green bell pepper, seeded and sliced
½ cup water
1 bay leaf
  Garlic salt and black pepper to taste
1 package (10 ounces) frozen zucchini

1. In a small bowl, mix meat and salad dressing and marinate, covered, at room temperature for 20 minutes. Drain and discard marinade. In a nonstick skillet prepared with cooking spray, sear meat cubes quickly over high heat, turning to brown evenly.

2. Add remaining ingredients except zucchini. Cover and simmer over moderately low heat until meat is tender—about 1 hour. Stir in zucchini. Simmer, uncovered, until most of the liquid evaporates. Remove bay leaf before serving.

MAKES 4 SERVINGS, 245 CALORIES EACH.

POLYNESIAN BEEF KEBABS

14 to 16 ounces lean roast beef or leftover steak, trimmed of fat and cut in 2-inch cubes
1 cup fresh pineapple (not canned)
1 teaspoon ground ginger
  Fresh basil leaves or ½ teaspoon dried basil
1 tablespoon lemon juice
2 teaspoons light soy sauce
2 teaspoons sesame oil

1. Stir beef with pineapple, ginger, and basil. Marinate for 20 minutes at room temperature or all day in refrigerator.

2. Drain and reserve marinade. Arrange alternate chunks of beef and pineapple on skewers (with fresh basil leaves between, if available). Combine lemon juice, soy sauce, and oil; brush on skewers. Place skewers on broiler rack 2 inches from heat source; broil for approximately 4 minutes. Turn and broil 3 to 4 minutes more.

MAKES 4 SERVINGS, 265 CALORIES EACH.

CROCKED CURRIED BEEF

2 pounds lean beef round, trimmed of fat and cut in 2-inch cubes
1 tablespoon curry powder
1 teaspoon cumin seeds
½ teaspoon ground cinnamon
¼ teaspoon each ground ginger, cloves, and allspice
1 onion, minced
1 clove garlic, minced
  Juice of 1 lemon
2 tablespoons raisins
1 tablespoon light soy sauce, or salt to taste (optional)
2 teaspoons cornstarch
¼ cup cold water
  Optional garnishes: yogurt, lemon wedges, and chopped fresh parsley or cilantro

1. Combine ingredients, except cornstarch and cold water, in a crock cooker. No pre-browning of the meat or pre-heating of the cooker is needed. Cover tightly and set on slow heat. Cook 16 to 18 hours or until meat is very tender. Gently stir meat once or twice during cooking time.

2. Twenty or 30 minutes before serving time, stir the cornstarch into cold water and stir this mixture into the crock cooker. Cover and continue to cook at lowest heat, stirring once or twice, until liquid thickens. Serve with dollops of yogurt, lemon wedges, and chopped fresh parsley or cilantro leaves as a garnish, if desired.

MAKES 8 SERVINGS, 175 CALORIES EACH.

Variation

Crocked Curried Lamb: Substitute lean lamb stew meat for the beef.

SPEEDY SUKIYAKI

Packaged shredded coleslaw can add crunch to hot dishes. This speedy version of the lean Japanese beef dish, sukiyaki, uses mixed frozen vegetables as well.

1 flank steak, trimmed of fat (about 1½ pounds)
1 large onion, sliced
1 cup sliced mushrooms
6 tablespoons light soy sauce
½ cup sake or sherry
1 package (10 ounces) frozen oriental vegetables, partly thawed
1 package (8 ounces) coleslaw vegetables (from supermarket produce department)

1. In a large nonstick skillet prepared with cooking spray, brown steak quickly over high heat, turning to brown evenly. Transfer to a cutting board. Slice diagonally into ⅛-inch-thick

strips. Slice strips in half width-wise; set aside.

2. Combine onion and mushrooms in the skillet; stir-fry for 3 minutes. Add soy sauce, sake, and all vegetables. Cook, stirring frequently, 4 to 5 minutes more. (Don't overcook; vegetables should be crisp.) Add steak strips; heat through.

MAKES 6 SERVINGS, 230 CALORIES EACH.

❦

SPICY SLOW-COOKED BEEF, MALAYSIAN STYLE

1   pound lean beef bottom round
    steak, trimmed of fat and
    cut in 1½-inch cubes
1   onion, chopped
1   clove garlic, finely chopped
1   tablespoon chopped fresh
    jalapeño pepper
1   tablespoon prepared mustard
1   tablespoon light soy sauce
1   teaspoon each coconut
    flavoring and ground
    coriander
½   teaspoon ground ginger
¼   teaspoon ground cumin

1. Combine ingredients in an electric crockery cooker and stir gently to coat meat evenly. Cover and cook at low setting according to manufacturer's directions, until meat is very tender—about 12 to 18 hours. Serve with brown rice and steamed vegetables if desired.

MAKES 4 SERVINGS, 175 CALORIES EACH.

SPICY LEAN CORNED BEEF

3   to 4 pounds lean corned beef
    round (not brisket)
    Water to cover
1   onion, sliced
5   cloves garlic, chopped
8   or 10 bay leaves
1   tablespoon each red pepper
    flakes, coriander seeds,
    black peppercorns, whole
    cloves, and ground ginger

1. To remove excess saltiness from corned beef, place in a pot with water, cover, and simmer for 30 minutes. Discard the cooking water and replace with fresh water. Add onion, garlic, and seasonings. Cover and simmer until meat is fork-tender—90 minutes or more, depending on size.

2. Let cool to room temperature, then discard water and spices. Chill. Slice very thin.

ABOUT 45 CALORIES PER OUNCE OF MEAT.

❦

CAJUN BEEF RAGOUT

1½ pounds lean beef bottom
    round steak, trimmed of fat
    and cut in 1½-inch cubes
1   can (8 ounces) tomatoes,
    undrained
2   ribs celery, sliced
2   onions, sliced
2   cloves garlic, minced
¼   cup dry red wine
¼   cup water
2   tablespoons raisins
1   tablespoon red wine vinegar
¼   teaspoon ground ginger
    Salt and pepper to taste
    Hot red pepper sauce to taste
    (optional)
4   carrots, sliced

1. In a nonstick frying pan, electric skillet, or Dutch oven prepared with cooking spray, brown beef cubes quickly over high heat, turning to brown

evenly. Drain fat, if any, from pan and discard.

2. Add remaining ingredients except carrots. Cover and simmer until meat is very tender—about 2 hours. Add carrots and simmer, covered, another 20 minutes or until carrots are tender. Uncover and simmer, stirring frequently, until nearly all liquid evaporates. Serve with brown rice, if desired.

MAKES 6 SERVINGS, 210 CALORIES EACH; BROWN RICE ADDS 115 CALORIES PER ½-CUP SERVING.

❦

BEEF POT ROAST TEX-MEX STYLE

4   to 5 pounds boneless beef
    bottom round roast,
    trimmed of fat
2   tablespoons Worcestershire
    sauce
2   tablespoons lime or lemon
    juice
1   tablespoon prepared mustard
2   cloves garlic, minced
1   can (6 ounces) spicy tomato
    juice
½   cup chili sauce
1   or 2 jalapeño peppers, finely
    chopped
2   tablespoons chopped fresh
    cilantro or parsley
2   teaspoons cumin seeds

1. Put meat in shallow plastic dish just large enough to hold it. Combine Worcestershire, lime juice, mustard, garlic. Spread mixture over meat. Cover and refrigerate overnight.

2. Roast meat in preheated 325-degree oven for 1 hour. Combine remaining ingredients; pour over meat. Cover and roast 3 to 4 hours more at 275 degrees, until meat is very tender. Baste occasionally with pan juices (thin with a little boiling water if necessary). Slice thinly to serve.

APPROXIMATELY 200 CALORIES PER 3½-OUNCE SERVING.

ROLLED BEEF FLANK STEAK, SPICY SAUERBRATEN STYLE

1½ pounds flank or top round steak, cut thin for rolling
1 tablespoon prepared mustard
6 tablespoons plain low-fat yogurt
3 tablespoons dried soup vegetables
1 teaspoon mixed poultry herbs
   Pinch each ground nutmeg, allspice, and cloves
1 cup dry red wine or tomato-vegetable juice

1. Spread mustard on one side of beef. Stir together remaining ingredients except wine; spread over mustard. Roll steak tightly; cover and refrigerate for 24 to 48 hours.

2. Pour on wine. Cover and roast in a preheated 350-degree oven for 1 hour. Uncover and roast until meat is very tender—30 to 45 minutes more. Baste occasionally and add more wine or a little water, if needed. Slice thinly to serve.

MAKES 6 SERVINGS, 185 CALORIES EACH.

❦

HOT 'N' SPICY CHILI MAÑANA

4 cups lean cooked diced beef or poultry
12 ounces light beer
1 can (8 ounces) plain tomato sauce
1 cup chopped onion
4 cloves garlic, minced
¼ cup chopped fresh jalapeño peppers
2 to 4 tablespoons chili powder, or to taste
2 tablespoons chopped fresh cilantro or parsley
1 teaspoon each dried oregano and ground cumin
   Salt to taste

1. Combine ingredients in a saucepan and simmer for 25 to 35 minutes or until thick. Serve with rice or beans, if desired.

MAKES 8 SERVINGS, 190 CALORIES EACH.

❦

CUBAN SPICY BEEF

1 pound lean roast beef, cut in cubes
1 can (8 ounces) stewed tomatoes, undrained
1 can (8 ounces) plain tomato sauce
¼ cup raisins
1 small onion, minced
1 clove garlic, minced
1 teaspoon cornstarch
1 teaspoon cumin seeds
1 teaspoon chili powder, or to taste
¼ teaspoon ground cinnamon

1. Combine all ingredients in a saucepan and stir well. Cover and bring to a slow boil. Simmer for 10 minutes. Serve with rice, if desired.

MAKES 4 SERVINGS, 230 CALORIES EACH.

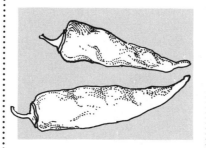

BEEF AND PEPPER CHILI

1¼ pounds beef top round steak, trimmed of fat
½ cup coarsely chopped onion
1 large clove garlic, minced
1½ teaspoons dried oregano
1 teaspoon ground cumin
½ teaspoon hot red pepper flakes
   Salt to taste
4 medium tomatoes, chopped
½ cup water
1 can (4 ounces) whole green chilies
1 tablespoon cornstarch
¼ cup sliced green onions

1. Brown beef in a non-stick Dutch oven well prepared with cooking spray. Add onion and garlic, and continue cooking, stirring occasionally, until browned. Combine the oregano, cumin, red pepper, and salt; sprinkle over beef. Stir in 3 cups tomatoes and the water. Cover tightly; bring to simmer. Cook 2 hours, until beef is tender.

2. Drain chilies and reserve liquid. Cut the chilies into ½-inch pieces; add to beef mixture. Combine cornstarch and reserved chili liquid; gradually stir into the pot until mixture thickens. Stir in remaining tomato, garnish with green onions, and serve.

MAKES 4 SERVINGS, 340 CALORIES EACH.

❦

BEEF TERIYAKI WITH MUSHROOMS

1½ pounds lean roast beef or leftover steak, trimmed of fat and cut in 2-inch cubes
½ cup pineapple juice
2 tablespoons Japanese-style soy sauce
1 clove garlic, minced
2 teaspoons ground ginger
12 ounces small whole mushrooms, washed
2 onions, quartered and separated into leaves
2 tablespoons salad oil

1. Combine beef with juice, soy sauce, garlic, and ginger in a plastic bag set into a bowl. Marinate for 2 hours or longer in refrigerator.

2. Drain and reserve marinade. Thread meat on skewers, alternating with mushrooms and onion leaves. Wipe lightly with oil. Broil about 4 inches from heat for 3 to 4 minutes. Turn and broil the other side 3 or 4 minutes more. Baste occasionally with reserved marinade.

MAKES 6 SERVINGS, 305 CALORIES EACH.

CURAÇAO-STYLE SPICY STUFFED PEPPERS AND EDAM CHEESE

One of my favorite hamburger dishes, this recipe was inspired by the Dutch West Indies specialty keshy yena, a favorite dish in Curaçao. In the original dish, a whole Edam cheese is hollowed out and filled with chopped peppers, onions, and a spicy ground beef mixture seasoned with raisins and spices. If you think that sounds like lots of calories . . . you're right!

This version turns the recipe "inside out"! We stuff peppers with a spicy lean meat mixture. More veggies, less fat, and fewer calories.

4   well-shaped bell peppers (green, red, and yellow)
1   pound lean ground beef
1   onion, chopped
½   cup chopped fresh mushrooms
2   hard-cooked eggs, coarsely chopped
1   large vine-ripe tomato, peeled and cubed
3   tablespoons white raisins
1   tablespoon chopped fresh jalapeño or other hot pepper
4   thin slices (2 ounces total) Edam cheese

1. Cut tops from bell peppers; discard stems but chop and reserve any pepper flesh surrounding stems. Remove seeds and membranes from pepper cases; stand cases in a small nonstick baking pan just large enough to hold them upright.

2. Prepare a nonstick skillet with cooking spray. Spread meat in a shallow layer and brown over moderate heat until underside is brown. Break into chunks; turn and brown lightly. Drain and discard any fat. Stir in onion and mushrooms; cook, stirring, just until beginning to brown. Remove from heat and stir in eggs, tomato, raisins, ja-lapeño, and reserved diced bell pepper. Spoon mixture into pepper cases.

3. Cover loosely with foil and bake in a preheated 350-degree oven for 35 to 40 minutes, until peppers are tender. Arrange Edam on top of each pepper case. Bake, uncovered, until cheese melts.

MAKES 4 SERVINGS, 360 CALORIES EACH.

❦

MEXICAN PIE

8   ounces lean ground beef round
    Garlic salt and black pepper to taste
5   tablespoons skim milk
1   cup biscuit mix (preferably whole wheat)
1   small onion, chopped
½   cup finely minced green bell pepper or fresh jalapeño or other hot pepper
2   vine-ripe tomatoes, peeled and diced
½   teaspoon each dried oregano and ground cumin
3   tablespoons light mayonnaise
½   cup plain low-fat yogurt
½   cup shredded part-skim mozzarella cheese

1. Spread meat in a shallow layer in a broiler pan and brown under the broiler. Drain and discard fat. Break meat into chunks; season with garlic salt and black pepper.

2. Prepare an 8- or 9-inch nonstick cake or pie pan with cooking spray. Using forks or a pastry blender, cut milk into biscuit mix until a soft dough forms. Spread dough in bottom and up the sides of pan. Put the browned beef in the bottom of the pie and sprinkle with onion, bell pepper, tomatoes, oregano, and cumin.

3. Blend mayonnaise with yogurt and spoon over top of pie; sprinkle with shredded cheese.

Bake in preheated 375-degree oven for 30 minutes. Remove from oven and wait 5 to 10 minutes before slicing into 6 wedges.

MAKES 6 SERVINGS, 220 CALORIES EACH.

❦

MEXICAN "PIÑATA-STYLE" MEATBALLS

Break them open and they're filled with flavor!

1½ pounds diet-lean ground beef
1   onion, minced
1   or 2 fresh jalapeño peppers, seeded and chopped, or 1 green bell pepper, seeded and chopped
6   tablespoons shredded extra-sharp Cheddar cheese
2   tablespoons fresh cilantro, chopped
1   clove garlic, minced
1   teaspoon ground cumin
    Pinch fresh or dried oregano
    Salt and pepper or lemon pepper to taste (optional)

1. Shape meat into 12 patties. Combine remaining ingredients. Divide mixture among tops of 6 flattened meat patties. Press another flattened patty on top of each; pinch edges together to enclose filling.

2. Broil or barbecue each filled patty for 2 to 3 minutes on each side.

MAKES 6 SERVINGS, 260 CALORIES EACH.

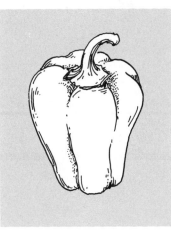

QUICK CURRIED BEEF

14 to 16 ounces lean roast beef or leftover steak
1 onion, sliced
1 clove garlic, minced (optional)
1 cup spicy tomato juice
2 tablespoons lemon juice
3 tablespoons raisins
1 teaspoon curry powder, or to taste
1 large firm red apple, cubed

1. On a cutting board, slice beef into 2-inch-long strips, discarding any fat; set aside. In a nonstick skillet prepared with cooking spray, heat onion and garlic, if desired, over moderately high heat until onion begins to brown lightly.

2. Stir in tomato and lemon juice, raisins and curry. Cook, stirring until most liquid evaporates and sauce thickens. At the last minute, stir in apple cubes and beef strips. Cook only until heated through. Apple should be crunchy and meat still pink in the middle. Serve immediately.

MAKES 4 SERVINGS, 285 CALORIES EACH.

VEAL

VEAL AND PIMIENTO PÂTÉ

8 slices high-fiber or whole wheat bread, dry or toasted
2 pounds lean veal, trimmed of fat and ground
2 eggs, beaten, or equivalent egg substitute
1 large red bell pepper (pimiento), seeded and minced
1 onion, minced
1 small pickle, minced
1 tablespoon minced fresh oregano or ½ teaspoon dried oregano
2 teaspoons garlic salt, or to taste
Pinch hot red pepper flakes or dash hot red pepper sauce

1. Moisten bread in tepid water; squeeze out moisture. Thoroughly mix with remaining ingredients; pack into a loaf pan to shape, smoothing the top flat. Invert on a shallow roasting pan; remove loaf pan. Bake in preheated 350-degree oven for 1 hour and 15 minutes or until meat thermometer inserted in center of loaf reads 170 degrees. Serve hot or chilled.

MAKES 10 DINNER SLICES, 205 CALORIES EACH, OR 15 SANDWICH SLICES, 135 CALORIES EACH; APPROXIMATELY 10 CALORIES LESS PER SLICE WITH EGG SUBSTITUTE.

❧

HUNGARIAN-SEASONED PAPRIKA VEALBURGERS

1 pound lean ground veal
½ cup plain low-fat yogurt
2 tablespoons Worcestershire sauce
1 tablespoon dried onion flakes
1 tablespoon paprika
Garlic salt and pepper to taste
2 cups sliced mushrooms

1. Combine all ingredients except mushrooms. Shape into 4 "cutlets." Arrange in a single layer on a baking pan; surround with mushrooms. Bake in preheated 475-degree oven, without turning, for 8 to 10 minutes.

MAKES 4 SERVINGS, 200 CALORIES EACH.

❧

ONE-PAN VEAL PAPRIKASH

12 ounces lean boneless veal stew meat, trimmed of all fat and cut in bite-size cubes
1 can (16 ounces) tomatoes, undrained
1½ cups water
½ cup red wine
3 ribs celery, sliced
1 large Spanish onion, chopped
1 clove garlic, minced
1 tablespoon paprika
2 teaspoons Worcestershire sauce
1 teaspoon prepared brown mustard
6 ounces uncooked curly noodles
½ cup plain low-fat yogurt
3 tablespoons minced fresh dill or parsley (optional)

1. Prepare a nonstick pan or pressure cooker with cooking spray. Brown meat over moderate heat, turning to brown evenly. Drain and discard any fat. Stir in remaining ingredients except noodles, yogurt, and dill. Cover and simmer until meat is tender—50 to 60 minutes in pan; 15 to 20 minutes in pressure cooker (follow manufacturer's directions).

2. Stir noodles into simmering liquid, a few at a time; simmer, uncovered, until noodles are tender and most liquid absorbed—12 to 15 minutes. Remove from heat and then stir in yogurt. Sprinkle with dill, if desired.

MAKES 4 MAIN-COURSE SERVINGS, 360 CALORIES EACH.

CHEESY VEAL LOAF

Yogurt makes this loaf taste even cheesier! Substitute ground turkey for the veal, if you like.

   1   pound ground veal
   ¾   cup rolled oats
   ½   cup plain low-fat yogurt
   1   egg, lightly beaten, or
        equivalent egg substitute
   ½   cup chopped onion
   ½   cup shredded extra-sharp
        American or Cheddar cheese
        Salt or garlic salt to taste
   3   tablespoons ketchup (optional)

   1. Combine all ingredients except ketchup; mix lightly. Pack into a nonstick loaf pan. Spread top with ketchup, if desired. Bake in preheated 350-degree oven for 1 hour.

MAKES 6 SERVINGS, 245 CALORIES EACH; 10 CALORIES LESS PER SERVING WITH EGG SUBSTITUTE; 10 CALORIES MORE PER SERVING WITH KETCHUP.

ITALIAN-SPICED VEAL "CUTLETS"

Ground veal shaped into the form of a "cutlet" is an easy and inexpensive stand-in for veal scaloppine.

   1   pound lean ground veal
   1   egg, beaten, or equivalent egg
        substitute
        Grated peel of 1 lemon
   ¼   teaspoon grated nutmeg
        Salt or onion salt and pepper
        to taste
   6   tablespoons Italian-seasoned
        bread crumbs
   2   teaspoons olive oil

   1. Combine all ingredients except bread crumbs and olive oil; mix lightly. Sprinkle the bread crumbs on a shallow plate. Divide the meat mixture in quarters and shape each into a flat "cutlet." Press cutlets into the bread crumbs, lightly coating both sides.

   2. In a large nonstick griddle or skillet prepared with cooking spray, heat 1 teaspoon of the olive oil over moderate heat. Brown cutlets on one side, add remaining teaspoon of oil, and turn cutlets to brown other side evenly. Cook for 2 to 3 minutes per side.

MAKES 4 SERVINGS, 235 CALORIES EACH; 10 CALORIES LESS PER SERVING WITH EGG SUBSTITUTE.

Variation

Poor Man's Veal Parmigiana: Follow preceding recipe. Top each serving with ½ cup oregano-seasoned tomato sauce and a thin (½-ounce) slice of part-skim mozzarella cheese.

ADDITIONAL CALORIES, 75.

※※

HAWAIIAN-STYLE VEAL "SPARERIBS"

Hawaiian barbecued ribs are usually high-calorie when they're made with fatty pork spareribs. This version is much leaner because it's made with low-calorie veal.

   2½   pounds lean breast of veal,
        trimmed of fat and cut in
        individual ribs
   1   can (8 ounces) crushed
        unsweetened juice-packed
        pineapple
   5   tablespoons ketchup
   ¼   cup vinegar
   3   tablespoons light soy sauce

   1. Place "riblets" in roasting pan in single layer. Bake in a preheated 425-degree oven for 20 to 25 minutes to brown meat and remove excess fat. Pour off all accumulated fat.

   2. Reduce oven temperature to 350 degrees. Combine remaining ingredients and pour over ribs. Cover pan with aluminum foil and return to oven. Bake for 1½ hours or until tender.

MAKES 8 SERVINGS, 240 CALORIES EACH.

Variation

Outdoor Cookout Version: Preheat hooded outdoor barbecue grill. Brown "riblets" on grill over moderate coals or heat. When well browned, transfer to shallow metal baking pan and add remaining ingredients. Cover pan with foil, close barbecue hood, and cook as above.

LAMB

DIJON-STYLE HERBED LAMB CHOPS

3   tablespoons white wine
2   tablespoons prepared Dijon-style mustard
1   clove garlic, minced
½   teaspoon each dried oregano and thyme
6   lean loin lamb chops, trimmed of fat (about 2 pounds total)

1. Mix well together wine, mustard, garlic, and herbs; brush on lamb chops. Broil 3 to 4 inches from heat source for 4 to 5 minutes per side depending on doneness desired. Best served rare.

EACH CHOP HAS APPROXIMATELY 75 CALORIES.

❦

CURRY-SPICED LAMB-STUFFED PEPPERS WITH RICE

4   well-shaped green bell peppers
1   can (8 ounces) tomatoes
1   small rib celery, minced
1   small onion, minced
5   tablespoons instant rice
¼   cup loosely packed chopped fresh cilantro or parsley
1   to 2 teaspoons curry powder, or to taste
1   teaspoon cumin seeds (optional)
    Salt or garlic salt and black pepper to taste
¾   cup lean ground lamb
¼   cup plain low-fat yogurt (optional)

1. Cut off and reserve tops of bell peppers; remove and discard seeds and membranes. Trim tops and mince usable pep-

per into a bowl. Drain tomatoes, reserving juice, and mash them. Add to minced pepper along with celery, onion, rice, cilantro, and seasonings and mix well.

2. Stand peppers in a shallow nonstick baking dish just large enough to hold them. Fill pepper cases with half the tomato-rice mixture. Stir ground lamb into remaining tomato-rice mixture and spoon into pepper cases so lamb mixture is on top and will brown. Bake in a preheated 350-degree oven for 1 hour, basting occasionally with reserved tomato juice. If desired, spoon on yogurt just before serving.

MAKES 4 SERVINGS, 145 CALORIES EACH; YOGURT ADDS 10 CALORIES PER SERVING.

Variation

Chili-Spiced Pork-Stuffed Peppers: Substitute fat-trimmed ground pork for lamb and chili powder for curry. Replace yogurt with 1 ounce shredded sharp Cheddar cheese, if desired. Cheddar adds 30 calories per serving.

❦

SKEWERED SESAME LAMB AND PINEAPPLE

1   can (20 ounces) juice-packed pineapple chunks
1   teaspoon ground ginger
    Fresh basil leaves or ½ teaspoon dried basil
1   pound leg-of-lamb steak, trimmed of fat and bone and cut in 1½-inch cubes
1   tablespoon lemon juice
2   teaspoons light soy sauce
2   teaspoons sesame oil

1. Drain pineapple juice into a bowl, reserving pineapple chunks in covered bowl in refrigerator until needed. Stir ginger and basil into juice and pour over lamb. Marinate, covered, 20

minutes at room temperature or all day in refrigerator.

2. Drain and reserve marinade. Arrange alternate chunks of lean lamb and pineapple on skewers, with fresh basil leaves between, if available. Combine lemon juice, soy sauce, and oil; brush over skewers. Place skewers on broiler rack 2 inches from heat source; broil for 4 minutes, just until heated through. Turn and broil 4 minutes more. Baste several times with reserved marinade.

MAKES 4 SERVINGS, 270 CALORIES EACH.

MEDITERRANEAN DILLED LAMB AND NOODLE CASSEROLE

3   cups uncooked curly noodles
2   cups boiling water
1   onion, chopped
2   cloves garlic, minced
    Juice and peel of 1 lemon
1   can (8 ounces) sliced stewed tomatoes
1   cup plain low-fat yogurt
1   pound lean lamb, trimmed of fat and ground
1½ cups mixed vegetable juice
2   tablespoons each chopped fresh dill and parsley
¼   teaspoon each dried oregano and savory
    Pinch each ground nutmeg and cinnamon
¼   cup bread crumbs

1. Layer ingredients in a 9-inch-square nonstick cake pan, adding them in the order given. Bake for 1 hour in a preheated 375-degree oven.

Note: This one-step recipe is a super time-saver, since neither noodles nor meat need to be precooked.

MAKES 6 SERVINGS, 315 CALORIES EACH.

※

MIDDLE EASTERN LAMB WITH PASTA PILAF

1	pound lean lamb, trimmed of fat and ground
5	tablespoons plain low-fat yogurt
1/4	cup wheat bran
2	cloves garlic, minced
2	tablespoons fresh or frozen mint or 2 teaspoons dried mint
2	teaspoons fresh oregano or 1/2 teaspoon dried oregano
1	teaspoon ground cinnamon
1/4	teaspoon ground nutmeg
	Salt and pepper to taste
	Lemon juice to taste
2	onions, halved and thinly sliced
6	ounces orzo (rice-shaped pasta)
1	ounce raisins
2	tablespoons chopped pistachio nuts or whole pine nuts
	Optional garnishes: lemon wedges, 6 tablespoons grated sharp Romano cheese

1. Combine lamb, yogurt, bran, and seasonings; shape into 18 small meatballs. Arrange in single layer on shallow nonstick roasting pan well prepared with cooking spray. Bake in a preheated 450-degree oven for 5 minutes, then turn meatballs. Add onion slices between meatballs. Return pan to oven and bake 5 minutes more.

2. Meanwhile, cook orzo in boiling, salted water according to package directions—8 to 10 minutes. Drain well. To serve, stir together hot drained orzo, raisins, pistachios, meatballs, and onions. If desired, serve with lemon wedges and a topping of cheese.

MAKES 6 SERVINGS, 265 CALORIES EACH; OPTIONAL INGREDIENTS ADD APPROXIMATELY 30 CALORIES PER SERVING.

※

LAMB SHISH KEBAB COOKED IN THE OVEN

1 1/2	pounds lean leg-of-lamb steak, trimmed of fat and bone and cut in 1 1/2-inch cubes
1/2	cup plain low-fat yogurt
1	clove garlic, minced
1/2	teaspoon each dried mint and dried marjoram or oregano
	Few drops liquid smoke seasoning or dash hickory-seasoned salt (optional)
	Black pepper to taste (optional)
2	onions
2	bell peppers (1 red, 1 green), seeded and cut in 1 1/2-inch squares

1. Combine lamb with yogurt, garlic, herbs, and seasoning. Refrigerate, covered, all day or overnight.

2. Peel and quarter onions, separate into leaves. On skewers, alternate the meat cubes with onion leaves and pepper squares. Brush skewers lightly with any remaining marinade. To oven barbecue: Suspend the skewers over the edges of a shallow baking pan. Roast in a preheated 450-degree oven for 30 to 40 minutes.

MAKES 6 SERVINGS, 190 CALORIES EACH.

PORK AND HAM

HAWAIIAN SWEET 'N' SOUR PORK

1	can (8 ounces) crushed juice-packed pineapple, with liquid
1/2	cup dill pickle relish or 1 dill pickle, chopped
2	tablespoons soy sauce
2	tablespoons sherry wine
4	cloves garlic, minced, or 1/2 teaspoon instant garlic
1	tablespoon molasses or 1 tablespoon plum preserves
1	can (2 ounces) sliced mushrooms (optional)
2	teaspoons fresh or dried ginger root (optional)
3	unpeeled purple plums, pitted and diced
1/4	cup water
3	ribs celery, sliced
2	onions, sliced
2	red or green bell peppers, seeded and sliced
12	ounces lean roast pork, trimmed of fat and cut in 1/2-inch cubes

1. In a nonstick skillet, stir together pineapple, relish, soy sauce, sherry, garlic, molasses, undrained mushrooms, if desired, and ginger, if desired. Add plums and water. Cover and simmer for 10 minutes.

2. Uncover and stir in celery, onions, and bell peppers. Return to a simmer, and cook for 5 minutes, stirring occasionally, until most liquid evaporates and mixture is quite thick. Stir in meat at the last minute, gently heating through.

MAKES 4 SERVINGS, 355 CALORIES EACH.

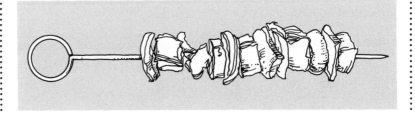

POLYNESIAN HAM WITH PINEAPPLE AND PEPPERS

1   can (6 ounces) unsweetened pineapple juice
1   tablespoon light soy sauce
4   teaspoons cornstarch
1   can (8 ounces) juice-packed pineapple chunks, with liquid
1   pound cooked lean ham, cut in 1-inch cubes
2   bell peppers (1 red, 1 green), seeded and cut in strips
1   onion, finely chopped
3   tablespoons golden raisins
1   tablespoon prepared mustard
1/4   teaspoon ground ginger

1. In a cold nonstick skillet, stir together juice, soy sauce, and cornstarch until cornstarch dissolves. Heat over moderately low heat, stirring, until thickened. Stir in remaining ingredients. Bring to a boil, cover, and simmer for 5 minutes or until heated through. Serve with rice, if desired.

MAKES 6 SERVINGS, 225 CALORIES EACH; RICE ADDS 110 CALORIES PER 1/2-CUP SERVING.

❧

SICILIAN-STYLE SAUSAGE PATTIES

2   pounds pork or veal shoulder, trimmed of fat and ground
1/2   cup Chianti wine
2   cloves garlic, minced
2   tablespoons minced fresh thyme or 2 teaspoons dried thyme
1   tablespoon paprika
2   teaspoons salt or smoke-flavored salt
1   teaspoon fennel seeds
1/4   teaspoon each black pepper and cayenne pepper, or to taste

1. Combine all ingredients and mix lightly. Shape into patties, 6 per pound of meat. (Raw patties may be frozen for later

use: Arrange them in a single layer on a cookie tin lined with aluminum foil. Cover with foil, label, and freeze. Patties may be barbecued or broiled without defrosting.)

2. Place patties 3 inches from heat source and broil or barbecue for 2 to 3 minutes per side (3 to 4 minutes per side if frozen). Be sure meat is cooked through.

MAKES 12 PATTIES, 130 CALORIES EACH WITH PORK; 110 CALORIES EACH WITH VEAL.

Note: It's not necessary to stuff meat mixtures into sausage casings. In fact, if you plan to barbecue, it's better to shape the meat into flat hamburgerlike sausage patties. Perfect in pita pockets, hamburger buns, or on thin rounds of French or Italian bread.

❧

LOW-CALORIE ITALIAN FRIED PEPPERS AND SAUSAGE PATTIES

12   Sicilian-Style Sausage Patties (recipe above)
10   sweet green frying peppers or 3 small green bell peppers, sliced
2   onions, sliced
4   cloves garlic, minced
1/4   cup dry red wine
2   tablespoons water
2   teaspoons salad oil
1   tablespoon minced fresh oregano or 1 teaspoon dried oregano or Italian seasoning
    Salt and pepper to taste

1. Prepare sausage patties according to recipe. While sausage patties cook under broiler or over barbecue, combine all remaining ingredients in a nonstick skillet. Cover and cook over low heat for 15 minutes. Arrange cooked patties on top of pepper

and onion mixture in skillet; serve from skillet.

MAKES 12 SERVINGS, 150 CALORIES EACH WITH PORK; 130 CALORIES EACH WITH VEAL.

❧

MEXICAN LIME-MARINATED PORK STEAK

1/2   cup lime juice
1   or 2 cloves garlic, minced
1   to 3 teaspoons chili powder to taste
1   teaspoon dried oregano
1   pound fresh ham steak (uncured pork slice, cut from leg), trimmed of fat

1. Combine juice, garlic, chili, and oregano; pour over pork. Refrigerate all day or overnight.

2. Remove pork from marinade. Broil 2 to 4 inches from heat source, for about 5 minutes per side, depending on thickness. Pork should be thoroughly cooked.

MAKES 4 SERVINGS, 260 CALORIES EACH.

❧

GRAPE PORK BURRITOS

1   teaspoon chili powder
1/2   teaspoon dried oregano, crushed
    Salt and black pepper to taste
1   pound lean fat-trimmed boneless pork, cut in strips
1   clove garlic, minced
1   tablespoon oil
1/4   cup water
1/4   cup chopped onion
1/4   cup chopped green or red bell pepper
1 1/2   cups halved grapes, seeded if necessary
1/4   cup chopped green chilies
    Dash hot red pepper sauce
8   corn tortillas, heated

1. Combine chili, oregano, salt, and black pepper; toss with

pork until coated. Cook seasoned pork and garlic in oil until browned. Add water, cover, bring to a simmer, and cook for 20 minutes.

2. Add remaining ingredients except tortillas. Cover and cook 5 minutes more. Divide filling among tortillas; roll. Serve with salsa and yogurt, if desired.

Makes 8 filled tortillas, 245 calories each.

PEANUTTY PORK, PEKING STYLE

¼ cup light soy sauce
¼ cup dry sherry wine
2 teaspoons peanut butter
2 teaspoons cornstarch
1 teaspoon prepared mustard
1 pound lean boneless pork leg steak, cut in ½-inch cubes
2 teaspoons toasted sesame oil
2 cups peeled carrots in ½-inch slices
2 cups green beans in 2-inch slices
½ cup canned bamboo shoots, drained
6 tablespoons dry roasted peanuts

1. Combine 2 tablespoons each of soy sauce and sherry with peanut butter, cornstarch, and mustard; blend well. Stir pork into mixture to coat; set aside.

2. Prepare a large nonstick skillet or electric frying pan with cooking spray. Add 1 teaspoon oil and the carrots; cook, stirring, over moderately high heat for 2 minutes. Add green beans; cook, stirring, for 1 minute. Add bamboo shoots; cook, stirring, 15 seconds more. Transfer vegetables to a bowl.

3. Add remaining oil and wine to skillet. Add pork; cook, stirring, until completely cooked through. Add vegetables and remaining soy sauce to skillet; cook, continuing to stir, just until

heated through. Serve sprinkled with peanuts.

Makes 6 servings, 220 calories each.

OVEN "STIR-FRY" PORK AND VEGETABLES

1 pound lean pork, trimmed of fat and cut in cubes
½ cup sherry wine
½ cup unsweetened pineapple juice
2 tablespoons soy sauce
¼ teaspoon each ground ginger and dried garlic
1 sweet onion, coarsely chopped
1 red or green bell pepper, seeded and cut in squares
1 medium zucchini, sliced
1 tablespoon quick-cooking tapioca

1. Combine pork cubes with wine, pineapple juice, soy sauce, ginger, and garlic. Bake, covered, in a preheated 275-degree oven for 3 hours, until nearly tender.

2. Stir tapioca into pan juices. Arrange onion and bell pepper on top of meat. Cover and bake for 40 minutes. Arrange zucchini on top of vegetables and bake, covered, 10 to 12 minutes longer, until heated through. Just before serving, stir well. Serve over plain cooked rice, if desired.

Makes 4 servings, 230 calories each; rice adds 110 calories per ½-cup serving.

HAWAIIAN SWEET 'N' SOUR HAM STEAK

1 can (8 ounces) juice-packed crushed pineapple, with liquid
4 cloves garlic, minced
2 tablespoons soy sauce
2 tablespoons sherry wine
2 tablespoons cider vinegar
2 tablespoons light apricot jam
1 can (2 ounces) sliced mushrooms, with liquid (optional)
2 teaspoons fresh or dried shredded ginger root or ½ teaspoon ground ginger (optional)
3 purple plums, pitted and diced
¼ cup water
3 ribs celery, sliced
2 onions, sliced
2 red or green bell peppers, seeded and sliced
1 slice cured ham, trimmed of fat and cut in ½-inch cubes (about 1½ pounds)

1. In nonstick skillet, stir together pineapple, garlic, soy sauce, sherry, vinegar, jam, mushrooms, ginger (if desired), plums, and water. Cover, bring to a boil over moderate heat, and simmer for 10 minutes.

2. Stir in celery, onions, and bell peppers. Simmer, uncovered, 5 minutes more, stirring occasionally, until most liquid evaporates and mixture is quite thick. Stir in meat at last minute, gently heating through.

Makes 6 servings, under 300 calories each.

PORK FRIED RICE

2   *eggs, lightly beaten, or equivalent egg substitute*
12   *ounces lean pork leg steak, cut in ½-inch cubes*
2   *large bell peppers (1 red, 1 green), seeded and cut in ¾-inch squares*
3   *scallions, diagonally cut in ½-inch slices*
2   *teaspoons oil*
3   *tablespoons light soy sauce*
2   *tablespoons dry white wine*
3   *cups cold cooked rice*

1. In a large nonstick skillet prepared with cooking spray, cook eggs undisturbed over low heat until set. Shred cooked eggs and set aside. Wipe skillet and spray again with cooking spray. Add 1 teaspoon oil and the pork; cook, stirring, until meat is cooked through. Remove pork and set aside.

2. Add remaining oil and the pepper squares to skillet; cook, stirring, for 1 minute. Add scallions; cook, stirring, 30 seconds more. Stir in soy sauce, wine, rice, pork, and shredded eggs. Toss to combine; cook, stirring frequently, until completely heated.

MAKES 4 SERVINGS, 340 CALORIES EACH; 310 CALORIES WITH EGG SUBSTITUTE.

❦

CAJUN SAUSAGE AND GREEN BEANS

1   *pound low-fat low-calorie breakfast sausage*
1   *can (16 ounces) sliced stewed tomatoes*
3   *tablespoons minced fresh parsley*
1   *clove garlic, minced*
¼   *teaspoon each dried thyme, dried marjoram, ground cloves, ground allspice, and cayenne pepper*
1   *bag (20 ounces) frozen green beans or 3 cans (8 ounces each) green beans*

1. In a nonstick skillet or under the broiler, brown the sausage, turning to brown evenly. Add remaining ingredients except green beans. (If using canned beans, drain liquid from beans and add it to mixture.) Simmer for 20 minutes.

2. Add green beans, and cook until crisp-tender (if frozen) or until just heated through (if canned).

MAKES 8 SERVINGS, 185 CALORIES EACH.

❦

SAUSAGE SICILIANO AND SPAGHETTI

1   *pound lean ground pork*
½   *teaspoon each dried sage, thyme, and hot red pepper flakes (all optional)*
    Salt and black pepper to taste
2   *onions, diced*
3   *tablespoons dry white wine*
1   *can (16 ounces) crushed tomatoes*
1   *can (8 ounces) plain tomato sauce*
1   *red bell pepper, seeded and diced*
1   *or 2 cloves garlic, minced*
12   *ounces uncooked spaghetti*

1. Combine ground pork with seasonings, if desired. Shape into flat patties. Prepare a large nonstick skillet generously with cooking spray; heat over moderate flame. Brown patties on each side. Remove from skillet and set aside.

2. In the skillet, cook onions and wine, stirring, until wine evaporates. Add remaining ingredients except spaghetti; cover and simmer for 30 minutes. Arrange browned patties on top of sauce mixture. Simmer, covered, 15 minutes more or until meat is completely cooked through and sauce thickens.

3. Meanwhile, cook spaghetti according to package directions until tender; drain well. To serve, spoon sauce and sausage patties over hot drained spaghetti.

MAKES 8 SERVINGS, 285 CALORIES EACH.

❦

YUGOSLAV PORK PATTIES

An adaptation of pljeskavica, the Yugoslavian "Big Mac"— these patties can be made with any lean ground meat.

1½   *pounds lean pork, trimmed of fat and coarsely chopped*
¼   *cup plain low-fat yogurt*
3   *tablespoons cooked rice*
1   *tablespoon lemon juice*
    Salt and pepper to taste
2   *teaspoons all-purpose flour*

1. Combine pork, yogurt, rice, lemon juice, salt, and pepper, mixing gently. Shape into 6 patties and coat very lightly with flour. In a nonstick skillet or electric frying pan well prepared with cooking spray, pan-fry until cooked through, turning once, or broil. Serve like burgers.

MAKES 6 PATTIES, 265 CALORIES EACH.

❦

PORK CHOPS DIABLO

6   *tablespoons plain low-fat yogurt*
6   *tablespoons dark spicy prepared mustard*
6   *center-cut pork chops, trimmed of fat (about 1½ pounds)*
    Salt or garlic salt and coarsely ground pepper to taste

1. Combine yogurt and mustard; spread mixture liberally on both sides of pork. Sprinkle with salt and pepper. Puncture all over with a fork. Leave at room temperature 30 minutes.

2. Arrange pork on rack in baking pan. Put pan in cold oven and set at 275 degrees. Bake for 2 hours or until tender, basting occasionally with pan juices.

MAKES 6 SERVINGS, 240 CALORIES EACH.

A Worldwide Collection of Poultry Dishes

POULTRY takes the prize for value and versatility . . . for easy adaptability into a whole world of spices and seasonings. Chicken and turkey are calorie light in comparison with most meats, and relatively inexpensive thanks to modern merchandising techniques.

Once upon a time chicken was reserved for Sunday (and turkey for Thanksgiving feasts), but the availability of chicken parts made chicken an anyday treat. Turkey producers soon followed the lead.

CHICKEN IS A FAVORITE

Chicken's flexible fixability—the ease with which it wears fancy dress one day and is comfortably "just folks" the next—makes chicken a dish you need never tire of.

World citizen that it is, chicken is uniquely multilingual, fluent in nearly every culinary tongue. It slips easily out of one language and into the next with a simple switch of seasonings: cook your chicken with tomatoes, onions, garlic, and thyme, and you evoke sunny images of southern France. Switch to basil, oregano, and rosemary, with a shake of shredded Parmesan for good measure, and the accent is decidedly Italian. Crossing the Adriatic, substitute mint for the basil, add some lemon juice, cinnamon, and nutmeg, and your dish takes on Hellenic flair. Move eastward into Turkey with more spices, hot peppers, and cool yogurt or sweet touches of fruit. Go southward into Africa and escalate the heat with more fiery seasonings. Carry these influences to the Caribbean and add tropical fruits for garnish. Wherever you are in the culinary world, there are scores of other ways to turn "Chicken again?" into "Chicken again!"

Luckily for cooks with the "light" idea, chicken is a beautiful bargain not only in cost but also in calories, so you can easily afford to dress it up with flourishes you—or your diet—might otherwise not be able to afford. Nearly everyone likes chicken . . . and nearly everyone can eat it, dieting or not. Its easy digestibility, low cholesterol content, and relative lack of saturated fat make chicken just what the doctor ordered for a variety of special diets.

Best of all, chicken is so available. There's no "season," and no reason to pay extra for "prime" or to mortgage the house at a boutique butcher. At its fanciest, chicken is a great entertainer! The best you can buy is right there in the supermarket waiting for you to pick and choose. And speaking of being choosy, today's chicken parts let every white- or dark-meat partisan pick the most loved parts . . . and every cook choose only the most suitable pieces to match the recipe.

CHICKEN NUTRITION

Low in calories, low in saturated fat and cholesterol content, chicken hits the mark for lean and healthful—it's "light" on target. Some types of chicken, though, are lighter than others. Young broiler-fryers are the leanest, tenderest chickens. They also have the most protein—and the least fat and calories. Choosing calorie-wise chicken, then, becomes simply a matter of age. The older and bigger, the fatter. (A little like people, unfortunately!) Here's a guide:

Type, Age, Market Weight	(Amounts per pound, boneless)		
	Protein	Fat	Calories
Broiler-fryer 7–12 weeks 2–4 pounds	57 g	46 g	664
Roaster 12 weeks 5–8 pounds	56 g	52 g	706
Stewing chicken 1½ years 4–6 pounds	56 g	65 g	820
Capons (neutered males) 16 weeks 4–7 pounds	61 g	56 g	765

The cut-up chicken parts so widely sold at poultry counters are invariably young broiler-fryer chickens, the least fattening kind. That means that you can choose the least fattening parts of the least fattening chicken. The amount of edible meat (and of protein), however, will vary, depending on both the fat and bone content. Here we list cut-up chicken parts in descending order, putting the least fattening parts first:

CUT-UP PARTS (Broiler-fryers; amounts per pound, with bone)			
	Protein	Fat	Waste	Calories per ounce
Wing	45 g	39 g	46%	34
Breast	76 g	34 g	20%	39
Leg	60 g	40 g	27%	39
Thigh	62 g	55 g	21%	47
Back	36 g	73 g	44%	51
Neck	41 g	76 g	36%	54

VERSATILE CHICKEN THIGHS

Thighs are meaty chicken pieces with moist, flavorful dark meat, the favorite part of the bird for many chicken lovers. Thighs average about 4 ounces each, with 20 grams of protein—enough for 1 serving. They also supply generous amounts of niacin, riboflavin, phosphorus, and other essential nutrients, yet they're low in calories and fat. One skinless thigh is approximately 120 calories.

Boned chicken thighs offer a whole new range of menu ideas, and boning is simple with this 3-step technique:

1. Cut along the bone from joint to joint.
2. Cut the meat from one joint, then pull or scrape the meat from the bone.
3. Cut the meat from the other joint. Keep a supply of boned thighs on hand in the freezer.

IS DARK MEAT FATTENING?

Calorie-conscious chicken lovers are frequently told that it is. Fattening compared to what? The edible portion of a chicken drumstick, without skin, contains only 115 calories per 100 grams (or 3½ ounces), compared with 250 to 400 calories for a similar quantity of hamburger or steak. The same quantity of chicken breast is 110 calories. So while white meat is less fattening, there's no reason for dark-meat lovers to avoid chicken drumsticks.

CAN YOU BROIL A FRYER?

Young chickens, 7 to 12 weeks old, comprise 90 percent of the chickens sold. Sometimes they're labeled "fryers," sometimes "broilers" . . . but

ROTISSERIE CHICKEN BASTES ITSELF!
—— ❖ ——

Whole chickens take a tender turn when roasted on a revolving spit. Rotisserie devices are frequently found on electric or gas barbecues, but many kitchen ovens or cooktops also feature rotisseries. Whatever way you set a chicken in motion, it's one of the most calorie-wise ways to cook. Your chicken literally self-bastes to a golden crispness in its own melting fat. And as the chicken turns, the fat drips off, out of harm's way.

For best flavor, about an hour before cooking, coat the chicken in a marinating combination of fruit juice or wine with spices and seasonings. Any leftover marinade can be used as a baste during cooking.

regardless of the label, you can cook them either way. The fact that they're called broiler-fryers doesn't mean that you can't roast, barbecue, bake, stuff, simmer, sauté, or sauce them. If you're weight wary, broilers or fryers are your best bet . . . no matter how you plan to cook them!

What about other chickens? Roasters are older, fatter chickens, too big to broil. They can be hens or cocks, and so can stewing chickens, which are generally too big, fat, and tough for anything but stew. Capons would have been cocks, except for an unfortunate (for them) operation. Although capon is very tender when roasted, it is, alas, too fattening for serious slimmers.

HANDLE WITH CARE

Chicken has many attractive qualities, but it has one characteristic that's cause for concern: susceptibility to bacterial growth. Though poten- tially very dangerous, contamination can be avoided or prevented by simple safeguards:

- *Date checking:* Look for a "Sell by" label. Avoid packages with an expired date.
- *Proper storage techniques:* Refrigerate in its store wrapping and use within 2 days. (Whole chickens packaged together in a plastic bag should be rinsed in cold water and wrapped individually in plastic wrap or put in fresh plastic bags; refrigerate and use within 2 days.) Or freezer-wrap tightly, seal, label, and freeze; use within 4 to 6 months. Let cooked chicken cool to room temperature before wrapping; refrigerate and use within 2 days. Or wrap, label, and freeze; use within 2 months.
- *Proper thawing techniques:* Thaw frozen chicken in the refrigerator, with the wrappings loosened. It will take 4 to 9 hours to thaw chicken parts, 12 to 16 hours for whole birds under 4 pounds. For quicker thawing, place wrapped chicken in cold water. Don't thaw chicken at room temperature.
- *Safe preparation:* Wash your hands, work surface, knives, and utensils scrupulously in soapy water both before and after you work with chicken; rinse well. To avoid the risk of bacterial growth, don't handle other foods at the same time. Rinse chicken carefully in cold running water before working with it. Cook as soon as possible after taking it from the refrigerator—and cook thoroughly.

SAVE $$ ON CHICKEN
—— ❖ ——

Really want to save? If you have more time than money, buy several whole birds on sale. Cut them into parts and package the parts together. You will have enough chicken for a recipe featuring breasts, one using drumsticks, another using thighs, still another with wings, and plenty of bony pieces for a large pot of soup . . . all at bargain prices!

CHICKEN

TEXAS CHICKEN ROLL-UPS

> 4 ounces extra-sharp Cheddar cheese, thinly sliced
> 4 chicken cutlets (2 boneless skinless breasts, halved) (about 1 pound)
> 1 can (8 ounces) Spanish-style tomato sauce
> 1 small onion, chopped
> 1 green bell pepper, seeded and chopped
> 1 ripe tomato, peeled and diced
> 2 teaspoons lime or lemon juice
> 2 teaspoons dried oregano
> 2 teaspoons chili powder, or to taste
> ½ teaspoon cumin seeds or ¼ teaspoon ground cumin

1. Top each cutlet with ¼ of the cheese. Roll up cutlets, securing with toothpicks, if necessary. Arrange in a single layer in a nonstick pot.

2. Combine remaining ingredients and pour over chicken. Heat to boiling, then lower to a simmer. Cover and simmer for 10 minutes. Uncover and continue simmering until sauce is thick. Serve with brown rice, if desired.

MAKES 4 SERVINGS, 290 CALORIES EACH; RICE ADDS 115 CALORIES PER ½ CUP.

LEMON CHICKEN

> 1 pound frying chicken pieces
> ½ teaspoon salt, or to taste
> ½ teaspoon onion salt, or to taste
> ½ cup water
> ⅓ cup fresh lemon juice
> 2 teaspoons grated lemon peel
> ½ teaspoon each dried crushed thyme and marjoram
>   Garnishes: paprika, lemon wedges, and snipped fresh parsley

1. Season chicken with salt; place in a nonstick baking pan, skin side down. Combine water, lemon juice, lemon peel, thyme, and marjoram and pour over chicken. Bake at 350 degrees for approximately 30 minutes, basting with pan liquid.

2. Turn chicken over and continue to bake, basting occasionally, 30 minutes more, until chicken is cooked through and the skin is crispy. Remove chicken to a heated platter; sprinkle with paprika and garnish with lemon wedges and parsley.

MAKES 4 SERVINGS, 180 CALORIES EACH.

SKILLET-EASY MEXICAN CHICKEN ENCHILADAS

> ½ pound chicken cutlets (boneless, skinless breasts), trimmed of fat and cut in ½-inch cubes
> ½ cup chopped onion
> ½ cup chopped sweet green pepper
> 1 tablespoon lime juice or vinegar
> 2 cups spicy tomato juice
> 1 cup water
> 1 tablespoon raisins
> ½ teaspoon cumin seeds
> ¼ teaspoon dried oregano
> 4 corn tortillas
> 2 tablespoons shredded sharp Cheddar cheese (optional)
> 4 tablespoons plain low-fat yogurt (optional)

1. Spread chicken in a shallow layer in a nonstick skillet prepared with cooking spray. Brown slowly over moderate heat; turn to brown evenly.

2. Stir in onion, green pepper, and lime juice; cook, stirring, for 1 minute. Add tomato juice, water, raisins, and seasonings. Simmer for 5 minutes or until sauce is thick.

3. Using a slotted spoon, fill the tortillas with chicken mixture, reserving the sauce in the skillet. Roll the tortillas and place in the skillet. (If the sauce has become too thick, first stir in a few tablespoons of boiling water.) Cover and simmer for 4 to 5 minutes or just until heated through. If desired, top each serving with 1 tablespoon Cheddar and 2 tablespoons yogurt.

MAKES 2 SERVINGS, 360 CALORIES EACH. CHEDDAR ADDS 30 CALORIES PER SERVING; YOGURT ADDS 20 CALORIES PER SERVING.

CAJUN-STYLE CHICKEN BREASTS

> 2 teaspoons diet margarine
> 8 chicken cutlets (4 boneless, skinless breasts, halved) (about 2 pounds)
> 1 large onion, chopped
> 2 green bell peppers, seeded and chopped
> 2 cups tomato juice
> ¼ teaspoon each cayenne pepper, dried thyme, garlic flakes, ground cloves, and ground allspice

1. Melt margarine in a heavy nonstick skillet. Add chicken and brown quickly on both sides over high heat. Remove to a platter.

2. Add onion and bell peppers; cook over moderate heat until soft. Add tomato juice and seasonings, return chicken to pan, and then simmer until sauce is thick.

MAKES 8 SERVINGS, 160 CALORIES EACH.

COCONUT CHICKEN

2   whole frying chicken breasts,
      split
2   cups water
4   small onions, quartered
1   clove garlic, minced (optional)
¼   cup golden raisins
2   tablespoons lemon or lime
      juice
2   teaspoons cumin seeds or 1
      teaspoon ground cumin
1   teaspoon each ground turmeric
      and pumpkin pie spice
4   tablespoons dried flaked
      coconut, divided
2   yellow summer squash, sliced

1. In a nonstick electric frying pan prepared with cooking spray, brown the chicken, skin side down, over moderate heat. When skin is crisp and well rendered of fat, drain and discard any fat.

2. Turn chicken, skin side up. Add garlic, raisins, lemon juice, cumin, turmeric, and pumpkin pie spice; sprinkle with 2 tablespoons of coconut. Cover and simmer for about 30 minutes, until chicken is tender. Add squash. Continue simmering, uncovered, stirring occasionally, until squash is crisp-tender and liquid has been reduced to a golden glaze. Before serving, sprinkle with the remaining coconut.

MAKES 4 SERVINGS, 295 CALORIES EACH.

❦

PHILIPPINE BREAST OF CHICKEN

3   large frying chicken breasts,
      split and trimmed of fringe
      fat
1   can (6 ounces) unsweetened
      pineapple juice
¼   cup vinegar
¼   cup light soy sauce
1   bay leaf

1. Place chicken, skin side up, in a single layer in a shallow roasting pan. Combine remain-

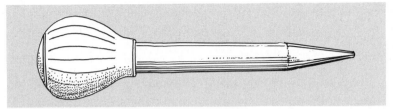

ing ingredients and pour over chicken.

2. Cover pan with aluminum foil and bake in preheated 425-degree oven for 30 minutes. Uncover and bake, basting frequently, an additional 20 minutes or until nearly all liquid evaporates and chicken has a rich, dark color. Remove bay leaf before serving.

MAKES 6 SERVINGS, 185 CALORIES EACH.

❦

MOROCCAN-STYLE CHICKEN KEBABS

1   can (8 ounces) low-salt tomato
        sauce
1   teaspoon ground turmeric
½   teaspoon ground pepper
½   teaspoon ground allspice
¼   teaspoon ground ginger
1¼   pounds chicken cutlets
        (boneless, skinless breasts,
        halved)
1¼   cups small white onions
1   large zucchini, cut in ½-inch
        chunks
8   cherry tomatoes
4   ounces fresh mushrooms,
        halved (about 1½ cups)

1. Combine tomato sauce and spices in a medium bowl. Pierce both sides of chicken with tines of a fork; cut into 1-inch pieces. Add chicken to tomato sauce mixture, stirring to coat thoroughly. Cover and refrigerate for 30 minutes.

2. Meanwhile, cook onions in boiling water for 2 to 3 minutes or until outer layers are tender. Drain; cut onions in half crosswise.

3. Alternate chicken and vegetables on skewers. Place on

a rack in a broiler pan and brush with marinade. Broil 4 inches from heat source until chicken is cooked through—8 to 10 minutes—basting with marinade and turning every 2 minutes.

MAKES 6 SERVINGS, 150 CALORIES EACH.

❦

CHICKEN BREASTS SEVILLANA

3   whole frying chicken breasts,
        split
3   tablespoons flour
1   can (10½ ounces) condensed
        chicken broth, skimmed of
        fat
3   tablespoons sherry or white
        wine
1   cup chopped peeled tomatoes
1   cup chopped onion
1   green bell pepper, seeded and
        sliced in strips
¼   teaspoon dried thyme
18   pimiento-stuffed green olives,
        sliced
½   pound fresh mushrooms, sliced

1. Shake chicken breasts and flour in a large bag until lightly coated. Place chicken, skin side up, in a shallow baking dish. Bake in a preheated 450-degree oven for 20 minutes or until well browned and rendered of fat. Drain and discard all fat.

2. Combine broth, sherry, tomatoes, onion, bell pepper, and thyme; pour over chicken. Cover with foil and bake at 350 degrees for 30 minutes. Stir in olives and mushrooms. Continue baking, uncovered, basting occasionally, until the liquid is reduced to a thick sauce.

MAKES 6 SERVINGS, 340 CALORIES EACH.

PORTUGUESE SPITTED CHICKEN

1   *frying chicken (3 pounds)*
3   *tablespoons Piri-Piri sauce (see page 82) or 2 tablespoons hot red pepper sauce mixed with 1 tablespoon vinegar*
2   *teaspoons olive oil*

1. Preheat oven equipped with electric rotisserie to 375 degrees. Affix chicken to spit, tying the drumsticks and wings together with kitchen twine.

2. Combine remaining ingredients and brush on chicken. Set up the spit in oven, with a pan beneath to catch drips. Roast the revolving chicken for 45 to 50 minutes or until it is cooked through. (Or roast on a rotisserie in a covered barbecue over coals until cooked through.)

EACH 3½ OUNCE SERVING HAS ABOUT 170 CALORIES.

❦

SAFFRON-SCENTED CHICKEN WITH SPICES AND PINE NUTS

1   *frying chicken (about 3 pounds), cut up*
2   *cups chopped onions*
1   *teaspoon saffron threads*
½   *cup chicken broth, skimmed of fat*
½   *teaspoon each ground cloves and paprika*
¼   *teaspoon ground cinnamon Salt and coarse pepper to taste*
6   *tablespoons pine nuts (pignoli nuts)*

1. Arrange chicken, skin side up, in shallow roasting pan. Roast in a preheated 350-degree oven for 25 to 30 minutes or until brown. Drain and discard fat.

2. Arrange onions in a shallow layer under and around chicken pieces. Bring broth to a slow boil, add the saffron, and simmer for 3 minutes. Pour broth over chicken; sprinkle with remaining seasonings.

3. Roast, basting occasionally, 25 minutes more. Sprinkle pine nuts over the dish during the last 5 minutes. Serve with toasted whole-grain pita bread, if desired.

MAKES 6 SERVINGS, 175 CALORIES EACH.

❦

TANDOORI-STYLE SPICED CHICKEN

4   *pieces frying chicken thighs (or equivalent chicken parts)*
4   *tablespoons plain low-fat yogurt*
2   *tablespoons lemon juice*
2   *tablespoons vinegar*
4   *teaspoons Tandoori Spice or 2 teaspoons each curry powder and paprika, plus optional pinch of ground ginger and cumin*

1. Pull skin of thighs away from meat but do not remove. With sharp-pointed knife, make several deep slits in the meat. Thoroughly combine remaining ingredients in a plastic bag. Add chicken, manipulating bag to cover meat with the marinade. Refrigerate for several hours.

2. Remove chicken from marinade and re-cover meat with skin. Coat skin with remaining marinade, shaking off excess. Arrange thighs in a shallow broiler tray. Broil 6 inches from heat source for 15 minutes, turning and basting frequently with pan juices. Move 3 inches closer to heat source. Broil, turning frequently, for another 12 to 15 minutes, until skin is very crisp.

MAKES 4 SERVINGS, APPROXIMATELY 215 CALORIES EACH.

❦

THAI-STYLE CHICKEN WITH BASIL

2   *tablespoons fish sauce (available in oriental groceries, or substitute additional soy sauce)*
2   *tablespoons light soy sauce*
2   *tablespoons plain low-fat yogurt Juice and grated peel of 1 lemon*
3   *cloves garlic, minced*
3   *tablespoons minced fresh basil or 1 teaspoon dried basil*
2   *teaspoons hot red pepper flakes*
1   *teaspoon ground ginger*
1   *frying chicken (about 3 pounds), cut up and trimmed of fat*

1. Put all ingredients except chicken in a plastic bag; knead bag lightly to mix. Add chicken and turn bag several times to coat pieces evenly. Marinate at room temperature for 30 minutes or for several hours in refrigerator.

2. Remove chicken pieces from bag and arrange, skin side up, in a shallow nonstick roasting pan. Roast in a preheated 375-degree oven for 50 minutes.

MAKES 6 SERVINGS, 190 CALORIES EACH.

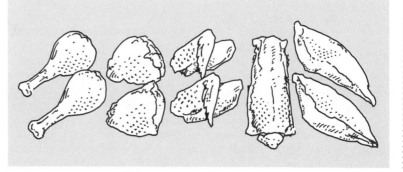

SPICY ORIENTAL CHICKEN WITH PEARS

3   whole frying chicken breasts, split
1   can (16 ounces) juice-packed pear halves
1   tablespoon lemon juice
1   tablespoon light soy sauce
½   teaspoon oriental 5-spice powder or pumpkin pie spice
    Paprika for garnish (optional)

1. Arrange chicken, skin-side up, in a shallow baking pan. Bake in a preheated 400-degree oven for 20 minutes or until skin is crisp and well rendered of fat. Drain and discard fat.

2. Drain pears and set aside; reserve juice. Pour pear juice, lemon juice, and soy sauce over chicken. Sprinkle with 5-spice powder. Bake for 25 minutes, basting often. Slice pear halves into quarters and arrange around chicken; baste with pan juices and bake 5 to 6 minutes more or until heated through. Sprinkle lightly with paprika, if desired.

MAKES 6 SERVINGS, 170 CALORIES EACH.

CHICKEN AND PEPPERS, ITALIAN STYLE

2   pounds chicken cutlets (boneless, skinless breasts), trimmed of fat and cubed
1   can (16 ounces) tomatoes, packed in purée
¼   cup dry white wine
1   large onion, chopped
2   cloves garlic, minced
2   tablespoons chopped fresh parsley
1   tablespoon chopped fresh basil or 1 teaspoon dried basil
1   teaspoon chopped fresh thyme or ¼ teaspoon dried thyme
4   green bell peppers, seeded and chopped

1. Prepare a nonstick skillet or electric frying pan with cooking spray. Add chicken cubes in a shallow layer, and cook slowly, turning to brown evenly on all sides.

2. Add all remaining ingredients except peppers. Cover and simmer over low heat for 10 minutes, stirring frequently. Add peppers, cover, and cook until tender—5 to 8 minutes more.

MAKES 8 SERVINGS, 180 CALORIES EACH.

CHICKEN ROLLS ACAPULCO

2   onions, chopped
1   clove garlic, minced
1   tablespoon olive oil
¼   cup liquid from container of olives
1   can (8 ounces) tomato sauce
1   can (8 ounces) stewed tomatoes, well broken up, or 1 large ripe tomato, chopped
1   large green bell pepper, seeded and thinly sliced
½   cup water
¼   cup coarsely chopped pimiento-stuffed green olives
3   tablespoons chopped fresh cilantro or parsley
2   tablespoons lemon or lime juice
1   tablespoon chili powder, or to taste
1   teaspoon ground cumin
    Pinch dried oregano
    Salt and freshly ground black pepper to taste
3   ounces part-skim queso blanco or light cheese
6   chicken cutlets (3 boneless, skinless breasts, halved) (about 1½ pounds)

1. Prepare a shallow nonstick roasting pan with cooking spray. Combine onions, garlic, oil, and olive liquid in pan. Place in a preheated 450-degree oven and bake for 5 minutes.

2. Combine remaining ingredients, except chicken and cheese, and pour over onion mixture. Bake 15 to 20 minutes longer, adding a little water if sauce becomes too thick.

3. Meanwhile, prepare chicken rolls: Cut cheese into 6 even slices and arrange 1 slice on each chicken cutlet. Roll up each cutlet with the cheese inside. Carefully place chicken rolls, seam side down, in the sauce and spoon some sauce on top. Bake for 8 to 9 minutes. Serve with rice, if desired.

MAKES 6 SERVINGS, 245 CALORIES EACH; RICE ADDS 110 CALORIES PER ½ CUP.

Variation

Chicken Rolls Italiano: Follow the preceding recipe, using part-skim mozzarella for the light cheese. Omit the cilantro, cumin, and chili powder; instead, add basil and hot red pepper flakes to taste.

DALMATIAN-STYLE CHICKEN

This dish normally calls for kaimack, a kind of fresh cheese popular in Yugoslav cooking. We use plain low-fat yogurt.

2   pounds young frying chicken, cut up
3   to 4 cloves garlic, finely minced
2   cups plain low-fat yogurt
2   tablespoons all-purpose flour
    Salt and pepper to taste

1. Arrange chicken pieces, skin side up, in a single layer in a nonstick pan. Bake in preheated 350-degree oven for 30 minutes until skin is crisp. Drain and discard fat.

2. Meanwhile, fold garlic into yogurt, along with flour. Add salt and pepper. Spoon yogurt mixture over chicken, cover, and bake 30 minutes more.

MAKES 6 SERVINGS, 280 CALORIES EACH.

CHINESE CHICKEN WITH SPICY SELF-MAKING PLUM SAUCE

2   *whole frying chicken breasts, split*
6   *ripe purple plums, pitted and thinly sliced*
1   *onion, halved and thinly sliced*
1   *clove garlic, minced*
3   *tablespoons water*
2   *tablespoons lemon juice*
2   *tablespoons light soy sauce*
1   *tablespoon honey or equivalent low-calorie sweetener*
1   *teaspoon oriental 5-spice powder*

1. Brown chicken, skin side down, in an ungreased non-stick skillet or chicken fryer. Drain and discard chicken fat. Blot chicken with paper toweling and return to the pan, skin side up.

2. Add remaining ingredients. Cover and simmer, stirring occasionally, until chicken is tender—40 to 45 minutes. Uncover and continue simmering until sauce is thick. (If using the low-calorie sweetener, do not add until cooking is complete and skillet has been removed from heat.)

MAKES 4 SERVINGS, 215 CALORIES EACH WITH HONEY; 200 CALORIES EACH WITH THE LOW-CALORIE SWEETENER.

ORIENTAL-STYLE "SESAME-FRIED" CHICKEN

6   *chicken cutlets (3 boneless, skinless breasts, halved) (about 1½ pounds)*
1   *tablespoon toasted sesame seed oil*
1   *tablespoon light soy sauce*
2   *tablespoons white wine*
2   *egg whites or egg substitute equivalent to 1 egg*
½   *teaspoon oriental 5-spice powder or ¼ teaspoon pumpkin pie spice and pinch anise seeds*
¼   *cup bread crumbs*
¼   *cup sesame seeds*

1. Place cutlets in plastic bag and add oil, soy sauce, wine, egg whites, and spice. Marinate for 1 hour in refrigerator.

2. Combine crumbs and sesame seeds on shallow plate; press each cutlet lightly into mixture, coating both sides. Arrange coated cutlets in single layer on a shallow nonstick baking pan prepared with cooking spray. Bake in a preheated 475-degree oven for about 8 minutes.

MAKES 6 SERVINGS, 205 CALORIES EACH.

CAJUN CHICKEN CASSEROLE

2   *cups diced cooked white-meat chicken or turkey*
2   *cups canned tomatoes, with liquid*
1   *cup cooked brown rice*
½   *cup chopped onion*
½   *cup minced celery*
½   *cup diced red or green bell pepper*
½   *cup cubed yellow squash*
1   *clove garlic, minced*
¼   *teaspoon each dried thyme, hot red pepper flakes, ground cloves, and ground allspice*
6   *tablespoons Italian-seasoned bread crumbs*

1. Combine all ingredients except bread crumbs in a casserole, mixing well. Top with bread crumbs and bake in preheated 350-degree oven for 35 to 40 minutes.

MAKES 6 SERVINGS, 195 CALORIES EACH.

CHICKEN CHINOISE WITH TRICOLOR PEPPERS

4   *frying chicken thighs*
1   *can (8 ounces) juice-packed pineapple tidbits*
2   *tablespoons light soy sauce, or to taste*
1   *clove garlic, minced*
¼   *teaspoon each ground ginger, pumpkin pie spice, and fennel seeds*
1   *large sweet onion*
1   *red, 1 yellow, and 1 green bell pepper, seeded and cut into 1-inch squares*
1   *cup water*
1   *teaspoon cornstarch*
2   *tablespoons ketchup or chili sauce*

1. Prepare a pressure cooker with a liberal amount of cooking spray. Brown chicken over moderate heat. Drain and discard fat. Arrange chicken in pressure cooker in a single layer.

2. Drain the pineapple juice into a small bowl and set the tidbits aside. Combine the juice, soy sauce, garlic, and spices and pour over chicken. Place a perforated metal trivet (or any small round metal rack or an unfolded steaming basket) on top of chicken. Add onion, peppers, and water.

3. Cover and pressure-cook at 15 pounds pressure for 10 minutes, then release pressure according to manufacturer's directions. Remove trivet and mix the vegetables lightly with chicken. Add reserved pineapple tidbits. Stir cornstarch into ketchup until smooth; combine

with chicken mixture. Warm over low heat, stirring gently, just until pineapple tidbits are heated and sauce thickens slightly.

MAKES 4 SERVINGS, 295 CALORIES EACH.

❦❦

CURRIED CHICKEN WITH RICE

2   pounds frying chicken breasts, split
1   cup chopped onions
1   clove garlic, minced
2   cans (10½ ounces each) condensed chicken broth, skimmed of fat
1½   cups uncooked long-grain rice
1   red or green bell pepper, seeded and cut in strips
1   teaspoon curry powder, or to taste
1   package (6 ounces) frozen pea pods, thawed
¼   pound fresh or canned sliced mushrooms
1   fresh vine-ripe tomato, chopped
     Salt and black pepper to taste

1. In a nonstick skillet prepared with cooking spray, arrange chicken breast halves, skin side down. Cook over moderate heat until skin browns. Drain and discard any fat. Remove chicken and set aside.

2. Combine onion and garlic with ¼ cup broth in the skillet and turn heat to high. Arrange chicken on top, skin side up. Cook until broth evaporates and onion is golden.

3. Add rice, pepper strips, remaining broth, and curry. Cover and lower heat. Simmer for 30 minutes. Add pea pods, mushrooms, tomato, salt, and black pepper. Cover and simmer just until heated through.

MAKES 8 SERVINGS, 330 CALORIES EACH.

❦❦

CHINESE CHICKEN WITH PEPPER AND PINEAPPLE

1   pound chicken cutlets (boneless, skinless breasts), cubed
2   red or green bell peppers, seeded and cut in squares
2   cups diagonally sliced fresh celery
1   onion, sliced
1   cup chicken broth, skimmed of fat
1   teaspoon 5-spice powder or 1 teaspoon pumpkin pie spice and pinch fennel seeds
2   cloves garlic, minced (optional)
1   can (16 ounces) juice-packed pineapple chunks
¼   cup light soy sauce
2   tablespoons vinegar
2   teaspoons cornstarch

1. In a nonstick skillet or electric frying pan prepared with cooking spray, arrange chicken in a shallow layer, and cook slowly, turning to brown evenly on all sides. Remove chicken from pan and set aside. Combine bell peppers, celery, onion,

broth, spice, and garlic, if desired, in pan. Cover and cook for 2 minutes; uncover and continue cooking, stirring often, until nearly all liquid evaporates.

2. Drain pineapple, reserving juice. Add pineapple and chicken to pan. Cook, stirring, until heated through and chicken is done. In a cup, thoroughly combine pineapple juice, soy sauce, vinegar, and cornstarch; stir mixture into pan. Cook and stir over high heat until mixture simmers, thickens, and clears.

MAKES 4 SERVINGS, 275 CALORIES EACH.

❦❦

CHICKEN AND MUSHROOM SUPREME WITH BLEU CHEESE SAUCE

2   teaspoons margarine
2   tablespoons dry white wine
8   ounces fresh mushrooms, sliced
1   pound chicken cutlets (boneless, skinless breasts), cubed
2   cups tender-cooked noodles
⅓   cup light bleu cheese salad dressing
2   tablespoons minced fresh parsley
2   tablespoons seasoned bread crumbs

1. Heat margarine in nonstick skillet; add wine and mushrooms. Sauté quickly over high heat until wine evaporates and mushrooms are lightly browned. Remove mushrooms and reserve; add chicken cubes to pan. Cook quickly over moderate heat until browned.

2. In a nonstick baking dish, combine all ingredients except bread crumbs. Sprinkle bread crumbs over top. Bake in preheated 350-degree oven for 20 minutes or until heated through.

MAKES 4 SERVINGS, 295 CALORIES EACH.

GOUDA-FILLED CHICKEN ROLLS

1   tablespoon lemon juice
2   teaspoons salad oil
1   teaspoon prepared mustard
     Pinch ground nutmeg
6   chicken cutlets (3 boneless
     skinless breasts, halved)
3   slices turkey ham, halved
3   ounces Gouda or Edam cheese,
     in 6 pieces
2   tablespoons herb-seasoned
     bread crumbs

1. Prepare a shallow nonstick pan liberally with cooking spray. Mix lemon juice, oil, mustard, and nutmeg in shallow dish. Lightly coat 1 side of each cutlet with lemon-mustard mixture. Arrange half a slice of turkey ham and a piece of cheese on the other side of cutlet, then roll with ham and cheese inside. Place the roll, seam side down, in pan.

2. Make remaining 5 chicken rolls and arrange in pan, not touching. Sprinkle each lightly with bread crumbs. Bake in preheated 450-degree oven for 9 to 10 minutes or until cheese begins to melt.

MAKES 6 SERVINGS, 215 CALORIES EACH.

Variation

St. Martin Style: On the Dutch Caribbean Island of St. Martin, Gouda cheese is combined imaginatively with curry and fruit in main courses with meat, poultry, or seafood, reflecting that island's international flavor. Here's how to make the preceding recipe St. Martin style, with raisins and spice as part of the filling: Substitute chili sauce or ketchup for the mustard and a generous shake of curry powder for the nutmeg. Also add 6 teaspoons white raisins to the ingredient list, and use 1 teaspoon in the filling for each of the chicken rolls.

EACH SERVING HAS 225 CALORIES.

TURKEY

OVERNIGHT TURKEY CHILI
(No beans)

Chocolate is an ingredient in many Mexican turkey dishes— the best known is Mole Poblano, turkey stewed in a rich, dark, and bitter sauce with lots of chocolate. Chocolate is also the "secret ingredient" that adds a counterpoint of bitterness to many Tex-Mex chili mixtures. Here's a slow-cooker chili that turns turkey thigh into a richly flavored chili overnight.

2   turkey thighs, skinned, boned,
     and cubed, or 1 pound
     boneless, skinless turkey
     thigh cutlets, cubed
1   can (8 ounces) sliced
     tomatoes, undrained
2   green bell peppers, seeded and
     chopped
1   or 2 fresh jalapeño peppers,
     seeded and chopped, or 1
     tablespoon chili powder, or
     to taste
1   onion, chopped
1   clove garlic, minced
¼   cup loosely packed chopped
     fresh cilantro leaves
1   tablespoon plain cocoa powder
2   teaspoons cumin seeds or ½
     teaspoon ground cumin
¼   teaspoon ground cinnamon

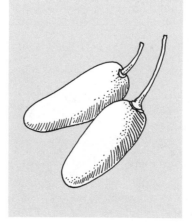

1. Combine ingredients in an electric crock cooker. Cover and cook for 14 to 16 hours at low heat.

Note: Double the recipe to make 8 servings, and then freeze the extras in single-serving portions, if desired.

MAKES 4 SERVINGS, 295 CALORIES EACH.

JAMBALAYA-SPICED TURKEY STEW

1   turkey thigh
2   tablespoons all-purpose flour
1   teaspoon each cayenne pepper,
     dried thyme, and sage
     Salt or garlic salt and coarsely
     ground black pepper to taste
1   cup chopped onions
1   cup chopped green bell peppers
1   cup chopped celery
½   cup diced lean cooked ham (2
     ounces)
½   cup chicken broth, skimmed of
     fat
2   bay leaves

1. Using a sharp, pointed knife, remove bone from turkey thigh. Cut thigh into 1½-inch cubes, leaving skin on. Trim and discard any fringe fat. Put turkey cubes in a bag with flour, cayenne pepper, thyme, sage, salt, and black pepper; shake until lightly coated.

2. Arrange turkey cubes in single layer, skin side up, in a nonstick roasting pan. Roast in preheated 425-degree oven until skin is crisp, well browned, and rendered of fat. Drain and discard any fat from pan, then add remaining ingredients. Cover pan loosely with foil and bake 20 minutes more. Lower heat to 350 degrees; bake until turkey is tender and most liquid evaporates. Discard bay leaves. Serve with plain cooked rice, if desired. Recipe may be doubled.

MAKES 4 SERVINGS, 295 CALORIES EACH; RICE ADDS 110 CALORIES PER ½ CUP.

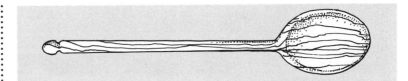

TURKEY BREAST WITH TEQUILA SUNRISE SAUCE

1 turkey breast (about 3 pounds)
2 large onions, sliced
1½ cups orange juice
½ cup tequila
1 clove garlic, minced, or pinch instant garlic
2 teaspoons dried oregano
2 teaspoons cumin seeds or ½ teaspoon ground cumin
   Salt and coarsely ground pepper to taste

1. In a nonstick roasting pan prepared with cooking spray, arrange turkey, skin side up. Bake, unseasoned, in a preheated 425-degree oven for 20 to 30 minutes, until skin is crisp. Drain and discard melted fat.

2. Spread onions under turkey. Combine remaining ingredients and pour over turkey. Lower heat to 350 degrees. Cover and bake for 1 hour or until turkey is tender. Uncover and bake until skin is crisp and liquid is reduced to a thick glaze. Baste frequently with pan liquid. (If needed, add a tablespoon of water.)

MAKES 10 SERVINGS, 235 CALORIES EACH.

᷍ᨏ᷍

MEXICAN POT-ROASTED TURKEY

1 turkey thigh and drumstick (about 2 pounds)
½ teaspoon poultry seasoning
2 cups peeled seeded diced tomatoes (fresh or canned)
1½ cups chopped onion
1½ cups diced green and red bell peppers (fresh or frozen)
1 cup turkey or chicken broth, skimmed of fat, or water
2 cloves garlic, minced
¼ teaspoon chili powder, or to taste
   Salt and black pepper to taste

1. Arrange turkey, skin side up, in a nonstick baking pan. Sprinkle with poultry seasoning. Bake in preheated 450-degree oven for 20 to 25 minutes, until skin is crisp. Drain and discard any fat.

2. Combine remaining ingredients and spoon over turkey. Reduce heat to 350 degrees. Cover and bake until tender, approximately 1 hour, basting occasionally with pan juices. (Add water, if needed.)

MAKES 6 SERVINGS, 365 CALORIES EACH.

᷍ᨏ᷍

TEX-MEX TURKEY TORTILLA CASSEROLE

2 cups plain tomato sauce
1 teaspoon dried minced garlic
1 teaspoon each dried oregano, chili powder, and cumin seeds, or to taste
1 jalapeño pepper, seeded and chopped (optional)
6 corn tortillas
1 cup pot-style low-fat cottage cheese
1 cup diced or shredded cooked turkey
1 onion, chopped
1 cup stewed tomatoes, with liquid
1 green bell pepper, sliced into rings
6 tablespoons shredded sharp Cheddar cheese

1. Combine tomato sauce with garlic, herbs, seasonings, and jalapeño pepper, if desired. Arrange 2 or 3 tortillas in the bottom of a nonstick baking pan or casserole prepared with cooking spray. Top with a little of the tomato sauce mixture, then spread the pot cheese in a layer.

Add another layer of tortillas and cover with turkey. If desired, set aside ½ tortilla for topping. Add remaining sauce, onion, and tomatoes. Top casserole with bell pepper rings.

2. Cover with a lid or foil and bake in a preheated 350-degree oven for 1 hour. Uncover and sprinkle with Cheddar (and reserved ½ tortilla torn into "chips," if desired). Bake 10 minutes more. Remove and let sit 10 minutes before serving.

MAKES 6 SERVINGS, 260 CALORIES EACH.

᷍ᨏ᷍

TURKEY CACCIATORE

2 teaspoons vegetable oil
1 cup chopped onion
2 cloves garlic, minced
8 ounces fresh mushrooms, sliced
1 can (28 ounces) whole tomatoes, drained and chopped
1 can (15 ounces) tomato sauce
2 ounces sliced ripe olives
2 teaspoons dried Italian herb seasoning, crushed
2 cups cubed cooked turkey
   Salt and black pepper to taste

1. Heat oil over moderately high heat in a Dutch oven or large saucepan. Add onion and garlic; cook until tender. Add mushrooms, tomatoes, tomato sauce, olives, and herbs.

2. Reduce heat and simmer for about 20 minutes, stirring occasionally. Stir in turkey; heat through. Add salt and black pepper. If desired, serve over spaghetti with a sprinkle of hot red pepper flakes.

MAKES 4 SERVINGS CACCIATORE, 300 CALORIES EACH.

TURKEY PICCADILLO

1 pound ground turkey
1 cup light beer
½ cup tomato juice
2 onions, halved and thinly
  sliced
1 rib celery, thinly sliced
¼ cup thinly sliced pimiento-
  stuffed green olives
¼ cup golden raisins
1 or 2 cloves garlic, chopped, or
  ¼ teaspoon instant garlic
2 teaspoons chili powder, or to
  taste
1 teaspoon cumin seeds or ¼
  teaspoon ground cumin
  Salt and pepper to taste

1. In a nonstick skillet prepared with cooking spray, brown the turkey over moderate heat, breaking it into chunks. Drain and discard any fat.

2. Add remaining ingredients. Simmer until most of the liquid evaporates. Stir frequently. If desired, serve over rice or pasta, or in tacos with shredded lettuce.

MAKES 4 MAIN-COURSE SERVINGS, UNDER 300 CALORIES EACH.

❧

MEXICAN FRUITED TURKEY BREAST

1 turkey breast (about 2½
  pounds)
  Salt to taste
  Cayenne pepper or chili powder
  to taste (optional)
½ cup juice-packed pineapple
  chunks, undrained
⅓ cup seedless raisins
¼ cup blanched almonds
½ teaspoon pumpkin pie spice or
  ¼ teaspoon each ground
  cinnamon and cloves
1 cup orange juice
2 tablespoons flour
  Orange sections for garnish
  (optional)

1. Season turkey to taste with salt and cayenne pepper. Ar-

range, skin side up, in a nonstick Dutch oven. Bake in preheated 450-degree oven for about 20 minutes or until skin is crisp. Drain and discard fat.

2. Add fruits, nuts, spices, and ½ cup orange juice. Cover and simmer (or bake in a 325-degree oven) for 1¾ to 2 hours or until meat is tender.

3. Remove turkey to serving platter. Combine flour with remaining ½ cup orange juice and stir into sauce. Cook, stirring, over low heat until sauce thickens. Pour over turkey. Garnish with fresh orange sections, if desired.

MAKES 8 SERVINGS, UNDER 300 CALORIES EACH.

❧

PRONTO TURKEY PUCHERO

This recipe takes its inspiration from a South American dish, puchero, a slow-cooked stew of fruit and meat. This quick and easy adaptation uses ground turkey, dried fruit, and other flavorful ingredients.

1 pound ground turkey
¾ cup turkey broth, skimmed of
  fat
¼ cup dry white wine
2 ripe tomatoes, peeled, seeded,
  and chopped
2 onions, halved and thinly
  sliced
3 tablespoons golden raisins
4 dried apricot halves
1 small bay leaf
¼ teaspoon poultry seasoning
2 red apples or 2 pears or 1 of
  each, cored and diced
  Salt and pepper to taste

1. Spread turkey in a large nonstick skillet or electric frying pan. Brown the underside over high heat, with no added fat. Break meat into bite-size chunks, turn, and brown other side. Drain fat from pan and discard.

2. Add broth, wine, tomatoes, onions, raisins, apricots, bay leaf, and poultry seasoning. Simmer, stirring frequently, until nearly all the liquid evaporates. Add apples (or pears), salt, and pepper. Continue to cook, stirring, until fruit is tender but not soft. Remove bay leaf before serving.

MAKES 4 SERVINGS, 320 CALORIES EACH WITH APPLES; 15 CALORIES MORE PER SERVING WITH PEARS.

❧

TURKEY ALL-MEAT "PIZZA"

Ground turkey forms the "crust" of this unusual meat loaf in the flat, round shape of a pizza, with mozzarella cheese and other pizza toppings of your choice.

1½ pounds ground turkey
1 clove garlic, minced
1 teaspoon salt, or to taste
¼ teaspoon black pepper
1 cup plain tomato sauce
3 ounces part-skim mozzarella
  cheese, shredded
1 tablespoon dried leaf oregano,
  crumbled
⅛ teaspoon hot red pepper flakes,
  or to taste

1. Combine turkey with garlic, salt, and black pepper. Gently pat into a 10-inch pie plate, overlapping the rim. Bake in preheated 425-degree oven for 15 minutes or until well browned. Drain and discard any fat.

2. Spread with tomato sauce; sprinkle with cheese, oregano, and red pepper. Bake 10 minutes longer until hot and bubbly. (Chopped bell peppers, mushroom slices, onions, or whatever low-calorie toppings you like on pizza are all good additions.)

MAKES 6 SERVINGS, 260 CALORIES EACH.

Fish and Seafood with Zest and Dash

⊓⊓⊓

FISH has always been prized among waistline watchers for its low fat content and light calorie count. But now it turns out that what little fat it does have is good for you . . . chockful of the Omega 3 fatty acids that can help protect against heart disease. Even shellfish, with its presumed high cholesterol content, turns out not to be so cholesterol-laden after all!

The news about fish and seafood keeps on getting better and better . . . no wonder they call it brainfood!

Unfortunately, a lot of slim-down plans make fish needlessly bland and boring, a pallid poached dish served with a stinting squirt of lemon and little else. But fish is so calorie-light that it can afford a few flourishes.

Coastline areas all over the world have exciting and imaginative ways of spicing fish and seafood. Their flavoring tricks are easily adapted to American kitchens, without unwanted extra calories.

The important precaution is to be mindful of the cooking method: breading and deep fat frying can double and triple the calorie count of fish and seafood because of the fat calories absorbed in cooking. Broiling, baking, and barbecueing are much better cooking choices. Slimmed-down stir-fry and oven-fry techniques can emulate the taste of frying with far less fat.

NUTS ABOUT NUTS?

You don't have to say "Nuts!" to nuts, even though they're half fat (that's what makes them high in calories). What better way to indulge your nutty passion than to pair your addiction with the leanest, least fattening food . . . fish! The French knew what they were doing when they dreamed up sole amandine.

You can combine any kind of fish with any kind of nutty topping, but it's more fun when there is some sort of ethnic geographic connection— Hawaiian macadamia nuts with mahi mahi, or southern catfish with cashews or peanuts. Sprinkle peanuts on fish seasoned with curry. Use pistachios with seafood in Italian pasta, or sprinkle them over swordfish barbecued Turkish style and seasoned with lemon and bay leaves. One tablespoon of chopped nuts adds about 50 calories, so use nuts judiciously!

ADD SOME CHEESE, PLEASE!

Cheese is another high-fat food that "light" cooks need to limit, but grated and sprinkled lightly on seafood, or rolled up in fish fillets, a little cheese can go a long way to making mildly flavored fish more interesting.

MAKE MINE VANILLA

In Provence they add a bit of vanilla to fish stews and mussel soup. They also add it very sparingly, along with allspice, when cooking chicken. A discreet touch of pure vanilla and grated orange rind is excellent in a stuffing for freshwater fish.

HADDOCK, VERA CRUZ STYLE

1 pound haddock or other fish
   fillets, fresh or defrosted
3 tablespoons lime or lemon
   juice
   Salt and black pepper to taste
2 onions, chopped
2 cloves garlic, minced
1 tablespoon salad oil
1 can (8 ounces) plain tomato
   sauce
1 can (8 ounces) stewed
   tomatoes, well broken up, or
   1 large ripe tomato, chopped
1 large fresh green bell pepper,
   seeded and thinly sliced
1 or 2 jalapeño peppers, to taste
   (optional)
½ cup water
¼ cup coarsely chopped pimiento-
   stuffed green olives
¼ cup olive liquid (from
   container)
¼ cup chopped fresh cilantro or
   parsley for garnish

1. Cut fish into serving-size pieces. Squirt with lime juice, season with salt and black pepper, and set aside. Combine onions, garlic, and oil in a large nonstick skillet or electric frying pan over medium heat. Cook, stirring, only until onions are golden. Stir in all remaining ingredients except cilantro, and heat to boiling.

2. Add fish to skillet and spoon on the sauce. Cook gently until fillets are cooked through and sauce is thick. (Or, to bake: Arrange fillets in a single layer in a nonstick baking dish and spoon the hot sauce mixture over them. Bake in a preheated 425-degree oven for 10 to 15 minutes or until fillets are opaque and flake easily.) Sprinkle with cilantro or parsley. Serve with Tabasco sauce and lemon wedges, if desired.

MAKES 4 SERVINGS, 220 CALORIES EACH.

❦

BARBADOS STEW, "FLYING FISH" STYLE

2 onions, chopped
½ cup white wine
2 bell peppers (red, green, or
   yellow), diced
1 jalapeño pepper, chopped, or
   generous pinch cayenne
   pepper (optional)
2 teaspoons fresh thyme or ½
   teaspoon dried thyme
1 can (8 ounces) sliced
   tomatoes, with liquid
   Pinch ground cloves
   Salt and black pepper to taste
6 fillets of flying fish, whiting, or
   other fish (about 1½
   pounds)
   Juice of 1 lime or ½ lemon
2 tablespoons chopped fresh
   parsley

1. Prepare a large nonstick skillet or electric frying pan liberally with cooking spray. Add onions, and cook over moderate heat just until they begin to brown. Add wine, bell peppers, jalapeño, if desired, and half the thyme. Cook until wine begins to simmer. Stir in tomatoes, cloves, salt and black pepper, if desired. Return to a simmer, and cook for 5 minutes.

2. Arrange fish fillets on top; sprinkle with lime juice and remaining thyme. Cover and simmer just until fish begins to flake—8 to 15 minutes, depending on variety. Serve from skillet; spoon sauce over fillets and sprinkle with parsley.

MAKES 6 SERVINGS, UNDER 165 CALORIES EACH.

❦

JAMAICAN-STYLE CURRIED COD STEAKS

1 can (16 ounces) sliced
   tomatoes, with liquid
2 potatoes, thinly sliced
1 green bell pepper, seeded and
   chopped
1 onion, chopped
2 teaspoons curry powder
2 tablespoons lime or lemon
   juice
1 teaspoon salad oil
½ teaspoon coconut flavoring
   (optional)
1 pound cod or other fish steaks
   or fillets
   Dash hot red pepper sauce

1. Combine tomatoes, potatoes, bell pepper, onion, and curry powder in a shallow nonstick baking dish well prepared with cooking spray. Cover with foil and bake in preheated 450-degree oven for 20 minutes.

2. Meanwhile, combine juice, oil, and coconut flavoring, if desired, in a plastic bag. Cut fish in serving-size pieces and add to bag; set aside while vegetables bake.

3. Uncover tomato-potato mixture. Arrange fish fillets on top, and spoon a little tomato mixture over them. Bake, uncovered, 4 to 5 minutes more or until fish flakes easily with fork. Serve with sauce and potatoes.

MAKES 4 SERVINGS, 210 CALORIES EACH.

MOCK-FRIED FLYING FISH, BARBADOS STYLE

1   egg or equivalent egg substitute
2   tablespoons lime or lemon juice
1   tablespoon salad oil
4   tablespoons bread crumbs
     Pinch each dried thyme and marjoram, onion powder, garlic powder, ground cloves, paprika, cayenne pepper
     Pinch salt and coarsely ground black pepper
8   fish fillets (1½ pounds)

1. Beat egg, juice, and oil together in a shallow dish; stir bread crumbs and seasonings together in another. Dip fish fillets first in egg mixture, then in crumb mixture. Arrange in a single layer on a nonstick baking tray well prepared with cooking spray.

2. Bake in a preheated 475-degree oven for 7 to 10 minutes without turning, until crisp and just cooked through. (Use an oven thermometer and don't put the tray in the oven until it has been thoroughly preheated.)

Makes 8 fillets, approximately 130 calories each.

BAKED COD FILLETS WITH BASIL

½   pound cod or other ocean fish fillets (haddock, lingcod, orange roughy, etc.)
1   teaspoon olive oil
1   teaspoon lemon juice
¼   teaspoon dried basil, crushed
⅛   teaspoon cracked black pepper
     Dash salt
2   plum tomatoes, cored and cut crosswise into thin slices
2   teaspoons grated Parmesan cheese

1. Pat fish dry and cut into two serving pieces. Combine oil

and lemon juice in a nonstick baking dish prepared with cooking spray. Add fish fillets and turn them to coat both sides lightly. Sprinkle with basil, coarse pepper, and salt. Overlap tomatoes in an even layer on fish and sprinkle with Parmesan cheese.

2. Cover with foil and bake at 400 degrees for 10 to 15 minutes, until fish flakes easily.

Makes 2 servings, 145 calories each.

ST. MARTIN SOUSED FISH

1   tablespoon mixed pickling spice (or 3 bay leaves, 5 cloves, 5 whole peppercorns, dash each ground ginger, nutmeg, and allspice)
2   or 3 thin slices onion
2   fish fillets or steaks (about ½ pound total)
3   tablespoons water
2   tablespoons lime or lemon juice
1   tablespoon vinegar

1. Put whole spices in bottom of glass pie pan and cover with a layer of thinly sliced onion. Place fish on top in single layer. Pour on water, then juice and vinegar. Cover and microwave for 5 to 6 minutes or bake in a preheated 350-degree oven for 20 minutes. Times are approximate; fish is done when it loses its translucence. Remove immediately.

2. Spoon liquid in pan over fish. Cool, then refrigerate,

covered, in cooking dish. At serving time, remove fish and discard onion, spices, and liquid. Fish will keep for 4 to 6 days in refrigerator.

Makes 2 servings, approximately 110 calories each.

ST. THOMAS–STYLE MICROWAVE POACHED FISH

1   onion, halved and thinly sliced
2   fish fillets or steaks (about 4 ounces each)
½   cup water
1   tablespoon minced fresh thyme or 1 teaspoon dried thyme
2   teaspoons butter or margarine
     Juice of 2 limes or 1 lemon
     Pepper or lemon pepper to taste
2   tablespoons chopped fresh parsley

1. Arrange onion in bottom of a shallow microwave dish and place fish on top in single layer. Pour on water and sprinkle with thyme. Microwave, covered, for 5 to 6 minutes, depending on your appliance's power—just until fish loses its translucence and begins to flake. Do not overcook.

2. Use spatula to transfer each serving to a plate. Put a dab of butter or margarine on top. With a slotted spoon, arrange onions on top of fish. Sprinkle with juice, pepper, and parsley.

Makes 2 servings, approximately 170 calories each.

BAY LEAF–SEASONED SWORDFISH STEAKS, TURKISH STYLE

1½ pounds swordfish or other fish steaks
10 or 12 bay leaves
¼ cup lemon juice
1 tablespoon soft butter or margarine
6 tablespoons plain low-fat yogurt, at room temperature
    Minced fresh parsley or chives for garnish

1. In a shallow nonstick baking pan prepared with cooking spray, arrange fish steaks on top of bay leaves in single layer. Sprinkle with lemon juice and dot lightly with butter. Bake in a preheated 450-degree oven just until fish flakes—15 to 20 minutes. Don't overcook. Transfer fish steaks to a platter.
2. Discard bay leaves. Fork-blend yogurt with lemon-butter pan drippings, and spoon over fish. Sprinkle with minced parsley and serve immediately.

MAKES 6 SERVINGS, 165 CALORIES EACH.

MICROWAVED ORIENTAL SWORDFISH STEAKS

1 pound swordfish steaks
2 tablespoons orange juice
1 tablespoon low-sodium soy sauce
1 tablespoon ketchup
1 tablespoon chopped parsley
1 small clove garlic, minced
2 teaspoons sesame oil
1 teaspoon lemon juice
¼ teaspoon dried oregano
    Pinch black pepper
1 can (8 ounces) sliced water chestnuts, drained
1 large orange, peeled, seeded, and sectioned

1. On a large, shallow, microwave-safe dish, arrange steaks with thickest areas to outside edges of dish. Combine remaining ingredients except water chestnuts and orange; pour over steaks. Cover with plastic wrap and refrigerate for 30 minutes, turning once.
2. Top steaks with water chestnuts. Re-cover dish with plastic wrap, turning back one corner to vent. Microwave on high power (100%) for 2 minutes; rotate dish ¼ turn. Top steaks with orange sections, re-cover, and microwave 2 to 3 minutes more, until fish is done. Let stand, covered, for 2 to 3 minutes.

MAKES 4 SERVINGS, 220 CALORIES EACH.

PORTUGUESE FISH STEW

2 cups chopped onions
6 cloves garlic, chopped
1 tablespoon olive oil
2 potatoes, peeled and cubed
2 green bell peppers, seeded and diced
2 cups peeled diced tomatoes or 1 can (16 ounces) tomatoes, diced
1 cup dry white wine
1 cup water
1 cup tomato juice
½ cup loosely packed cilantro or parsley, or ¼ cup each
2 bay leaves
¼ teaspoon ground nutmeg
    Salt and coarsely ground black pepper to taste
1½ pounds boneless fish, cut in large cubes (see Note 1 below)
1 tablespoon Piri-Piri (see Note 2 below) or hot red pepper sauce, or to taste (optional)

1. Combine 1 cup of onions, the garlic, and olive oil in large nonstick pot. Cook over low heat, stirring often, just until onions start to brown. Stir in remaining onions and all remaining ingredients except fish and Piri-Piri. Cover and simmer for 30 minutes.
2. Arrange fish carefully on top of simmering stew. Cover and simmer an additional 5 to 8 minutes, just until fish begins to flake. To serve, discard bay leaves and spoon the stew into soup plates. Piri-Piri may be added individually at the table. Serve with crusty Italian-style bread, if desired.

Notes: (1) Use at least 4 kinds of fish steaks or fillets; choose from among cod, swordfish, hake, halibut, fresh tuna, and mackerel, for example. (2) Piri-Piri sauce is a hot condiment on every table in Portugal; it's made from fiery Angola peppers. The closest substitute would be a Louisiana-style hot red pepper sauce.

MAKES 6 SERVINGS, APPROXIMATELY 375 CALORIES EACH.

OVEN-FRIED CAJUN-STYLE BLACKENED REDFISH

1 pound redfish, tilefish, red snapper, bluefish, or salmon fillets, ¾ inch thick
¼ cup diet margarine
    Juice of ½ lemon
4 teaspoons dried powdered thyme
1 tablespoon flour
1 teaspoon cayenne pepper, or to taste
½ teaspoon coarsely ground black pepper
½ teaspoon salt or garlic salt, or to taste (optional)
    Pinch ground cloves

1. Place cast iron skillet (or griddle or baking pan) with oven-safe iron handle in oven. Set oven at highest temperature setting, 475 to 500 degrees, and let skillet heat until oven reaches temperature.

2. Meanwhile, wash fillets in cold water and pat dry. Melt diet margarine with lemon juice. Combine remaining ingredients, mixing well; sprinkle on a shallow plate. Dip fillets first in lemon-margarine mixture, then in dry mixture, coating both sides.

3. Slide out oven rack and arrange fillets, skin side down, in a single layer in the hot skillet. Pour any remaining lemon-margarine mixture on top and sprinkle on any remaining seasoning mix. Slide rack back into oven and close door. Set a timer for 12 minutes; do not open oven. When timer rings, use a spatula to transfer fish to plates. Serve with lemon wedges and chopped parsley.

MAKES 4 SERVINGS; PER SERVING: 160 CALORIES WITH REDFISH; 150 CALORIES WITH TILEFISH; 165 CALORIES WITH RED SNAPPER; 195 CALORIES WITH BLUEFISH; 305 CALORIES WITH SALMON.

❧

AEGEAN-STYLE SWORDFISH WITH MUSSELS

1 pound swordfish or shark steaks, cut in 4 pieces
1 tablespoon instant-blending flour
1 tablespoon extra-virgin olive oil
4 ounces fresh mushrooms, sliced
1 clove garlic, minced
½ cup dry white wine
2 bay leaves
1 tablespoon minced fresh thyme or dill
2 pounds live mussels, washed
¼ cup loosely packed chopped fresh parsley

1. Coat fish lightly with flour. Heat oil in a large nonstick pan over moderate heat. Add fish, mushrooms, and garlic, and cook for about 6 minutes, turning fish once. Add wine, bay leaves, and thyme. Bring to a sim-

mer, and cook for 3 minutes.

2. Meanwhile, rinse mussels in cold tap water and pull off any clinging seaweed. Discard any mussels that are open and don't close when insides are tickled with tip of knife. Arrange mussels over swordfish. Cover pan and steam for 3 to 4 minutes, until mussels are open. Before serving, discard bay leaves and any mussels that fail to open; sprinkle with parsley.

MAKES 4 SERVINGS, 270 CALORIES EACH.

❧

ITALIAN-STYLE SEAFOOD STEW

1 medium onion, chopped
2 cloves garlic, minced
1 tablespoon olive oil
2 cups water
1 cup dry white wine
2 plum tomatoes, diced
½ teaspoon dried basil
¼ teaspoon crushed hot red pepper flakes
1 bay leaf
   Salt and black pepper to taste
1 pound mixed firm fish (such as halibut, sea bass, red snapper, rockfish), cut into 1½ inch chunks
½ pound raw medium shrimp, peeled and deveined, or 24 mussels, scrubbed and debearded, or a combination of both

1. In large soup kettle, combine onion, garlic, and oil. Sauté for 5 minutes or until onion is soft. Add water, wine, tomatoes, basil, red pepper, bay leaf, salt, and black pepper. Bring to a simmer, partially covered, and cook for 10 minutes.

2. Add seafood and simmer, covered, for 8 to 10 minutes or until fish flakes when tested with a fork. Remove and discard bay leaf.

MAKES 4 MAIN-COURSE SERVINGS, 215 CALORIES EACH.

BAKED SCROD ESPAÑOL

4 ounces fresh mushrooms, sliced
1 tablespoon olive oil
1 can (16 ounces) stewed tomatoes, well broken up
¼ cup dry sherry
1 onion, minced
1 green bell pepper, seeded and diced
1 clove garlic, minced
1 small bay leaf
1 pound scrod or cod fillets or steaks

1. Combine mushrooms and olive oil in a nonstick skillet. Cook, stirring, over high heat until mushrooms brown. Stir in all remaining ingredients, except fish. Bring to a simmer and cook for 5 to 6 minutes. Remove and discard bay leaf.

2. Arrange fish in a single layer in a shallow nonstick baking pan. Cover with sauce. Bake in a preheated 375-degree oven for 15 to 25 minutes, basting occasionally, until fish flakes easily.

MAKES 4 SERVINGS, 185 CALORIES EACH.

❧

GARLIC-BROILED BLUEFISH

8 ounces bluefish fillets
2 tablespoons lemon juice
2 teaspoons olive oil
2 small cloves garlic, minced
   Pinch each dried thyme and paprika (optional)

1. Arrange fish in a single layer in a nonstick broiler-proof pan. Combine lemon juice, oil, garlic, and thyme, if desired. Spread fish with garlic mixture. Sprinkle with paprika, if desired.

2. Broil or barbecue about 4 inches from heat source for 5 to 6 minutes without turning, until fish flakes easily. Baste with pan juices every 2 minutes.

MAKES 2 SERVINGS, 180 CALORIES EACH.

SAUTÉED CATFISH WITH RED PEPPER CREAM

    4   skinless catfish fillets (about 1 pound)
         Salt and black pepper to taste
    1   teaspoon lemon juice
    1   teaspoon finely chopped shallots
    1   clove garlic, minced
         Flour
    1   tablespoon sesame oil
    1   tablespoon olive oil or additional sesame oil
    1   cup Red Pepper Cream (recipe follows)

1. Rinse catfish and pat dry. Season with a little salt, black pepper, and lemon juice. Rub with shallots and garlic. Dust with flour and shake off excess.

2. Heat sesame oil and olive oil in large heavy skillet. Cook fillets until lightly golden on both sides, allowing about 10 minutes cooking time per inch of thickness (measured at thickest part of fillet). Place catfish over a small amount of Red Pepper Cream on individual serving plates.

MAKES 4 SERVINGS CATFISH, 190 CALORIES EACH.

☆

RED PEPPER CREAM

    3   red bell peppers (about 1 pound) or 1 cup red pepper purée
    1   teaspoon minced shallots or onions
    1   small clove garlic
    1   teaspoon olive oil
    2   tablespoons white wine vinegar
    2   tablespoons white wine
    1   tablespoon light cream cheese, diced
         Salt and black pepper to taste

1. To make red pepper purée: Broil peppers on foil-lined baking sheet, turning frequently, for about 10 minutes or until blistered and blackened.

Wrap in foil and set aside. When cool enough to handle, remove and discard skins, ribs, and seeds. Purée in blender or food processor until smooth. Set aside.

2. In a heavy saucepan over moderate heat, sauté shallots and garlic in olive oil until soft but not brown. Add vinegar, wine, and cheese. Bring to boil and stir in red pepper purée. Simmer for 5 minutes.

3. In blender or food processor, blend for 10 to 15 seconds, until mixture is smooth. Strain into a saucepan. Season to taste with salt and black pepper. Heat and serve warm.

MAKES ABOUT 1¼ CUPS, UNDER 15 CALORIES PER TABLESPOON.

☆

SALMON TERIYAKI

    ¼   cup dry white wine
    4   tablespoons water
    1   tablespoon sugar
    2   tablespoons light soy sauce
    ¼   teaspoon ground ginger or 1 teaspoon grated ginger root, or to taste
    1   teaspoon cornstarch
    4   salmon steaks (about 4 ounces each)

1. Combine wine, 3 tablespoons water, sugar, soy sauce, and ginger in saucepan; bring to a boil. Dissolve cornstarch in remaining water and add to soy sauce mixture. Cook, stirring, until thickened. Baste salmon with mixture.

2. Broil 5 inches from heat, allowing 10 minutes cooking time per inch of thickness. Baste several times during cooking. Do not turn salmon. Serve with remaining sauce.

MAKES 4 SERVINGS, 270 CALORIES EACH.

☆

MICROWAVED FILLET OF SOLE MEDITERRANEAN

    3   tablespoons finely chopped onion
    2   cloves garlic, minced
    1   tablespoon olive oil
    1   can (16 ounces) whole tomatoes or 2 large tomatoes
    ¾   cup sliced ripe black olives, well drained
    ½   teaspoon dried oregano, crushed
    1   tablespoon minced fresh parsley
         Salt and pepper to taste
    1   pound sole or flounder fillets, in 4 pieces

1. Combine onion, garlic, and oil in 4-cup glass measure. Microwave on high power (100%) for 2 minutes or until soft. Drain tomatoes, reserving juice; seed and chop. Reserve a few olive slices for garnish. Add the remaining olives, as well as the tomatoes, oregano, parsley, salt, and pepper, to the onion mixture.

2. Pat fillets dry. Spread tomato mixture on fillets and roll up from narrow end. Arrange, seam side down, in microwave-safe baking dish prepared with oil or cooking spray. Cover with

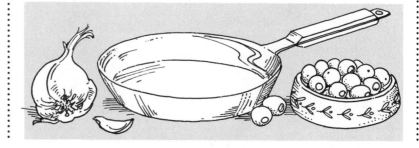

vented plastic wrap, and microwave on high power (100%) for 3 minutes, rotating the dish once. Then let this stand, covered, for 3 minutes to finish cooking. Fish is cooked when it just flakes with a fork.

3. Place reserved tomato liquid in a 2-cup measure; microwave on high power (100%) for 2 minutes. Spoon some of tomato liquid over fish and garnish with reserved olives.

MAKES 4 SERVINGS, 190 CALORIES EACH.

❧

CHEDDAR AND FLOUNDER FLORENTINE

2   packages (10 ounces each) frozen chopped spinach, thawed
4   flounder fillets (4 ounces each), fresh or defrosted
2   tablespoons minced fresh onion or 2 teaspoons instant onion (optional)
½   cup skim milk
    Generous pinch ground nutmeg
4   slices extra-sharp Cheddar cheese (½ ounce each), crumbled
2   teaspoons lemon juice
    Seasoned salt and pepper to taste
    Paprika to taste

1. Mix spinach with onion, if desired; spread over bottom of a shallow, 8-inch nonstick baking dish prepared with cooking spray. Pour milk over spinach and sprinkle with nutmeg. Arrange cheese over spinach. Place fish fillets over cheese in a single layer and then sprinkle with lemon juice, salt, pepper, and paprika.

2. Cover pan tightly with foil. Bake in a preheated 400-degree oven until fish flakes easily—about 20 minutes.

MAKES 4 SERVINGS, 195 CALORIES EACH.

MARINATED BLUEFISH, MIDDLE EASTERN STYLE

1   small onion, thinly sliced
8   to 10 bay leaves
1   pound bluefish fillets
2   tablespoons lemon juice
    Salt or garlic salt and pepper to taste
1   teaspoon olive oil

1. Arrange onion slices and bay leaves in a shallow non-stick pan. Add fish in a single layer and sprinkle with lemon juice, salt, and pepper. Cover and refrigerate for several hours, turning occasionally.

2. Remove and discard bay leaves. Brush fish with ½ teaspoon of the oil; broil 3 to 4 inches from heat source for 3 to 4 minutes. Turn fish, brush with remaining oil, and broil 3 to 4 minutes more or until fish flakes easily.

MAKES 4 SERVINGS, 155 CALORIES EACH.

❧

BLUEFISH ROLL-UPS

2   pounds bluefish fillets, cut into 12 strips
1   cup white wine
½   cup salt-free almonds, crushed to crumbs
½   cup loosely packed, finely chopped fresh parsley
1   teaspoon each dried oregano and lemon pepper
12 cherry tomatoes

1. Soak fish strips in wine for 5 to 10 minutes in refrigerator. Mix almonds, parsley, oregano, and pepper in a small bowl. Dip fish strips in almond mixture, then roll each strip around a cherry tomato.

2. Place rolls on a nonstick baking dish prepared with cooking spray. Bake in a preheated 400-degree oven for 10 to 14 minutes.

MAKES 8 SERVINGS, 200 CALORIES EACH.

CURRIED CATFISH, THAI STYLE

2   tablespoons light soy sauce
1   tablespoon salad oil
2   teaspoons curry powder
½   teaspoon ground ginger
    Lemon pepper to taste
¼   teaspoon coconut extract (optional)
1   pound catfish fillets
¼   cup dry-roasted peanuts

1. Combine all ingredients except fillets and peanuts in a plastic bag. Add fillets and toss to coat evenly.

2. Arrange fillets in single layer on a nonstick pan coated with cooking spray. Bake in a preheated 475-degree oven for 8 minutes. Top with peanuts.

MAKES 4 SERVINGS, 200 CALORIES EACH.

❧

MAHI MAHI, POLYNESIAN STYLE

1   pound mahi mahi
1   tablespoon light soy sauce
    Pinch each ground cinnamon, ginger, and cloves
1   can (8 ounces) juice-packed pineapple chunks, drained, with juice reserved
2   teaspoons curry powder
2   bell peppers (1 red, 1 green), seeded and thinly sliced

1. Combine fish with soy sauce, cinnamon, ginger, and cloves in a nonmetallic bowl. Marinate for 30 minutes at room temperature.

2. Remove fish from marinade; arrange in nonstick baking pan prepared with cooking spray. Combine pineapple juice with curry and pour over fish. Add pineapple chunks and bell pepper. Cover pan tightly with foil.

3. Bake in a preheated 350-degree oven for 15 minutes. Uncover and bake 5 minutes more, or until cooked through.

MAKES 4 SERVINGS, APPROXIMATELY 150 CALORIES EACH.

CRAB IMPERIAL–STUFFED FLOUNDER

1 pound flounder fillets, in 4 pieces

CRAB IMPERIAL MIXTURE:

1½ teaspoons flour
¼ cup low-fat milk
1 egg white, well beaten
2 tablespoons finely chopped red or green bell pepper
1 tablespoon light mayonnaise
1 tablespoon finely chopped fresh parsley
¾ teaspoon lemon juice
¼ teaspoon dry mustard
¼ teaspoon Worcestershire sauce
⅛ teaspoon seasoned salt
⅛ teaspoon celery salt
⅛ teaspoon black or white pepper
Generous dash cayenne pepper
½ pound crabmeat, flaked
¼ cup dry bread crumbs
Paprika for garnish
Lemon wedges for garnish

1. Rinse flounder fillets and pat dry; set aside.

2. In a saucepan, stir flour into milk. Heat and stir until thickened; cool. Add egg, bell pepper, mayonnaise, parsley, lemon juice, and seasonings (except paprika). Gently fold in crabmeat. Divide the crab mixture and spoon onto each fillet. Roll into pinwheel shape starting at the narrow end. Secure with toothpick if needed. Stand up in a nonstick baking pan prepared with cooking spray. Sprinkle with bread crumbs and garnish with paprika.

3. Bake in a preheated 400-degree oven for 12 to 15 minutes or until fish is opaque and begins to flake. Garnish with lemon wedges to serve.

MAKES 4 SERVINGS, 195 CALORIES EACH.

MEXICAN GARLIC-BROILED HADDOCK

1 pound fresh haddock or other fish fillets
4 or 5 cloves garlic, coarsely chopped
3 tablespoons butter or margarine
3 tablespoons lime juice
2 tablespoons water
Pinch cumin seeds
Salt and pepper to taste
2 tablespoons chopped fresh cilantro or parsley for garnish

1. In a shallow nonstick roasting pan prepared with cooking spray, arrange fillets in a single layer. In a small saucepan over moderate heat, cook garlic, butter, juice, and water, stirring until butter melts; pour mixture over fish. Sprinkle with cumin, salt, and pepper. Broil 4 to 5 inches from heat source, occasionally spooning pan liquid over fish, until fish flakes easily.

MAKES 4 SERVINGS, 175 CALORIES EACH.

MEXICAN GARLIC BASTE FOR BROILED FISH FILLETS

1 large clove garlic, mashed and finely minced
2 tablespoons lime or lemon juice
1 tablespoon soft butter or margarine
1 pound fish steaks or fillets
¼ cup loosely packed minced fresh parsley (optional)

1. Blend garlic with juice and butter, using the back of a tablespoon. Spread mixture over

fish. Broil 3 to 4 inches from heat source just until fish flakes—5 to 8 minutes, depending on thickness. Sprinkle with fresh parsley, if desired.

MAKES 4 SERVINGS, UNDER 125 CALORIES EACH (WITH SOLE, FLOUNDER, OR COD).

ITALIAN-STYLE MICROWAVED HALIBUT STEAKS

1 pound halibut steaks, approximately 1 inch thick
⅓ cup light Italian dressing
1 tablespoon lemon juice
¼ teaspoon pepper
¼ teaspoon paprika

1. Place steaks in a microwave-safe dish. Combine remaining ingredients and pour over fish. Cover dish with plastic wrap and refrigerate for 30 minutes, turning once.

2. Turn back one corner of plastic wrap for venting. Cook 4 to 5 minutes on high power (100%), rotating dish ¼ turn after 2 minutes. Let stand 2 to 3 minutes before serving.

MAKES 4 SERVINGS, 115 CALORIES EACH.

HONG KONG GROUPER IN SWEET 'N' SOUR PLUM SAUCE

1 dressed whole fresh grouper (about 2 pounds) or 1 pound fish steaks or fillets, in 4 serving pieces
5 tablespoons unsweetened plum purée
¼ cup white wine
3 tablespoons light soy sauce
Dash hot red pepper sauce or pinch hot red pepper flakes
¼ cup water (approximate)
2 tablespoons minced fresh cilantro or parsley for garnish
2 tablespoons thinly sliced green onions for garnish

1. Arrange fish in a baking dish. Stir together plum purée, wine, soy sauce, and hot red pepper sauce and add water to make 1 cup basting sauce. Pour sauce over fish.

2. Bake in preheated 400-degree oven just until fish begins to flake—about 15 minutes for whole fish, 8 to 10 minutes for fillets or steaks. Baste once or twice as it cooks. Serve with pan juices. Garnish with cilantro and green onion slices.

MAKES 4 SERVINGS, 120 CALORIES EACH.

❧

MUSSELS AU GRATIN

4   pounds fresh live mussels
½   cup water
4   cloves garlic, minced
1   teaspoon pepper
2   tablespoons olive oil
¼   cup finely chopped onion
½   cup finely chopped parsley
2   tablespoons lemon juice
¾   cup cracker crumbs
½   cup grated Parmesan cheese
    Lemon wedges for garnish

1. Wash mussels under cold running water; pull off beards. Discard any mussels that do not close tightly when the insides are lightly tickled with the tip of a knife.

2. In large pot, combine water, half of the garlic, and half the pepper. Bring to a boil. Add mussels and cook until they open, about 7 to 10 minutes. With slotted spoon, transfer mussels from broth onto rimmed baking sheets. Break off top halves of shells and discard along with any unopened shells.

3. Heat oil in medium skillet. Sauté the remaining garlic and the onion until soft. Add parsley and lemon juice. Combine with cracker crumbs and Parmesan. Sprinkle mixture over mussels.

4. Bake in preheated 400-degree oven for about 5 minutes

or until crumbs are lightly browned. Serve warm with lemon wedges.

MAKES 6 MAIN-COURSE SERVINGS, 220 CALORIES EACH.

❧

SHRIMP, BROCCOLI, AND RED PEPPER, STIR-FRY STYLE

2   teaspoons cornstarch
½   cup chicken broth
4   tablespoons dry sherry
1   pound medium-size shrimp, shelled and deveined, with tails left on
½   teaspoon salt, or to taste
¾   cup unsalted cashew nuts
4   tablespoons vegetable oil
2   cups broccoli florets plus 1 cup broccoli stems sliced ¼ inch thick
1   red bell pepper, seeded and cut into 1-inch squares (about 1 cup)
1   tablespoon finely chopped fresh ginger root
1   clove garlic, crushed

1. In a small bowl, combine cornstarch, chicken broth, and 2 tablespoons sherry, stirring until well blended; set aside. In a medium-size bowl, combine shrimp, remaining sherry, and salt, tossing to coat; set aside. In a 12-inch skillet or wok over medium heat, toast cashew nuts until golden brown, shaking pan frequently—about 3 minutes. Remove nuts from skillet and set them aside.

2. In same skillet over moderately high heat, warm 2 tablespoons oil. Add broccoli florets and stems and bell pepper; cook for 2 minutes, stirring constantly, or until vegetables are crisp-tender. With a slotted spoon, transfer vegetables to a large bowl. In skillet over moderately high heat, warm remaining 2 tablespoons oil. Add shrimp; cook, stirring constantly, until shrimp turn pink. With a

slotted spoon, transfer shrimp to the large bowl.

3. Add ginger root and garlic to skillet; cook for 1 minute, stirring constantly, or until golden. Stir cornstarch mixture again. Add quickly to skillet, and cook, stirring constantly, until mixture comes to a boil and thickens. Return shrimp, vegetables, and cashews to skillet; cook for 2 minutes, stirring constantly, until heated through.

MAKES 4 SERVINGS, 474 CALORIES EACH.

❧

SPICY CAJUN SHRIMP

2   dozen fresh or thawed large shrimp or 1 pound medium shrimp
1   teaspoon dried basil, crushed
1   teaspoon ground cayenne pepper
½   teaspoon black pepper
½   teaspoon crushed red pepper
½   teaspoon dried thyme, crushed
½   teaspoon dried oregano, crushed
½   teaspoon salt, or to taste
2   tablespoons margarine
1½ teaspoons minced garlic
1   teaspoon Worcestershire sauce
1   large tomato, peeled and coarsely diced
4   tablespoons beer, at room temperature
3   cups cooked rice (optional)

1. Clean and devein the shrimp under cold running water. Drain well, then set aside.

2. In a small bowl, combine basil, cayenne, black pepper, crushed red pepper, thyme, oregano, and salt. In a large nonstick skillet over high heat, combine these with margarine, garlic, and Worcestershire sauce.

3. When margarine melts, add the tomato, then the shrimp. Cook and stir for 2 minutes. Add the beer; cover and cook 1 minute more. Remove from heat. Serve with rice, if desired.

MAKES 4 SERVINGS, 175 CALORIES EACH.

SZECHUAN-STYLE SNOW CRAB

1 pound Alaska snow crab or
  other crab meat
¼ cup water
2 tablespoons Hoisin sauce or
  ketchup
2 tablespoons dry sherry
2 teaspoons Worcestershire sauce
2 teaspoons cornstarch
2 teaspoons sugar (optional)
  Salt to taste (optional)
1 onion, cut into 8 wedges, with
  layers separated
1 green bell pepper, seeded and
  cut into ¼-inch slices
2 teaspoons oil
1 clove garlic, minced
  Dash ground hot red pepper
¼ cup sliced green onion,
  including tops

1. Thaw crab, if necessary;
cut in chunks and set aside.

2. In a small jar, combine
water, Hoisin, sherry, Worcestershire sauce, cornstarch,
sugar and salt, if desired. Cover,
shake well, and reserve.

3. Sauté onion and green
pepper in 1 teaspoon oil for 2
minutes or until onion is tender;
remove from skillet. Add garlic,
red pepper, and remaining oil;
sauté for 10 seconds. Add water
mixture; cook, stirring, until
mixture thickens. Add crab and
sautéed vegetables; cook 1 minute longer or until heated
through. Sprinkle with green
onion.

MAKES 4 SERVINGS, 180 CALORIES EACH.

✦

SCALLOP SEVICHE

1 pound fresh bay or sea scallops
1 small onion, thinly sliced
½ cup fresh lemon juice
7 or 8 bay leaves
  Salt and coarsely ground black
  pepper to taste
1 clove minced garlic (optional)
  Pinch hot red pepper flakes
  (optional)

1. Combine ingredients in
nonmetallic bowl or container.
Cover and refrigerate for 24
hours. Discard bay leaves. Remove scallops from marinade
and serve chilled.

MAKES 12 APPETIZER SERVINGS, 35 CALORIES EACH.

✦

SZECHUAN SCALLOPS WITH SWEET PEPPERS

**Sweet peppers replace Chinese
chili peppers in this dish, made
hot with red pepper flakes and
a dash of hot red pepper sauce,
if you like.**

3 sweet bell peppers (red, green,
  yellow, or 1 of each), seeded
  and cut in 1-inch squares
1 large sweet onion, halved, cut
  in 1-inch cubes, layers
  separated
¾ cup spicy tomato juice
2 tablespoons dry sherry or other
  white wine
2 tablespoons light soy sauce
½ teaspoon ground ginger
1 teaspoon hot red pepper flakes,
  or to taste
  Hot red pepper sauce to taste
  (optional)
2 cups fresh or thawed scallops
  (about 10 ounces)

1. Arrange all ingredients
near stove. Prepare a large nonstick skillet or electric frying pan
liberally with cooking spray. Arrange onion leaves in skillet in a
single layer. Cook over medium
heat just until onion begins to
brown.

2. Combine all ingredients, except scallops, in skillet;
cover, bring to a simmer, and
cook for 5 minutes. Uncover and
simmer until sauce thickens—4
or 5 minutes more. Stir in scallops, and cook just until heated
through and coated with sauce.
Serve with plain rice if desired.

MAKES 4 SERVINGS, 175 CALORIES EACH;
RICE ADDS 110 CALORIES PER ½-CUP.

CRAB IMPERIAL– STUFFED SHRIMP

1½ pounds large shrimp

CRAB IMPERIAL MIXTURE:
1 tablespoon flour
½ cup low-fat milk
1 egg, well beaten, or equivalent
  egg substitute
2 tablespoons light mayonnaise
2 tablespoons finely chopped fresh
  parsley
1½ teaspoons lemon juice
½ teaspoon dry mustard
¼ teaspoon Worcestershire sauce
¼ teaspoon seasoned salt
¼ teaspoon celery salt
¼ teaspoon black or white pepper
⅛ teaspoon cayenne pepper
1 pound crabmeat, flaked
½ cup dry bread crumbs
  Paprika for garnish

1. Peel and devein the
shrimp, leaving tail intact. Butterfly the shrimp by splitting
them down the back; do not cut
all the way through. Arrange,
split side up, in nonstick baking
pan prepared with cooking spray.
Set aside.

2. In a 1-quart pot, stir
flour into milk. Heat and stir until thickened; cool. Add egg, mayonnaise, parsley, lemon juice,
and seasonings (except paprika).
Gently fold in crabmeat. Spoon
equal portions of crabmeat mixture into each shrimp. Sprinkle
with bread crumbs and paprika.

3. Bake for 2½ minutes on
lower rack of preheated 500-degree oven. Then broil about 5
inches from the heat source for
1½ minutes, until golden brown.

MAKES 6 SERVINGS, 215 CALORIES EACH
WITH EGG; 205 CALORIES EACH WITH EGG
SUBSTITUTE.

Barbecue Ideas from Every Corner of the Globe

COOKING over coals is a calorie-wise way to prepare food. Unlike most other cooking methods, barbecuing (as well as broiling) subtracts fat rather than adding it. The sight of fat dripping into the coals is reassuring evidence that calories are going up in smoke!

There are, however, two calorie-enhancing pitfalls waiting to trap the health-minded backyard chef: choosing high-fat meat and adding more fat and calories in the form of marinades or bastes. To get around these traps:

- *Avoid* high-fat marbled steaks, greasy ribs, and those fat-fringed chops.
  Instead, choose lean meats, poultry, and seafood. Combine cubes of meat with lots of crunchy veggies on skewers.
- *Avoid* oily bastes and sugary barbecue sauces that obliterate natural flavors under a blanket of unneeded calories.
  Instead, choose fruit or tomato juices for bastes. Add flavor with fresh herbs, hickory chips, or mesquite.
- *Avoid* fatty hamburger meat. The higher the fat content, the higher the calories. Resist the urge to buy "inexpensive" fatty chopped meat, with maybe 1,200 calories per pound.
  Instead, choose lean ground meat. It's not as expensive as it seems because hamburgers made from lean beef shrink less—you get more patties per pound!
- *Avoid* high-fat frankfurters. Traditional wienies can contain as much as 27 percent fat and as much as 140 to 150 calories each.
  Instead, choose chicken and turkey franks.

- *Avoid* high-calorie toppings. Sweet relishes can add 21 calories per tablespoon. Chili sauce is 16 calories per tablespoon. That innocuous slice of Cheddar that turns a meat patty into a cheeseburger can add 96 calories to the count. Ketchup is 16 calories per tablespoon.
  Instead, choose leaner toppings. Mustard is about 15 calories a tablespoon, but the hotter it is, the less you'll use. Sour or dill pickle relish is lower than sweet relish. Sauerkraut is a good bet at only 3 calories per tablespoon. If you must cover your hamburger with cheese, select part-skim varieties—mozzarella, for example. Ketchup contains sugar; why not use fresh tomato slices instead? Serve burgers California-style, with tomato slices, crisp lettuce, and fragrant sweet onion.

Here's another tip—for cooking chicken on the grill. To preserve its natural flavor and moisture, cook it slowly over glowing coals with no flames. Start with the skin side down and the grill about 2 inches above the coals; turn the chicken once at this level to seal in juices. Raise the grill and complete cooking, turning and basting often. To test for doneness, insert a fork; when the juices run clear, cooking is complete.

What makes barbecuing especially appealing is its long and varied tradition. It's the most fundamental way to cook, so every culinary culture has its special contribution that can be borrowed for American backyards.

HAWAIIAN BROIL FOR THE BARBECUE

½ cup white wine
½ cup water
3 tablespoons soy sauce
3 tablespoons thawed pineapple juice concentrate
2 cloves garlic, minced
1 tablespoon ground ginger
1 teaspoon each curry powder and pumpkin pie spice
3 pounds thick boneless top round steak, trimmed of fringe fat

1. Put meat in a plastic bag and place bag in a shallow bowl (to catch any drippings). Combine remaining ingredients and add mixture to bag. Refrigerate for 24 hours. If meat is frozen, put frozen meat in the bowl and let it defrost in mixture.

2. Remove meat from the marinade and broil or barbecue 4 inches from heat source, turning once, until medium rare—12 to 14 minutes. (Use a meat thermometer to check doneness: 130 degrees is medium rare, 140 degrees is medium. The U.S. Department of Agriculture suggests 140 degrees for safety.) Thick marinated round steak can also be affixed inside a revolving rotisserie basket in a covered grill over the coals. Add some hickory or mesquite chips to the coals to flavor the meat with fragrant smoke as it turns. To serve, remove the meat to a cutting board and slice very thinly against the grain.

EACH 3½-OUNCE SERVING HAS APPROX-IMATELY 155 CALORIES.

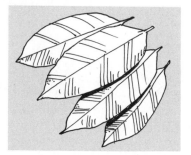

SPICY CAJUN KEBABS

1½ pounds round steak, trimmed of fringe fat and cut in 1½-inch cubes
¾ cup plain or spicy tomato juice
3 tablespoons Worcestershire sauce
3 tablespoons lemon juice
2 cloves garlic, minced
2 teaspoons fresh thyme or ½ teaspoon dried thyme
1 to 2 teaspoons hot red pepper sauce (optional)
3 onions, quartered, layers separated
3 bell peppers (1 red, 1 green, 1 yellow), seeded and cut in squares

1. Combine meat with remaining ingredients except onions and peppers. Refrigerate, covered, for 6 to 8 hours.

2. Thread the cubes of meat on skewers, alternating with pieces of onion and pepper. Brush vegetables with reserved marinade. Broil or barbecue 3 to 4 inches from heat source for 12 to 14 minutes, turning once.

MAKES 6 SERVINGS, 210 CALORIES EACH.

SPICY MARINATED FLANK STEAK

½ cup apple juice
½ cup cider vinegar
1½ pounds beef flank steak
2 cloves garlic, chopped
¼ cup chopped bay leaves
1 tablespoon whole peppercorns
2 teaspoons cumin seeds
1 teaspoon olive oil

1. Pour apple juice and vinegar over flank steak. Sprinkle with garlic and all seasonings. Roll steak and place in plastic bag in refrigerator all day or leave overnight.

2. Scrape bay leaves and other seasonings from steak with a knife. Brush steak lightly with oil. Broil or barbecue 3 inches from heat source until done to taste—about 4 minutes per side for medium rare. Save leftover steak for sandwiches.

MAKES 6 SERVINGS, 205 CALORIES EACH.

LAMB SHISH KEBAB ON THE GRILL

2 pounds lean lamb, cut from leg of lamb, trimmed of fat, and cut in 2-inch cubes
1 cup dry white wine
2 tablespoons fresh oregano or 2 teaspoons dried oregano
2 or 3 cloves garlic, minced
2 teaspoons salt
½ teaspoon pepper

1. Put meat cubes into a plastic bag set in a deep non-metallic bowl. Combine remaining ingredients and pour over meat. (Meat should be just covered; add a little water to marinade, if necessary). Marinate in refrigerator for at least 5 hours.

2. With a slotted spoon, remove meat from bowl, reserving marinade. Skewer meat and grill over hot coals for 20 minutes, turning frequently. Baste occasionally with reserved marinade.

EACH 4-OUNCE SERVING HAS APPROX-IMATELY 230 CALORIES.

BARBECUED LEG OF LAMB

1 leg of lamb, boned
Garlic salt and coarse ground pepper to taste
1 can (8 ounces) plain tomato sauce
½ cup ketchup
¼ cup chopped onion
1 tablespoon brown sugar
1 tablespoon oil

1. Sprinkle lamb with garlic salt and pepper. Secure lamb on rotisserie. Combine remaining ingredients and brush

on lamb frequently as it revolves on rotisserie. Continue to barbecue lamb until a meat thermometer registers internal temperature as 125 to 130 degrees for medium rare, 145 degrees for medium.

EACH 4-OUNCE SERVING HAS APPROXIMATELY 250 CALORIES.

❦

BARBECUE LONDON BROIL DIABLO

3	to 4 pounds boneless beef top round (London broil), trimmed of fat
1	cup dry red wine
1	cup beef broth, skimmed of fat
1	onion, halved and thinly sliced
2	cloves garlic, minced
2	tablespoons chopped fresh parsley
2	tablespoons ketchup
2	teaspoons liquid smoke seasoning (optional)
2	tablespoons Dijon-style mustard
2	tablespoons Worcestershire sauce

1. Combine all ingredients except mustard and Worcestershire sauce in a shallow nonmetallic bowl. Cover and refrigerate for 24 hours.

2. Drain marinade. Mix mustard with Worcestershire sauce and spread lightly on both sides of meat. Put meat on grid and adjust heat to low setting if using a gas barbecue; otherwise, raise grid 5 to 6 inches from heat source so meat cooks slowly. Close barbecue cover or tent meat loosely with aluminum foil. Barbecue for 20 to 25 minutes, then turn meat and insert meat thermometer. Continue cooking until desired degree of doneness is reached.

EACH 4-OUNCE SERVING HAS ABOUT 100 CALORIES.

POLYNESIAN-STYLE SKEWERED TURKEY

1	pound turkey breast tenderloin, cut in 2-inch cubes
1	cup sliced onions
½	cup dry white wine
⅓	cup water
¼	cup light soy sauce
2	cloves garlic
1	teaspoon curry powder
1	tablespoon honey (optional)

1. Put turkey cubes in a shallow nonmetallic bowl. In an electric blender or a food processor, purée the remaining ingredients. Pour over turkey and mix well. Refrigerate for several hours or overnight.

2. Drain and reserve marinade. Thread turkey on skewers. Broil or barbecue 3 inches from heat source, turning frequently and basting with marinade, until cooked through.

MAKES 4 SERVINGS, 170 CALORIES EACH; HONEY ADDS 15 CALORIES PER SERVING.

❦

CHINESE CHICKEN ON SKEWERS

1¼	pounds boneless chicken breasts, flattened and cut lengthwise into strips ¾ inch wide
4	ounces Canadian-style bacon or ham, diced
1	large onion, coarsely chopped
2	green bell peppers, seeded and coarsely chopped
8	ounces small fresh mushrooms
1	tablespoon salad oil
2	tablespoons light soy sauce
1	teaspoon ground ginger
	Garlic salt to taste
	Dash cayenne pepper

1. Wrap chicken strips around bacon cubes and vegetable chunks; thread on 6 skewers. Combine oil, soy sauce, and seasonings; brush over skewers, coating evenly.

2. Barbecue over hot coals for 15 minutes, turning frequently. Or place skewers on a shallow nonstick roasting pan or cookie tin and pour on marinade. Place pan in preheated 450-degree oven and bake for 15 minutes, turning once or twice during cooking.

MAKES 6 SERVINGS, 225 CALORIES EACH.

❦

TEXICANA OVEN-BARBECUED CHICKEN

1	frying chicken, cut up (about 3 pounds)
1	cup fresh or canned chicken broth or beef broth, skimmed of fat
1	can (6 ounces) tomato paste
¼	cup minced fresh or frozen green bell pepper or 2 tablespoons dried green bell pepper flakes
1	tablespoon vinegar or lemon juice
1	teaspoon dried oregano
1	teaspoon chili powder, or to taste
½	teaspoon cumin seeds

1. Arrange chicken skin side up, under broiler; broil for 15 to 20 minutes, until skin is crisp and well rendered of fat. Drain and discard fat.

2. Combine remaining ingredients; spoon over browned chicken pieces. Bake in a preheated 350-degree oven for 35 to 40 minutes, until sauce is thick and chicken is tender. Baste often.

MAKES 8 SERVINGS, 275 CALORIES EACH.

SOUTH PACIFIC HAM AND CHICKEN BROCHETTES

8 ounces cooked cured ham steak, trimmed of fat and cut in 1-inch cubes
2 chicken cutlets (1 boneless, skinless breast, halved), cut in 1-inch cubes
2 bell peppers (1 red, 1 green), seeded and cut in 1-inch squares
1 can (16 ounces) juice-packed pineapple chunks, drained, with juice reserved
¼ cup light soy sauce
2 tablespoons salad oil

1. Thread skewers, alternating ham, chicken, pepper, and pineapple pieces. Combine ⅓ cup juice from pineapple with soy sauce and oil; pour some of the mixture over skewers, rotating them.

2. Broil or barbecue for 10 minutes, turning to cook evenly and basting often with pineapple-soy marinade.

MAKES 6 SERVINGS, 225 CALORIES EACH.

❦

DILLED FISH IN FOIL

FOR EACH 1-SERVING PACKET:
4 ounces fish fillet (flounder, sole, fluke, etc.)
3 slices vine-ripe tomato, peeled
2 or 3 thin onion slices
1 tablespoon chopped fresh dill leaves
1 tablespoon lemon juice
  Salt and pepper to taste
1 small clove garlic, minced (optional)
1 bay leaf (optional)

1. Apply cooking spray to the shiny side of a sheet of heavy-duty aluminum foil large enough to hold the ingredients. (A double layer of lighter-gauge foil can be substituted.) Place fish in center, top with remaining ingredients, and fold foil loosely

to close. Crimp edges to contain liquid.

2. For barbecuing: Place on rack in a preheated covered barbecue. Cook undisturbed for 12 to 15 minutes (depending on thickness of fish), then open foil carefully. Continue to cook until fish flakes easily. Remove from foil and spoon cooking sauce over fish. Discard bay leaf before serving.

3. For oven cooking: Follow barbecuing directions in a preheated 425-degree oven, increasing cooking time to 15 to 20 minutes.

EACH 1-SERVING PACKET HAS APPROXIMATELY 155 CALORIES.

❦

SKEWERED SEA SCALLOPS

1 pound sea scallops
4 ounces small fresh mushrooms
2 bell peppers (red or green or 1 of each), seeded and cut in squares
½ cup light French dressing

1. Alternate scallops with vegetables on skewers; coat lightly with some of the dressing. Grill over charcoal or under broiler for approximately 10 minutes, turning and basting frequently with remaining dressing.

MAKES 4 SERVINGS, 180 CALORIES EACH.

Variation

Sea Scallops Satay: Add 2 tablespoons light soy sauce, ½ teaspoon ground ginger, and ¼ teaspoon curry powder to French dressing in previous recipe.

EACH SERVING HAS 190 CALORIES.

❦

SMOKY MESQUITE TUNA STEAKS

  Handful mesquite, hickory, or other hardwood chips, soaked in warm water for 1 hour
2 pounds thick tuna steaks or fillets
2 teaspoons olive oil

OPTIONAL SEASONINGS:
  Lemon juice to taste
  Salt and pepper to taste
  Bay leaves or any fresh herbs to taste

1. Preheat covered charcoal, gas, or electric grill according to manufacturer's directions. If possible, heat only one side of grill, or arrange charcoal on one side so that fish can be cooked on the other, not directly over heat. In single-burner gas or electric grill, raise grid as far from heat as possible. (Fish should cook in heat and smoke accumulated inside covered grill, rather than broiling.) Charcoal is ready when flame dies and coals are covered with white ash. When gas or electric grill is hot, turn heat control to low. Drain wood chips and sprinkle them on top of charcoal or ceramic coals.

2. Lightly coat fish with oil and arrange on grill in single layer—if possible, not directly over heat. If desired, sprinkle fish with lemon juice, salt, and pepper; arrange herbs on top. Close lid and let fish cook in smoke, without turning. Timing will depend on thickness of fish and barbecue temperature;

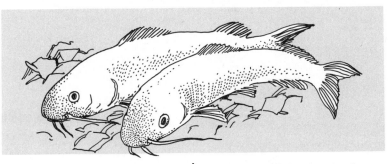

longer, slower cooking is preferable. Allow about 20 minutes, less for thinner fish or hotter grill. Fish is done when firm, opaque, and just beginning to flake; if it flakes easily or falls apart, it's overcooked. Good hot or cold.

Note: If using dark meat tuna, you can lessen the fishy taste by first brining the fish. (This step isn't necessary for albacore tuna.) Combine 1 quart of water with a tray of ice cubes and 3 heaping tablespoons of salt. Mix well, then submerge the tuna steaks for 1 to 2 hours. Add more ice if needed, to keep the fish cold. Drain well, then grill.

MAKES 8 SERVINGS, UNDER 215 CALORIES EACH.

❦

NEW ORLEANS–STYLE BLACKENED CATFISH

1	tablespoon paprika
2½	teaspoons salt
1	teaspoon granulated onion powder
1	teaspoon cayenne pepper
¾	teaspoon each ground white pepper and ground black pepper
½	teaspoon each powdered dried thyme and powdered dried oregano
8	catfish fillets (2 pounds)
¼	cup butter or margarine, melted

1. Prepare a heavy nonstick griddle or nonstick all-metal skillet liberally with cooking spray.

Place on grill in a covered, gas-fired barbecue as close as possible to heat source. Cover barbecue and let pan get very hot while you prepare fish.

2. Mix seasonings well and sprinkle on a shallow plate. Dip each fillet in melted butter, then in seasoning mix until well covered. Open barbecue cover and arrange fillets in a single layer on hot skillet. Cook briefly, only 1 minute per side for small catfish fillets, up to 2 minutes per side for thicker fillets.

Note: Pan must be all metal—no wooden, plastic, or other non-flameproof handles.

MAKES 8 SERVINGS, 170 CALORIES EACH.

❦

HAWAIIAN SEARED TUNA STEAKS, AHI STYLE

2	pounds thick tuna steaks
2	teaspoons salad oil
	Light soy sauce to taste
	Chopped fresh cilantro or parsley for garnish (optional)

1. Preheat charcoal, gas, or electric grill according to manufacturer's directions. If grill is uncovered, lay foil over grids to speed heating and to make grids hot enough to leave sear marks. Lower grids as close to heat source as possible. The object is to cook fish quickly, like steak, directly over flames or heat, with grill uncovered.

2. Lightly coat fish with oil; arrange on grill in a single layer,

directly over heat. Sprinkle fish lightly with soy sauce. Grill for 2 to 3 minutes depending on thickness, turn, and grill other side an additional 2 minutes or to desired doneness. Fish should still be pink in the middle and have a single set of grill marks. Timing will depend on thickness of fish and closeness to heat. Sprinkle with cilantro, if desired.

MAKES 8 SERVINGS, 175 CALORIES EACH.

❦

MIDDLE EASTERN BARBECUE BASTE

1	cup plain low-fat yogurt
¼	cup fresh lemon juice
2	tablespoons fresh mint or 2 teaspoons dried mint, crushed
1	teaspoon ground cumin
¼	teaspoon each ground cinnamon and nutmeg
1	clove garlic, minced (optional)

1. Fork-blend ingredients, cover, and refrigerate. Stir before using. This is a perfect marinade or basting liquid for chicken, lamb, beef, hamburger, or fish.

MAKES APPROXIMATELY 1⅓ CUPS, UNDER 10 CALORIES PER TABLESPOON.

❦

SPICY CURRIED LIME MARINADE FOR BARBECUED SEAFOOD

⅓	cup plain low-fat yogurt
⅓	cup light French salad dressing
⅓	cup lime juice
1	clove garlic, minced
1	to 2 tablespoons curry powder

1. Blend ingredients together and use as a marinade or baste for thick, firm fish fillets or steaks.

MAKES 1 CUP MARINADE, UNDER 20 CALORIES PER TABLESPOON.

Sauces, Salsas, Marinades, and Bastes

TODAY, most Americans avoid traditional sauces and gravies, and the big roasts and mashed potatoes that normally go with them. Most gravies and sauces are loaded with fat, usually the worst kind: highly saturated animal fat found in butter, cream, or the drippings from a roast.

But what good is such a virtuously sauceless approach if the roast chicken and gravy are replaced by fried chicken and french fries . . . if the vegetables are slathered with butter instead of hollandaise sauce? Sauces, minus the unwanted fat, can make the leanest and healthiest foods appealing.

It's the fat rather than the flour that makes gravies and sauces so fattening. They don't have to be off limits for calorie and cholesterol watchers. Sauces can actually save you calories—by replacing butter on mashed potatoes and vegetables, for example. The leanest and least-fattening meats, as well as poultry, taste better with the added moistness of a well-seasoned gravy or a spicy salsa topping.

GRAVY WITH NO ADDED FAT

Take away the fat and what do you have? Low-calorie gravy . . . with none of the flavor missing. Low-fat meat and poultry gravies are made the same way. Both have two main components: fat-skimmed drippings from the roasting pan (broth or stock can substitute) plus flour.

Defat the drippings. The intensely flavorful, richly colored residue that remains in the pan after roasting is a combination of condensed browned meat or poultry juices and melted fat. The melted fat is what you want to eliminate. Fat is close to 1,600 calories a cupful, while the broth is less than 100!

If you have time, pour the drippings into a container and chill until the fat congeals on the surface and is easily removed. Last minute? Pour drippings into a glass jar. In 2 minutes the fat will separate. Suction off the clear fat on top with a bulb baster.

Thicken without fat. The old-fashioned thickening method calls for combining fat with flour as a paste, but the new way calls for making a paste with cold water. Follow these directions:

1. Combine flour with cold water in a covered jar. Use 2 tablespoons flour and ¼ cup cold water for each cupful of gravy you want. Shake vigorously until the flour is completely blended into the cold water. Never use hot water; it will cause the flour to lump.
2. Measure the fat-skimmed broth and/or drippings—you need about 5 ounces for each cup of gravy desired. Heat to boiling in a nonstick saucepan and gently but thoroughly stir the flour paste into the simmering stock and drippings. Cook and stir until gravy simmers and thickens.

Too thick? You can thin the gravy by adding a little more hot or cold water. If it's not thick enough, simply simmer until it reduces to the desired consistency.

Season to taste. Taste the gravy and add seasonings to suit yourself. Salt or seasoned salt, pepper, hot red pepper, herbs, minced parsley, white wine, and soy sauce are some of the favorites. Some people like to intensify the natural poultry flavor with a dash of soy sauce or MSG (*monosodium glutamate;* be aware, however, that some people are sensitive to it). A few drops of commercial gravy seasoning will make the color darker.

LEANER "CREAM" SAUCE

Cream sauce is an amalgamation of fat and flour slowly stirred over very low heat with milk or cream. Fresh herbs and other seasonings are often added to provide flavor. Herbs aren't fattening . . . but the butter and cream are!

It's possible to make a "cream sauce" by omitting the butter or other fat and using skim milk instead of whole milk or cream. In this case, the fresh, cold skim milk would be combined with the flour and mixed thoroughly—shaken in a tightly covered jar—before cooking over very low heat. The "cream" sauce that this method yields really requires the quotation marks, because it's not very creamy. Both the texture and dairy flavor are a bit thin and disappointing.

Our leaner "cream" sauce is made by combining easy-blending flour with part-skim ricotta cheese to create a smooth paste as a base. Ricotta is the fresh sweet cheese that's used in making lasagna, and its rich dairy flavor creates the rich taste and texture of cream sauce—without cream, butter, or other added fat. We use the quotation marks because there is no cream—and no cream calories—in sauces made with this base.

❖

LEANER "CREAM" SAUCE BASE

2   *cups part-skim ricotta cheese*
¼   *cup easy-blending flour*
2   *tablespoons fresh nonfat milk*

1. Combine ingredients in a food processor or electric blender and process until completely smooth. Spoon the mixture into a covered container (or return to the cheese container), label, and store in the refrigerator. Use by the tablespoon as a thickener for soups, sauces, stews, or other dishes.

EACH TABLESPOON HAS 20 CALORIES.

For even greater convenience—and longer storage—you can freeze this base: Spread the ricotta mixture in an ice cube tray and put the tray in your freezer. When the cubes are frozen, take them out of the tray, repack in a labeled plastic bag, and return them to the freezer. Now you can take out only what you need, reseal the bag, and put the rest back in the freezer.

To thicken liquids, sauces, soups, or stews with the cubes, remove the cooking pan from the heat and put the frozen cubes on the surface of the liquid, allowing them to thaw off-heat. When the white sauce concentrate has thawed, stir it into the liquid, then gently reheat until the mixture begins to simmer and thicken. (If the mixture is too thick, thin with a little hot water.) As a general rule, allow approximately 1 cube per serving. (For instance, if you are thickening a sauce or stew that serves 4, use 4 cubes.)

Leaner "Cream" Sauce Base can add a touch of class almost anywhere. The examples below should help get your imagination going.

Mock sour-cream sauce: Add a squirt of lemon juice to any of the following cream sauce suggestions, and they will have the taste of a sauce made with sour cream. (Great on noodles or baked potatoes . . . add a generous sprinkle of parsley and paprika.)

Creamy gravy: For a creamy gravy to go with roast beef or poultry, skim the drippings from the roast. Let the fat rise to the top, then suction it off with a bulb-type baster and discard. Heat the drippings over a low flame. Thin with a little boiling water if needed, then stir in a few tablespoons of the sauce base (or frozen cubes) to make a dairy-rich creamy gravy. Allow approximately 4 tablespoons of the sauce base or 2 frozen cubes per cup of drippings.

Creamy mustard or horseradish sauce: For a great sauce with roast beef, follow the preceding directions, using beef broth or fat-skimmed drippings from a lean roast of beef. Add 1 or 2 tablespoons prepared mustard or horseradish (or to taste) per cup of sauce.

Self-sauced veggies: After cooking the vegetables, blend 2 or 3 tablespoons (or 1 or 2 frozen cubes) sauce base into the reserved vegetable cooking water. For even more flavor, first cook the veggies in fat-skimmed chicken broth and add a few leaves of fresh basil.

Leaner "cream" soup: Almost any soup can be made into a "cream" soup without creaming the calorie count! Spoon a few tablespoons or 1 or 2 frozen cubes of sauce base into the soup just before serving; stir well over low heat until thickened.

Delicate sauce for seafood: Reserve the poaching liquid from fish. Season it to taste with lemon juice and chopped fresh parsley, thyme, tarragon, or dill. Heat gently and stir in 2 or 3 tablespoons or 1 or 2 frozen cubes of cream sauce base. Try poaching the fish in some dry white wine and using that as a base for a creamy wine sauce.

Saucy encores: Use cream sauce to recycle leftover roast chicken or turkey. First heat the meat gently in fat-skimmed chicken broth. Season with grated nutmeg, lemon peel, and fresh herbs, if desired, or spice lightly with mild curry powder. Then thicken the mixture with cream sauce base. Serve over hot drained pasta or brown rice. Or use as a filling for crêpes.

SIMPLE SALSAS: SOME LIKE IT HOT . . . SOME NOT

When it comes to culinary BTUs, there's no pleasing everyone at the same table. If you have to tend to asbestos tongues and velvet palates at the same time, my suggestion is to make food spicy but not hot, and serve the "heat" separately in the form of homemade hot pepper relish.

Hot or not, peppers are a dieter's delight—only about 10 calories an ounce.

The simplest fresh pepper relish is made merely by chopping up hot green chilies or red peppers in the food processor or by hand. Fire-eaters can spoon the fresh minced pepper on their food to suit their taste. Fresh chopped chili peppers will keep 3 or 4 days in a covered jar in the refrigerator. If you make more than you can use in that amount of time, you can freeze it.

To make a hot pepper mixture that will keep longer in the refrigerator, mince hot peppers and put them in a jar with twice as much white vinegar. Store the jar in the refrigerator and the minced pepper will be usable for a month. (The vinegar will become hot and spicy; use a few drops to perk up salad dressings if you like.) Green chilies will lose their bright green color when stored in vinegar, but hot red peppers will keep their bright tone.

Use the hot pepper as a seasoning ingredient in cooking, or serve it at the table to add heat to milder versions of Mexican, Indian, Szechuan, and other fiery cuisines.

TWENTY-ONE WAYS TO SEASON TOMATO SAUCE

In the "light and spicy" kitchen, tomato sauce replaces the rich bland "white sauce" as the basic sauce. While "white sauce" is generally a cholesterol-laden, calorie-rich concoction of flour, cream, and butter, tomato sauce can be virtually fat free. Plain canned tomato sauce is a good starter for cooks in a hurry. Be sure to check the label and buy a brand with no added fat or oil; then season it to suit yourself.

- *À l'américain:* onion, a little garlic, white wine or cognac, tarragon, bay leaf, parsley; optional: a little butter or margarine. Serve with lobster or other shellfish, or over seafood pasta.
- *Alla puttanesca (Italian):* garlic; a small amount of anchovies, black olives, and/or capers (all are very salty); parsley; optional: a small amount of olive oil. Serve with pasta.
- *Armenian:* onion, garlic, paprika, allspice, cinnamon, black pepper, parsley; optional: a little butter or margarine. Serve with lamb or poultry.
- *Cacciatore (Italian, hunter's style):* onions, garlic, dry white wine, sweet peppers, oregano, basil. Use as a cooking sauce for cut-up chicken or turkey; serve with pasta, if desired.

- *Chinese:* a few drops of toasted sesame oil, green onions, garlic, light soy sauce, fresh or ground ginger, a pinch of anise or fennel seeds.
- *Chinese Szechuan:* to the Chinese sauce above, add cayenne pepper, red pepper flakes, or hot red pepper sauce to taste.
- *Cuban:* the basic seasoning mixture, known as *sofrito*, combines tomatoes with garlic, onion, and green bell peppers.
- *Curry:* onion, garlic, lemon juice, raisins, cumin seeds, cilantro, diced crisp apple; optional: a little butter. Serve with lamb, poultry, vegetables, rice.
- *Greek:* onion, green bell pepper, green olives, brown stock, cinnamon, nutmeg, mint, oregano, parsley; optional: a small amount of olive oil.
- *Hungarian:* onion, garlic, green bell pepper, paprika. Serve with meat or poultry, noodles.
- *Marinara (Italian):* a small amount of olive oil, garlic, parsley.
- *Louisiana Creole:* garlic, onion, green bell pepper, chopped celery, brown stock, thyme, parsley, pinch ground cloves, hot red pepper sauce to taste. Serve with seafood, meat, or poultry.

- *Mexican:* onion, garlic, chili powder, cumin, oregano, cilantro.
- *Mexican mole:* onion, garlic, hot peppers, chili powder, cocoa powder, cumin, oregano, cilantro, cinnamon. Use as a cooking sauce for cut-up chicken or turkey.
- *Milanese (Italian):* garlic, anchovies, white wine, grated Parmesan cheese; optional: a small amount of olive oil.
- *Mushroom:* a little sautéed smoked lean ham or Canadian-style bacon, nutmeg, mushrooms, white wine, parsley, black pepper.
- *Niçoise (French):* garlic, anchovies, white wine, capers, lemon slices, black pepper; optional: a small amount of olive oil. Serve with fish or seafood, pasta.
- *Pizzaiola (Italian):* garlic, anchovies, parsley, black and green olives, white wine, brown stock, oregano; optional: a small amount of olive oil. Serve with meat.
- *Provençale (French):* garlic, basil, thyme, black pepper; optional: a small amount of olive oil. Use as cooking sauce for meat or poultry; serve with pasta.
- *Spanish:* onion, garlic, bay leaf (remove before serving), parsley; optional: a small amount of olive oil.
- *Turkish:* onion, garlic, hot pepper, cumin, cinnamon, black pepper, parsley; optional: a small amount of olive oil. Serve with lamb or poultry.

MARINADE, CUBAN STYLE

This basic marinade is called *adobo*; it combines the juice of bitter oranges (shades of Seville!) plus garlic and pepper, augmented with cumin seeds. A good substitute for bitter orange juice: combine equal parts orange and grapefruit juice plus a little grated grapefruit rind.

Put chicken or lean beefsteak in a nonmetallic bowl; add the fruit juice, some mashed garlic cloves, and a generous pinch of cumin seeds or ground cumin. Refrigerate, covered, for several hours before broiling or barbecuing.

PESTO WITH ZEST

Pesto is an Italian word meaning "crushed." It's related to the English word *pestle*—as in mortar and pestle—the pestle being the blunt rounded object that does the crushing in the bowl-shaped mortar. In the language of food, however, *pesto* has come to mean fresh basil sauces, "crushed" in the food processor with lots of oil—so much that you could be crushed by the calorie count! Today's more calorie-conscious versions substitute other ingredients for the oil: flavorful chicken broth, for example. Creamy versions made with low-fat ricotta cheese or yogurt are particularly healthy and calcium rich.

FRESH TOMATO SAUCE

3   vine-ripe tomatoes, peeled and diced
2   cloves garlic, minced
2   teaspoons olive oil
    Salt and coarse pepper to taste
¼   cup chopped fresh basil or parsley
½   cup shredded part-skim mozzarella cheese

1. Combine garlic and olive oil in a nonstick pan. Heat over moderate heat until garlic begins to brown. Stir in tomato, salt, and pepper. Reduce heat and warm just until heated through. Spoon over hot drained spaghetti; top with chopped basil and mozzarella.

MAKES 4 SERVINGS, 90 CALORIES EACH.

❦

FRESH SPICY SALSA

For the hottest sauce, use whole hot chili peppers, including the seeds. If you prefer to reduce the heat, however, use only the pepper part and discard the seeds. To tame the fire even more, chop the chili peppers and rinse them in cold water for several minutes before combining with the remaining ingredients. For no heat at all, substitute sweet bell peppers.

6   tablespoons minced fresh hot peppers or ½ cup chopped sweet bell peppers
1   cup peeled cubed vine-ripe tomatoes
1   onion, minced
1   or 2 cloves garlic, chopped
5   or 6 tablespoons chopped fresh cilantro
    Juice of 1 lime
    Salt and black pepper to taste

1. Combine ingredients and store in the refrigerator. Serve this tasty fresh salsa on any-

thing mild and low-calorie . . . try it on a baked potato!

MAKES APPROXIMATELY 2 CUPS, 5 CALORIES PER TABLESPOON.

❦

RED PEPPER SALSA

½   cup fresh lemon juice
¼   cup chopped sweet red pepper
¼   cup chopped hot red pepper (fresh or canned)
¼   cup chopped onion
¼   cup chopped fresh parsley or cilantro
2   cloves garlic, minced
2   teaspoons cumin seeds (optional)

1. Combine ingredients and refrigerate, covered, until serving time. Spoon over broiled chicken, fish, or meat, or serve over black beans or rice.

MAKES 8 SERVINGS, UNDER 15 CALORIES EACH.

Variation

Sweet Pepper Salsa: Use all sweet red pepper, ½ cup total (omitting the ¼ cup of hot pepper).

❦

GAZPACHO SALSA

½   cup peeled cubed vine-ripe tomato
½   cup chopped peeled cucumber
½   cup chopped green bell pepper
½   cup chopped onion
1   tablespoon chopped garlic
1   tablespoon green olive oil
1   tablespoon vinegar
    Salt and black pepper to taste

1. Combine ingredients. Spoon over broiled lean hamburger or other meat, or on chicken or fish. Pour over pasta, rice, or baked potato. Spoon over cold flaked tuna or combine with tuna in pita pockets.

MAKES 2 CUPS, UNDER 10 CALORIES PER TABLESPOON.

MIDWINTER SALSA

1   can (8 ounces) stewed tomatoes
1   green bell pepper, seeded
1   onion
1   clove garlic
2   or 3 fresh or canned jalapeño peppers, seeded
2   tablespoons minced parsley
1   tablespoon lime or lemon juice
1   teaspoon chili powder, or to taste (optional)

1. Combine ingredients in an electric blender or food processor and process until coarsely chopped. (Or chop food by hand and mix together.) Refrigerate, covered, for 30 minutes or more. Serve as a dip for raw vegetables, or heat gently and serve as a hot sauce over steamed seafood, baked or broiled chicken, or lean roast beef.

MAKES 6 SERVINGS, 25 CALORIES EACH.

❦

MILD MEXICAN SALSA
(More tomato than chili pepper)

6   vine-ripe tomatoes, peeled and diced
1   onion, peeled and minced
1   rib celery, minced
1   jalapeño pepper, seeded and minced
3   tablespoons lime or lemon juice
1   tablespoon each minced fresh oregano and minced fresh cilantro or parsley
1½ teaspoons cumin seeds or ½ teaspoon ground cumin

1. Stir ingredients together and refrigerate for 24 hours before serving. (Recipe may be halved.) Store in refrigerator. Spoon chilled salsa over broiled chicken, fish, or lean hamburgers.

MAKES 1 QUART (16 SERVINGS), 20 CALORIES EACH.

GARDEN SALSA

4   vine-ripe tomatoes, peeled and
       diced
2   jalapeño peppers, seeded and
       minced
1   large onion, minced
1   red, yellow, or green bell
       pepper, seeded and chopped
3   tablespoons lime or lemon
       juice
3   tablespoons chopped fresh
       cilantro or parsley
1   tablespoon minced fresh
       oregano
1   teaspoon ground cumin

1. Mix all ingredients thoroughly in a small nonmetallic bowl. Cover; refrigerate for at least 2 hours for flavors to blend.

MAKES 1¾ CUPS, 10 CALORIES PER TABLESPOON.

❧

MUSTARD-MAYONNAISE SAUCE FOR COLD CRAB

½   cup plain low-fat yogurt
½   cup light mayonnaise
2   tablespoons Dijon-style
       mustard
       Salt and pepper to taste

1. Gently fold ingredients together until blended; serve with cold crab or other chilled seafood.

MAKES 1 CUP, 25 CALORIES PER TABLESPOON.

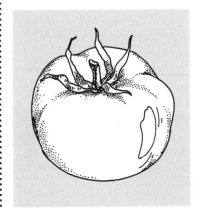

LOUIS DRESSING FOR SEAFOOD

½   cup light mayonnaise
¼   cup plain low-fat yogurt
3   tablespoons chili sauce
1   tablespoon water
1   tablespoon lemon juice
1   tablespoon minced fresh onion,
       or 1 teaspoon dried onion
       flakes
1   teaspoon prepared horseradish
½   teaspoon minced fresh
       tarragon or pinch dried
       tarragon
       Salt and pepper to taste

1. Fork-blend ingredients. Refrigerate, covered, until serving time. Good with cold cooked shrimp or other shellfish.

MAKES APPROXIMATELY 1 CUP, 25 CALORIES PER TABLESPOON.

❧

COLD CRAB SAUCE

⅓   cup light mayonnaise
⅓   cup plain low-fat yogurt
3   tablespoons prepared mustard
1   tablespoon lemon juice
       Dash hot red pepper sauce

1. Gently fold ingredients together. Cover and store in the refrigerator. Great with cold lobster, shrimp, fish, or crab.

MAKES APPROXIMATELY 1 CUP, 25 CALORIES PER TABLESPOON.

❧

LIGHT TARTAR SAUCE

1   cup light mayonnaise
3   tablespoons finely chopped
       pickles or 3 tablespoons
       pickle relish
2½   tablespoons finely chopped fresh
       parsley
1   tablespoon capers (½ ounce)
1   tablespoon lemon juice
1   teaspoon Dijon-style mustard
1   teaspoon grated onion

1. Blend all ingredients together, cover, and refrigerate.

About 1 hour before serving, set sauce out to come to room temperature.

MAKES 1¼ CUPS, 35 CALORIES PER TABLESPOON.

❧

MARTINIQUE LIME SAUCE FOR FISH

Widely used in Mexico and the Caribbean, lime juice adds its own special piquancy to slim seafood dishes. In this Martinique-inspired recipe, light mayonnaise substitutes for oil, saving more than 300 calories. If you substitute lemon, use the juice of only 1 lemon. The juices of both citrus fruits are similar in calories—about 4 per tablespoon.

¼   cup light mayonnaise
       Juice of 2 limes
3   tablespoons minced fresh
       parsley
2   tablespoons chopped scallion
1   to 3 teaspoons minced fresh
       jalapeño pepper

1. Whisk all ingredients together.

MAKES APPROXIMATELY ½ CUP, 25 CALORIES PER TABLESPOON.

❧

LOUISIANA HOT SAUCE

1   tablespoon butter
1½   tablespoons fresh lemon juice
1½   tablespoons Worcestershire
       sauce
½   teaspoon salt, or to taste
⅛   teaspoon pepper
⅛   teaspoon Tabasco sauce, or to
       taste

1. Melt butter and add remaining ingredients. Serve with seafood.

MAKES ⅓ CUP, UNDER 10 CALORIES PER TEASPOON.

LIGHT STONE CRAB SAUCE

6 tablespoons light mayonnaise
1 tablespoon Dijon-style mustard, or to taste
  Juice of 1 lime or ½ lemon

1. Mix ingredients together thoroughly.

MAKES APPROXIMATELY ½ CUP, 35 CALORIES PER TABLESPOON.

CHINESE CRANBERRY-PLUM SAUCE FOR POULTRY

6 fresh purple plums, pitted and thinly sliced
1 cup fresh cranberries
1 onion, finely chopped
1 clove garlic, finely minced
1 can (6 ounces) apricot or peach nectar or pineapple juice
2 tablespoons light soy sauce
1 tablespoon fennel or anise seeds
4 packets low-calorie sweetener (optional)

1. Combine all ingredients except optional sweetener in a heavy saucepan over moderate heat. Cover and cook for 10 minutes.
2. Uncover and simmer until sauce is thick. Remove from heat and add sweetener, if desired. Serve hot or chilled with chicken, pork, hot or cold meats.

MAKES 8 SERVINGS, 45 CALORIES EACH.

TIGER MUSTARD

¼ cup light mayonnaise
¼ cup spicy brown mustard
¼ cup vinegar
3 tablespoons prepared white horseradish, or to taste

1. Combine ingredients and mix thoroughly with a fork until blended smooth. Cover and store in refrigerator. Serve with hot or cold lean roasted meat.

MAKES ABOUT 1 CUP, 15 CALORIES PER TABLESPOON.

SZECHUAN-STYLE BASTING SAUCE

6 ounces regular or spicy tomato juice
6 ounces apricot or pineapple juice
2 tablespoons light soy sauce
2 tablespoons white or cider vinegar
1 teaspoon ground ginger
¼ to ½ teaspoon cayenne pepper, or to taste

1. Combine ingredients, bring to a simmer, and cook for 5 minutes. Spoon over broiled chicken or fish. (Or combine ingredients in a bowl and pour over chicken while it bakes.)

MAKES 6 SERVINGS, 30 CALORIES EACH.

CANARY ISLANDS MOJO SAUCE

½ cup loosely packed fresh parsley
½ cup cider vinegar
4 cloves garlic, finely minced
2 tablespoons each cumin seeds and Spanish paprika
2 tablespoons olive oil
  Salt and coarsely ground pepper to taste

1. Finely mince parsley by hand or in an electric blender or food processor. Add remaining ingredients and mix well. Spoon over baked potatoes or boiled new potatoes, or use on fish, chicken, or rice.

MAKES APPROXIMATELY 1 CUP, 20 CALORIES PER TABLESPOON.

APPLE CURRY COOKING SAUCE FOR CHICKEN

1 cup unsweetened applesauce
3 tablespoons minced fresh onion or 1 tablespoon dried onion flakes
1 to 2 teaspoons curry powder, or to taste
½ teaspoon ground ginger
1 tablespoon soy sauce (optional)

1. Stir ingredients until smooth. Spoon over chicken breasts before baking.

MAKES 4 SERVINGS, UNDER 35 CALORIES EACH.

SWEET 'N' SOUR PICKLED PINEAPPLE SAUCE

1 can (10 ounces) condensed beef or chicken broth, skimmed of fat
1 cup unsweetened crushed pineapple
1 can (6 ounces) tomato paste
½ cup dill pickle relish
1 onion, minced
1 clove garlic, minced
  Salt and pepper to taste

1. Combine ingredients in a saucepan. Simmer for 15 minutes, stirring occasionally. Serve over lean cooked meat, poultry, or vegetables.

MAKES 8 SERVINGS, 70 CALORIES EACH.

THAI-STYLE SALSA

½ cup sherry or other white wine
    (not too dry)
2 tablespoons soy sauce
2 tablespoons fish sauce
    (available in oriental
    groceries, or substitute
    additional soy sauce)
½ cup fresh parsley, minced
2 tablespoons each minced fresh
    basil, cilantro, and mint, or
    2 teaspoons each dried
    basil, cilantro, and mint
1 or 2 jalapeño peppers, coarsely
    chopped
1 tablespoon shredded fresh
    ginger or 1 teaspoon
    ground ginger

1. Combine ingredients;
toss with hot noodles or rice.

Makes 6 servings, 35 calories each.

❦

SPICY MOROCCAN
SAUCE FOR CHICKEN

6 tablespoons light mayonnaise
1 tablespoon lemon or lime juice
2 cloves garlic, finely minced
1 fresh or canned hot cherry
    pepper or jalapeño pepper,
    seeded and minced
1 tablespoon chopped fresh
    cilantro or parsley
2 teaspoons ground cumin
1 teaspoon paprika
½ teaspoon cayenne pepper

1. Combine ingredients
and store, covered, in refrigerator. Serve with cold
chicken.

Makes approximately 1 cup, 20 calories per tablespoon.

❦

CURRY BASTE

1 cup plain low-fat yogurt
¼ cup fresh lemon juice
1 to 2 tablespoons curry powder
1 clove garlic, minced (optional)

1. Fork-blend ingredients.
Cover and refrigerate. Stir before using. Makes a great marinade or baste for chicken, lean
lamb, beef, hamburger, or fish.

Makes approximately 1⅓ cups, under
10 calories per tablespoon.

❦

SPEEDY MUSHROOM-
TOMATO-WINE SAUCE

1 cup plain tomato sauce
1 cup dry white wine
1 cup canned stewed tomatoes,
    with liquid
1 cup mushroom stems and caps
1 teaspoon each dried oregano
    and dried thyme
1 clove garlic, minced (optional)

1. Combine ingredients in
a saucepan and simmer for 20 to
25 minutes or until sauce is reduced and thick. Spoon over
pasta.

Makes 6 servings, 40 calories each.

❦

MINT SAUCE FOR
GREEN PASTA

½ cup chicken broth, skimmed of
    fat
½ cup minced fresh mint
    Juice of 1 lemon
1 clove garlic
    Pinch grated nutmeg
    Salt and coarse pepper to taste

1. Heat broth to boiling.
Process all ingredients in an elec-

tric blender or a food processor.
Toss sauce with hot drained
green pasta.

Makes 4 servings, under 15 calories
each.

Variation

Cream-Style Mint Sauce: Substitute plain low-fat yogurt for
the chicken broth. Let yogurt
warm to room temperature; do
not cook.

Makes 4 servings, 25 calories each.

❦

SICILIAN SWEET
PEPPER SAUCE

2 teaspoons olive oil
1 onion, minced
1 clove garlic, minced
1 cup chicken broth, skimmed of
    fat
3 green or red bell peppers,
    seeded and diced or
    shredded
2 tablespoons each minced fresh
    basil and minced fresh
    parsley
    Salt and coarsely ground black
    pepper to taste (optional)

1. In a nonstick skillet prepared with cooking spray, combine olive oil, onion, and garlic.
Cook, stirring, over moderate
heat for 2 minutes.

2. Add remaining ingre-
dients; cover, bring to a simmer,
and cook for 7 to 8 minutes. Toss
with hot drained pasta.

Makes 4 servings, 70 calories each.

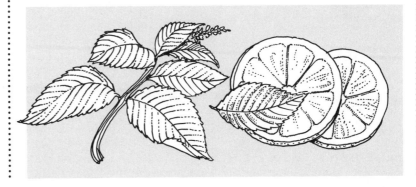

SPANISH "PESTO" SAUCE

3/4 cup undiluted chicken broth
1/4 cup wine vinegar
2 tablespoons olive oil
1/2 cup loosely packed fresh cilantro
1/2 cup loosely packed fresh parsley
2 to 4 cloves garlic
1/2 teaspoon ground cumin
1 tablespoon minced sweet or hot fresh pepper (optional)

1. Heat broth, vinegar, and olive oil to boiling. Mince cilantro, parsley, and garlic and stir in. (Or pour hot mixture over remaining ingredients in an electric blender or food processor and process until chopped.) Spoon over baked potatoes, hot drained pasta, plain cooked rice, or broiled chicken. To make a sauce for poached seafood, substitute the poaching liquid for the chicken broth.

MAKES 6 SERVINGS, 55 CALORIES EACH.

꙳

SLIM PESTO SAUCE

3/4 cup chicken broth, skimmed of fat
1/2 cup loosely packed fresh basil
3 cloves garlic, peeled
1/4 cup grated Parmesan cheese
1 tablespoon olive oil
Salt and pepper to taste

1. Heat broth to boiling. Combine all ingredients in an electric blender or a food processor; process until basil and garlic are minced. (Or use a mortar and pestle: mash basil and garlic together, then mix with remaining ingredients.) Serve tossed with hot drained pasta.

MAKES 4 SERVINGS, 65 CALORIES EACH.

Variation

Creamy Pesto Sauce: Replace the broth and olive oil with 1/2 cup part-skim ricotta cheese and 1/3 cup water. Blend all ingredients in an electric blender or a food processor until smooth.

MAKES 4 SERVINGS, 75 CALORIES EACH.

꙳

PARSLEY-YOGURT PESTO

6 ounces plain low-fat yogurt, at room temperature
1/2 cup packed fresh parsley, minced
1/2 cup packed fresh basil or spinach, minced
1 clove garlic, minced
5 tablespoons grated Parmesan cheese
1/4 teaspoon grated nutmeg
Salt and coarse pepper to taste

1. Combine yogurt, parsley, basil, and garlic. Fold in Parmesan, nutmeg, salt and pepper to taste. Stir into hot drained green pasta just before serving.

MAKES 6 SERVINGS, 45 CALORIES EACH.

꙳

IBERIAN CILANTRO SAUCE

3/4 cup condensed chicken broth
1/4 cup wine vinegar
2 tablespoons olive oil
1/2 cup loosely packed fresh cilantro
1/2 cup loosely packed fresh parsley
2 to 4 cloves garlic
1 tablespoon minced fresh bell pepper or hot pepper (optional)
1/2 teaspoon ground cumin

1. Heat broth, vinegar, and oil to boiling. Mince cilantro, parsley, and garlic; stir into broth mixture with pepper, if desired, and cumin. (Or pour hot mixture over remaining ingredients in an electric blender or a food processor and process until chopped.) Spoon over baked potatoes, hot drained pasta, plain cooked rice, or broiled chicken. (To make a sauce for poached seafood, substitute the poaching liquid for the chicken broth.)

MAKES 6 SERVINGS, 55 CALORIES EACH.

꙳

CREAMY SPINACH-RICOTTA SAUCE

1 cup part-skim ricotta cheese, at room temperature
1 cup loosely packed spinach leaves
1 clove garlic
Grated nutmeg and grated lemon peel to taste
Salt and pepper to taste

1. Combine ricotta, spinach, and garlic in a food processor and process until completely smooth. Season to taste. Toss with hot drained pasta.

MAKES 4 SERVINGS, 90 CALORIES EACH.

꙳

MOCK HOLLANDAISE SAUCE

1/2 cup cooking liquid (from seafood or vegetables)
6 tablespoons light mayonnaise
2 tablespoons lemon juice

1. Combine all ingredients and whisk until well blended. Great served over hot steamed fish . . . or vegetables!

MAKES 1 CUP, 15 CALORIES PER TABLESPOON.

Pasta, Potatoes, Rice, and Beans

PASTA, potatoes, beans, and rice were once strictly avoided by the weight-wary on the grounds that they were "fattening carbohydrates." Now, with updated nutritional knowledge, "starchy foods" have resumed their place as an important part of the menu.

Virtually fat free, these foods become fattening only when excess calories are added . . . usually in the form of butter, gravy, or fat-rich sauces.

In the old meat-and-potatoes days of "plain home cookin,' " potatoes and rice were usually served buttered. Pasta was macaroni and cheese, or spaghetti and meatballs. Beans? They were rarely served at all . . . except for the syrupy baked beans at the Fourth of July picnic! No wonder these foods were thought to be fattening.

This chapter shows you how to spice up these healthy complex carbohydrate foods without all that unwanted excess sugar and fat.

SPICY PASTA, EAST AND WEST

Pasta is extremely versatile and popular in many cuisines beyond Italian. In the Orient, where spaghetti was said to originate, noodles are made from rice and other grains. Most American supermarkets offer a staggering variety of pastas in every conceivable shape. Ethnic markets and gourmet shops offer oriental noodles in all their varieties. And health food stores provide pastas made from whole wheat and other whole grains.

Gourmet shops and some supermarkets offer freshly made northern Italian–style pasta, still moist and straight out of the pasta maker or freshly packaged and refrigerated. In northern Italy, most homemade pasta is really what Americans would call egg noodles because whole eggs are added to the dough. Regular machine-made dry pasta is simply flour and water. So, northern Italian–style pasta dishes will taste more authentic if you use packaged egg noodles rather than packaged spaghetti or macaroni.

Uno momento, you may say, aren't noodles *molto* high in cholesterol? The addition of one egg, spread over many servings, does not make noodles a high-cholesterol food. One-half cup of cooked noodles contains 25 milligrams of cholesterol, compared with 250 in a whole egg—only $\frac{1}{10}$ the cholesterol. Noodles come in a variety of sizes and shapes, from whisker thin (use in place of angel hair pasta or oriental noodles) to flat broad noodles that can substitute for lasagna.

Almost all pasta and noodles have roughly the same calories per dry ounce—100 to 110. Their shape and the source of the grain won't change the values much. What does make a difference is how long the pasta is cooked and how much water it absorbs. Spaghetti cooked only till *"al dente"*—firm to the teeth—has 192 calories a cup, while a cup of pasta cooked till tender has only 155 calories, according to government estimates. Noodles aren't any more fattening, really. Their calorie count, 200 per cupful, is about the same as *al dente* macaroni.

POTATOES ARE SOUL PLEASING

If you think spuds are duds where dieting is concerned, think again! Only 115 calories each, potatoes don't deserve their dumpy-frumpy image. Potatoes have such an appetite-appeasing, soul-pleasing nature that they can help keep you from overdoing it on other, far more fattening foods that might appear on the same menu.

In the past, potatoes have gotten bad press from the company they keep: calorie-rich toppings like butter, sour cream, and cheese. Or they're stripped of their skins, sliced, and deep fat fried. French frying is a caloric catastrophe that can more than triple the calorie cost of potatoes with added fat—often saturated fat, at that!

This chapter features methods that minimize the fat and calorie content while boosting nutrition. Its emphasis is on spicy salsas and pestos for toppings instead of butter and fat.

RICE IS RIGHT

Despite its starchy image, rice is actually the waistline watcher's friend: filling but nonfattening. Brown rice is best because it's highest in appetite-appeasing natural bran and fiber. It's the bran-rich outer layer that gives brown rice its distinctively delicious nutty taste and texture.

Contrary to commonly held belief, you can't "wash away" the calories or starch from rice. Rinsing cooked rice flushes the vitamins down the drain but doesn't reduce the calorie count. The best way to prepare rice is to cook it so that all the cooking liquid is absorbed.

GOOD NEWS BEANS

Low in calories, high in fiber, virtually fat free, beans are rich in lean vegetable protein. Combined with rice or other grains, beans can be the protein equal of meat . . . without the fat and cholesterol. That's why beans have always figured prominently in spicy ethnic cuisines.

"Light and spicy" cooks have a whole rainbow of colors, sizes, and shapes to choose from. Beans even come patterned—speckled and "black-eyed," for example. There are actually more than a thousand kinds!

Despite this vast variety, beans can be accommodatingly interchangeable, and if you lack a package or can of the "correct" type of bean a certain ethnic recipe calls for, substituting another kind will usually yield a dish that tastes every bit as good. Only a stickler for authenticity is likely to complain.

While beans vary in appearance and texture, the truth is that they all pretty much taste the same. It's their bland taste and mealy, absorbent texture that help to make beans so versatile: they suck in the flavor of the foods they're cooked with. That can be fat, sugar, and salt on the one hand—Boston baked beans cooked with molasses and fatty salt pork—or it can be fragrant combinations of garlic, onions, spices, and herbs.

Beans are filling and nonfattening because of their high residue of indigestible fiber, a feature that is both an asset and a liability. The ability of beans to produce intestinal gas—and its embarrassingly noisy and unpleasantly fragrant consequences—can be minimized by soaking dried beans overnight in cold water, then discarding that water, along with the soluble components responsible for most of the distress. An alternative to overnight soaking: cover beans with water and cook them for 20 minutes; then drain and discard the cooking water before proceeding with the final cooking.

The actual cooking time for beans will vary with their size and type, so when substituting one variety of dried bean for another, it's best to consult the package and use its suggested cooking time as a guide. In the final analysis, beans are "done" when they "feel done," tender but not mushy.

PASTA

CREOLE SPAGHETTI SAUCE

    3   onions, chopped
    2   teaspoons oil
   10   ounces clam broth or chicken
        broth, skimmed of fat
  ½   cup dry red wine or water
    1   can (16 ounces) plum
        tomatoes, with liquid
    1   can (6 ounces) tomato paste
    2   ribs celery, chopped
    1   green bell pepper, seeded and
        chopped
  ½   cup chopped fresh parsley
    2   or 3 fresh basil leaves or ½
        teaspoon dried basil
    1   teaspoon fresh thyme or ½
        teaspoon dried thyme
        Dash Worcestershire sauce
        Dash each ground cumin and
        cayenne pepper
    2   tablespoons flour
  ¼   cup cold water

1. Combine onions and oil in a large nonstick pan prepared with cooking spray. Cook, stirring, over moderate heat just until onions begin to brown; stir in remaining ingredients except flour and water. Cover and simmer 1 hour or more, stirring occasionally.

2. Mix flour with cold water until smooth. Stir into simmering sauce. Simmer, uncovered, until sauce is thick. Spoon over hot drained pasta.

MAKES 6 SERVINGS, 115 CALORIES EACH; TENDER-COOKED PASTA ADDS 155 CALORIES PER CUP.

Variation

Shrimp Creole and Pasta Shells: Wash, shell, and devein 2 pounds shrimp. Prepare sauce as directed. Arrange shrimp on top of sauce during the last 5 or 10 minutes of cooking, depending on size. (Be sure shrimp are cooked through but avoid overcooking, which causes shrimp to become rubbery.) Spoon shrimp sauce over hot drained macaroni shells. Shrimp adds 95 calories per serving to sauce.

❖

TEX-MEX TORTILLA "LASAGNA"

Corn tortillas replace pasta in this tasty variation.

    2   cups plain tomato sauce
    1   teaspoon each chili powder,
        cumin seeds, and dried
        oregano
    1   teaspoon minced garlic, or to
        taste
    1   jalapeño pepper, seeded and
        chopped (optional)
    6   corn tortillas
    1   cup pot-style low-fat cottage
        cheese
    1   cup diced or shredded cooked
        white-meat chicken or
        turkey
    1   onion, chopped
    1   cup stewed tomatoes, with
        liquid
    1   green bell pepper, sliced in
        rings
  ½   cup shredded part-skim
        mozzarella cheese
  ¼   cup crushed tortilla chips for
        garnish (optional)

1. Combine tomato sauce, chili, cumin, oregano, garlic, and jalapeño pepper, if desired; set aside. In the bottom of a nonstick baking pan or casserole prepared with cooking spray, arrange 3 tortillas; add a little

tomato sauce. Spread pot cheese in a layer and add another layer of tortillas. Top with chicken. Add remaining sauce, the onion, and stewed tomatoes. Top with bell pepper rings.

2. Cover and bake in a preheated 350-degree oven for 1 hour. Uncover; sprinkle with mozzarella and crushed tortilla chips, if desired, and bake 10 minutes more. Remove from oven and wait for 10 minutes before serving.

MAKES 6 SERVINGS, 270 CALORIES EACH; TORTILLA CHIPS ADD APPROXIMATELY 10 CALORIES PER SERVING.

❖

LINGUINE LOUISIANA STYLE

    6   ounces linguine or spaghetti,
        cooked according to package
        directions until tender
    2   ounces lean diced ham or
        Canadian-style bacon
    1   clove garlic, minced
  ½   cup chopped onion
    2   tablespoons dry white wine
    8   ounces stewed tomatoes
  ½   cup chopped red and green
        bell pepper
  ½   cup minced celery
   12   ounces spicy tomato juice
  ½   teaspoon each ground allspice
        and ground cloves
        Hot red pepper sauce to taste
        (optional)
    1   cup cooked crabmeat or tiny
        shrimp

1. While pasta is cooking, prepare a large nonstick skillet or electric frying pan with cooking spray and brown the ham and garlic. Stir in the onion and wine, and cook, stirring, for 1 minute.

2. Add remaining ingredients except crabmeat. Simmer 5 minutes more, then stir in crabmeat and cook until heated through. Spoon over hot drained linguine.

MAKES 4 SERVINGS, 270 CALORIES EACH.

NORTH PACIFIC PASTA PRIMAVERA

This dinner typifies what's so great about American cuisine: an Alaskan salmon grilled over mesquite from the Southwest, served on Italian pasta from Boston, with vegetables from Florida, California, and Mexico—and everything available in the corner supermarket! This is a great way to serve any leftover cooked fish.

1½	cups sliced mushrooms
2	tablespoons chopped onion
2	tablespoons diet margarine
1	tablespoon flour
⅛	teaspoon each dried basil, oregano, and thyme
½	cup low-fat milk
12	ounces salmon, cooked and flaked
1	small yellow squash or zucchini, sliced thin
1	carrot, peeled and shredded
½	cup fresh peas or frozen peas, thawed
½	cup diced tomato
2	tablespoons minced parsley
2	tablespoons white wine (optional)
8	ounces spinach fettucine or spaghetti, cooked according to package directions until tender
	Salt and pepper to taste
	Lime or lemon wedges for garnish

1. Sauté mushrooms and onion in margarine. Add flour and herbs; cook, stirring for 1 minute. Gradually add milk; continuing to stir, cook until thickened.

2. Add salmon, squash, carrot, peas, tomato, parsley, and wine, if desired, and heat thoroughly. Toss hot drained pasta with vegetable mixture and season to taste with salt and pepper. Garnish with lime.

MAKES 6 SERVINGS, APPROXIMATELY 270 CALORIES EACH.

PETALUMA PEPPER PASTA

1	tablespoon corn oil
3	large cloves garlic, minced
½	cup finely chopped onion
½	cup minced red bell pepper
½	cup minced yellow bell pepper
⅓	cup strong chicken broth, skimmed of fat
2	tablespoons chopped fresh basil or 2 teaspoons dried basil
¼	teaspoon hot red pepper flakes
7	ounces ruffled noodles, cooked and drained

1. In large nonstick skillet, heat oil over moderately high heat. Add garlic, onion, and bell peppers; sauté for 4 minutes.

2. Stir in broth, basil, and red pepper flakes. Bring to a boil, stirring occasionally. Reduce heat and simmer for 4 minutes. Spoon over pasta; toss to coat. If desired, serve over assorted salad greens.

MAKES 6 SERVINGS, 175 CALORIES EACH.

THAI NOODLES, BROCCOLI, AND PRAWNS

3	ounces egg noodles, cooked according to package directions until tender
1	pound fresh broccoli
1	onion, thinly sliced
¾	cup chicken broth, skimmed of fat
8	ounces shelled raw shrimp
4	cloves garlic, finely chopped
1	tablespoon toasted sesame oil
2	tablespoons chopped fresh cilantro or parsley
1	jalapeño pepper, seeded and chopped, or to taste
1	tablespoon oyster or fish sauce (available in oriental groceries) or soy sauce
	Juice of 1 lemon
	Lemon pepper to taste

1. While noodles are cooking, trim broccoli florets and cut stems thinly into rounds. In a saucepan, combine onion, broth, and sliced broccoli stems, then arrange florets on top. Cover, bring to a simmer, and cook for 6 to 8 minutes, just until crisp-tender. Combine shrimp, garlic, and oil in nonstick skillet. Sauté just until shrimp turn opaque— 2 to 4 minutes, depending on their size.

2. Drain noodles and return to cooking pan. Stir in the broccoli mixture, sautéed garlic and shrimp, cilantro, and jalapeño pepper. Season with oyster sauce, lemon juice, and lemon pepper.

MAKES 4 SERVINGS, 245 CALORIES EACH.

MEXICAN TURKEY MOLE SAUCE FOR SPAGHETTI

1	pound lean ground turkey
3	pounds canned tomatoes, with liquid
2	cups water or 2 cups chicken or turkey stock, skimmed of fat
½	cup light beer
1	can (6 ounces) tomato paste
2	large onions, chopped
2	or 3 fresh jalapeño peppers, seeded and chopped
3	cloves garlic, minced
¼	cup minced fresh cilantro
3	tablespoons raisins
1	tablespoon plain cocoa powder
2	teaspoons cumin seeds
¼	teaspoon each dried oregano and ground cinnamon
	Salt and black pepper to taste

1. In a nonstick skillet prepared with cooking spray, brown the turkey, breaking it into chunks as it cooks. Drain and discard fat, if any.

2. Add tomatoes and break up well with a fork. Add remaining ingredients, cover, and simmer for 3 hours, stirring occasionally, until thick. Serve over

hot, drained, tender-cooked protein-enriched spaghetti.

MAKES 8 SERVINGS, 195 CALORIES EACH; CHICKEN OR TURKEY STOCK ADDS 10 CALORIES PER SERVING. EACH ¾ CUP OF TENDER-COOKED SPAGHETTI (ABOUT 1 OUNCE DRY) ADDS 115 CALORIES.

❧

SPICY ONE-STEP LASAGNA WITH LEAN SAUSAGE TOPPING

No precooking of the lasagna pasta needed . . . no prebrowning of the meat. Simply assemble and bake!

7	ounces uncooked lasagna noodles
½	cup boiling water
2	cups part-skim ricotta cheese
2	cups uncreamed pot-style cottage cheese
2	beaten eggs or equivalent egg substitute
¼	cup minced fresh parsley
¼	cup minced chives or onion
1	teaspoon each dried oregano and dried basil
	Dash each garlic salt and ground nutmeg
3½	cups canned tomatoes in purée
12	thin slices part-skim mozzarella cheese (about 6 ounces)
12	ounces lean ground pork or veal
1	teaspoon fennel seeds
⅓	teaspoon each dried sage and dried thyme
3	tablespoons Italian-seasoned bread crumbs
3	tablespoons grated Romano cheese

1. Arrange half of the noodles in a single layer in the bottom of a 9- by 13-inch nonstick baking pan, breaking up the noodles to fit. Pour on the boiling water. Set aside.

2. Stir together the ricotta, cottage cheese, eggs, parsley, chives, oregano, basil, garlic salt, and nutmeg. Reserve ½ cup of the ricotta mixture; spread the rest evenly over the layer of noodles. Cover with remaining noodles, arranged in a single layer. Pour on 3 cups of tomatoes, reserving ½ cup of the purée. Add the mozzarella in a single layer and cover with remaining tomato purée.

3. Combine the ground meat with the fennel seeds, sage, thyme, and the reserved ½ cup of the ricotta mixture; mix lightly. Arrange the meat mixture in chunks on top. Sprinkle with bread crumbs and Romano.

4. Bake in a preheated 350-degree oven for 1 hour and 45 minutes or until topping is crusty. Let stand at room temperature for 15 minutes before cutting.

MAKES 12 SERVINGS, 305 CALORIES EACH; 265 CALORIES PER SERVING WITH EGG SUBSTITUTE AND VEAL.

❧

QUICK BROCCOLI PASTA

1	tablespoon corn oil
2	tablespoons coarsely chopped walnuts
2	cups broccoli florets
3	large cloves garlic, minced
⅓	cup strong chicken broth, skimmed of fat
	Dash of ground hot red pepper
7	ounces pasta swirls, cooked and drained

1. In large nonstick skillet, heat oil over moderately high heat. Add nuts; sauté for 1 to 2 minutes, shaking pan occasionally, until lightly browned. Remove nuts with slotted spoon and set aside.

2. Add broccoli and garlic to skillet; sauté for 3 to 4 minutes or until broccoli is tender. Stir in broth and red pepper. Cook for 2 minutes. Add pasta and nuts; toss to coat.

MAKES 4 SERVINGS, 265 CALORIES EACH.

❧

SPAGHETTI WITH SWEET PEPPER CONFETTI

5	ounces spaghetti, cooked according to package directions until tender, and drained
1	large red onion, halved and thinly sliced
½	cup each shredded red, green, and yellow bell peppers
½	cup shredded carrot
½	cup light mayonnaise
	Juice of 1 lemon
	Fresh basil and oregano to taste
	Paprika, hot red pepper flakes, salt, and coarsely ground black pepper to taste

1. Combine ingredients and heat gently in a shallow, nonstick, covered skillet or in the microwave on the lowest heat setting. Stir often and cook only until it is heated through—approximately 4 to 5 minutes in the skillet.

MAKES 10 SERVINGS, 95 CALORIES EACH.

TURKEY LASAGNA SWIRLS

1	pound ground turkey
2	cloves garlic, minced
2	tablespoons minced fresh basil or 1 tablespoon dried basil, crushed
3	cups tomato-vegetable juice
2	tablespoons cornstarch
10	ounces part-skim ricotta cheese
4	ounces shredded part-skim mozzarella cheese
1½	cups finely chopped cooked broccoli
¼	cup grated Romano cheese
½	teaspoon ground nutmeg
8	lasagna noodles, cooked and drained
	Fresh basil for garnish

1. Prepare a large nonstick skillet with cooking spray. Cook turkey with garlic and basil, breaking up meat and turning until browned evenly. Drain any melted fat from pan and discard.

2. In a small bowl, stir juice and cornstarch together until smooth; gradually stir into turkey. Cook and stir over moderate heat until mixture boils and thickens. Reduce heat to low; cover and simmer for 5 minutes.

3. In medium bowl, combine ricotta, half of the mozzarella, the broccoli, Romano, and nutmeg. Spoon some of the cheese mixture down center of each lasagna noodle; roll up. Cut each roll-up in half crosswise, making 2 swirls.

4. On bottom of 13- by 9-inch nonstick baking dish, spread 2 cups of the turkey sauce. Arrange roll-up halves, cut side down, in sauce. Spoon on remaining sauce.

5. Cover and bake in preheated 350-degree oven for 30 minutes. Uncover; sprinkle with remaining cup of mozzarella. Bake 10 minutes more or until cheese melts. Garnish with basil.

MAKES 8 SERVINGS, 345 CALORIES EACH.

❦

ONE-PAN PASTA WITH MEAT SAUCE AND ZUCCHINI

12	ounces beef round, trimmed of fat and ground
1	cup boiling water
3	cups cold water
1	can (20 ounces) tomatoes, broken up
1	can (6 ounces) tomato paste
1	onion, chopped
2	cloves garlic, minced
1½	tablespoons minced fresh oregano or 1½ teaspoons dried oregano
½	teaspoon salt, or to taste
¼	teaspoon pepper
6	ounces vermicelli (thin spaghetti), broken up
2	cups thinly sliced zucchini

1. Brown meat in nonstick skillet with no added fat, breaking it up as it browns. Add boiling water, then drain liquid into a container; set aside for fat to rise to surface.

2. In the skillet, combine cold water, tomatoes, tomato paste, onion, garlic, and seasonings; heat to boiling. With bulb-type baster, remove and discard surface fat from liquid drained from browned meat. Add skimmed liquid to skillet and bring to a simmer.

3. Add vermicelli a little at a time. Simmer, stirring occasionally, until vermicelli is tender and most liquid evaporates. Ar-

range zucchini slices on top in single layer. Simmer 4 to 6 minutes more or until sauce is thick and zucchini is crisp-tender.

MAKES 4 SERVINGS, 370 CALORIES EACH.

❦

FAJITA-STYLE BEEF AND PASTA

1	pound beef flank steak
½	cup brine from jar of hot peppers
¼	cup lime or lemon juice
2	cloves garlic, finely minced
1	tablespoon cumin seeds
2	teaspoons minced fresh oregano or ½ teaspoon dried oregano
8	ounces thin spaghetti
1	cup plain low-fat yogurt
2	onions, halved and very thinly sliced
2	jalapeño or other hot peppers, thinly sliced, or 2 teaspoons thin dill pickle slices
4	ripe tomatoes, diced
2	cups shredded iceberg lettuce
1	cup shredded Monterey Jack cheese
¼	cup loosely packed fresh cilantro or parsley

1. In a nonmetallic bowl, combine meat with brine, lime juice, garlic, cumin seeds, and oregano. Cover and marinate for 30 minutes at room temperature or all day or overnight in the refrigerator.

2. One hour before dinner, remove any refrigerated ingredients, except meat mixture, from refrigerator so they reach room temperature. Cook spaghetti in unsalted water according to package directions. Marinating liquid from beef may be added to spaghetti cooking water.

3. While pasta cooks, broil or barbecue flank steak 3 inches from heat source for 4 or more minutes per side, depending on desired doneness (rare is best). Slice cooked beef very thinly

against grain; cover with foil to keep hot.

4. Drain cooked pasta and return to cooking pot. Over very low heat, stir in yogurt, onions, peppers, and tomatoes, and cook just until heated. Arrange pasta mixture on platter or individual plates; pile on sliced beef. Add shredded lettuce, cheese, and parsley. Serve with tabasco or chili sauce, if desired.

MAKES 6 SERVINGS, 320 CALORIES EACH.

※

LEMON LINGUINE WITH LAMB AND YOGURT SAUCE

8   ounces lean lamb or beef, ground
1   large onion, halved and sliced
1   medium zucchini, sliced
3/4 cup water
3   tablespoons minced fresh parsley
2   tablespoons chopped fresh mint or 2 teaspoons dried mint
2   teaspoons minced fresh oregano or 1/2 teaspoon dried oregano
1/4 teaspoon each ground cinnamon and nutmeg
    Garlic salt and pepper to taste
1   teaspoon cornstarch
3/4 cup plain low-fat yogurt
3   cups linguine, cooked until tender
    Juice of 2 lemons

1. In a large nonstick skillet prepared with cooking spray, brown the meat and onion over moderate heat. Drain and discard any fat. Stir in the zucchini, water, herbs, spices, and seasonings. Cover, bring to a boil, and simmer for 5 minutes.

2. Combine cornstarch with yogurt and stir until smooth. Gently stir into the skillet, and cook until sauce simmers and thickens. Spoon over hot drained linguine and season to taste with lemon juice.

MAKES 4 SERVINGS, 250 CALORIES EACH.

MEATLESS VEGETABLE PASTITSIO

6   ounces large macaroni
2   eggs, lightly beaten, or equivalent egg substitute
1/4 cup plain low-fat yogurt
2/3 cup grated Parmesan cheese
1   cup sliced fresh mushrooms
1   can (8 ounces) plain tomato sauce
1/4 cup minced onion or 2 tablespoons dried onion flakes
3   tablespoons chopped fresh parsley
1   teaspoon dried mint
1/2 teaspoon each dried oregano and ground cinnamon
    Pinch ground nutmeg
1 1/2 cups skim milk
3   tablespoons instant-blending flour
    Salt or butter-flavored salt and freshly ground pepper to taste
    Lemon wedges for garnish

1. Cook macaroni according to package directions until tender—16 to 18 minutes. Drain but don't rinse. Stir beaten eggs into hot macaroni, then stir in yogurt and half the Parmesan. Set aside.

2. Combine mushrooms, tomato sauce, onion, parsley, mint, oregano, cinnamon, and nutmeg. Set aside.

3. In a saucepan, combine milk, flour, salt, and pepper. Cook, stirring, over moderate heat until simmering. Set aside.

4. To assemble: Layer half of macaroni mixture in a nonstick 8-inch square cake pan. Top with mushroom mixture. Add remaining macaroni mixture; cover with milk mixture. Sprinkle with remaining Parmesan. Bake in a preheated 350-degree oven for 40 to 50 minutes, until set. Cut in squares and serve with lemon wedges.

MAKES 6 SERVINGS, 225 CALORIES EACH

※

LINGUINE A QUATRE SAISONS

1/2 cup sliced onion
1   cup thinly sliced fresh mushrooms
1/4 cup white wine or water
1   can (16 ounces) sliced stewed tomatoes
1   package (10 ounces) frozen artichokes, partly thawed
10 pitted black olives, thinly sliced
2   tablespoons olive liquid from container
2   teaspoons Provençale herbs or 1/2 teaspoon each dried rosemary, savory, basil, and thyme
1   clove garlic, minced
12 ounces linguine or spaghetti, cooked according to package directions until tender

1. In a large nonstick skillet or electric frying pan prepared with cooking spray, spread onion in a shallow layer and brown. Stir in the mushrooms and white wine. Cook over moderate heat until most of the liquid evaporates.

2. Stir in remaining ingredients except linguine. Cover and simmer for 20 minutes. Pour over hot drained pasta and toss.

MAKES 8 SERVINGS, 200 CALORIES EACH.

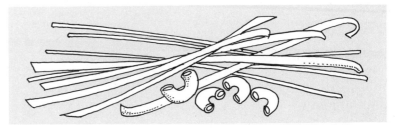

BONELESS CHICKEN CACCIATORE WITH PASTA

12 ounces chicken cutlets or 2 small breasts, skinned and boned
1 tablespoon low-calorie margarine
1 small green bell pepper, seeded and chopped
1 small onion, sliced
1 can (2 ounces) sliced mushrooms, drained
2 cloves garlic, minced
1 can (20 ounces) tomatoes, broken up
1 can (6 ounces) tomato paste
1½ cups water
1 can (10 ounces) condensed chicken broth, skimmed of fat
2 tablespoons dry white wine
1½ tablespoons minced fresh oregano or 1½ teaspoons dried oregano
  Salt and black pepper to taste
6 ounces vermicelli (thin spaghetti), broken up

1. Cut chicken in bite-size chunks. Heat margarine in a non-stick skillet and brown chicken quickly over high heat. Stir in bell pepper, onion, mushrooms, and garlic. Brown lightly, stirring.

2. Add tomatoes, tomato paste, water, broth, wine, oregano, salt, and pepper; heat to simmering. Add vermicelli a little at a time. Simmer, stirring occasionally, until vermicelli is tender and most liquid evaporates to a thick sauce. (Add a little water, if needed.)

MAKES 4 SERVINGS, 360 CALORIES EACH.

POTATOES

SPANISH EGG AND POTATO PIE

6 eggs or equivalent egg substitute
2 cups peeled cubed cooked potatoes
1 onion, finely chopped
1 green bell pepper, seeded and finely chopped
12 pimiento-stuffed green olives, sliced
1 or 2 cloves garlic, minced
4 ounces lean ham or Canadian-style bacon, cubed

1. Beat eggs well; fold in remaining ingredients. Prepare a round nonstick baking pan with cooking spray. Spoon in egg mixture and bake in a preheated 350-degree oven for 25 to 30 minutes, until eggs are set. Cut into wedges to serve.

MAKES 4 SERVINGS, 265 CALORIES EACH WITH EGGS; 185 CALORIES EACH WITH EGG SUBSTITUTE.

SCALLOPED POTATOES

2 cups thinly sliced potatoes
½ cup dried mushrooms
½ cup thinly sliced onions
1¼ cups condensed beef or chicken broth
1 teaspoon olive oil
  Pinch grated nutmeg
  Dash paprika
3 tablespoons finely chopped parsley

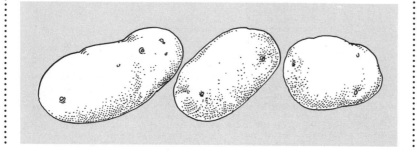

1. Combine all ingredients except parsley in a covered baking dish and bake in a preheated 350-degree oven for 45 minutes. Uncover and bake, basting occasionally, 10 to 15 minutes longer. Sprinkle with parsley before serving.

MAKES 6 SERVINGS, 65 CALORIES EACH.

THICK OVEN FRIES

2 potatoes
2 tablespoons salad oil

1. Scrub potatoes but do not peel. Cut in half lengthwise, then evenly cut each half lengthwise into 5 or 6 thick wedges, all with some peel. Put wedges in a bowl of cold water for 15 to 20 minutes.

2. Drain potato wedges and pat dry with paper towels. Put them in a plastic bag and add salad oil. Shake, coating wedges lightly with oil.

3. On a nonstick cookie tin prepared with cooking spray, arrange potato wedges in a single layer. Bake in a preheated 500-degree oven for 12 to 15 minutes, until potatoes are crisp and browned outside. Season to taste with salt or seasoned salt, paprika, lemon pepper, etc.

MAKES 4 SERVINGS, 120 CALORIES EACH.

DILLED POTATOES

6 potatoes, peeled and sliced thin
½ cup minced onion
1 clove garlic, minced
1 cup chicken broth, skimmed of fat
1 tablespoon lemon juice
1 tablespoon olive oil
  Salt and pepper to taste
6 tablespoons chopped fresh dill leaves

1. Place all ingredients except dill in a saucepan. Cook

over moderate heat for 10 minutes or until potatoes are tender; drain. Toss with dill.

MAKES 12 SERVINGS, 65 CALORIES EACH.

❦

HOT POTATO CURRY

1 tablespoon diet margarine
1 onion, halved and sliced
1 green bell pepper, seeded and diced
3 potatoes, peeled and quartered
1 cup chicken broth, skimmed of fat, or 1 cup water
1 or 2 teaspoons curry powder, or to taste
3 tablespoons minced fresh parsley or cilantro

1. In a saucepan, melt the margarine over moderate heat. Add onion, and cook, stirring, until translucent. Stir in pepper and potatoes. Add broth and curry. Cover and simmer until potatoes are nearly tender—about 20 minutes.

2. Uncover and simmer until most of liquid evaporates. Add minced parsley just before serving.

MAKES 6 SERVINGS, 85 CALORIES EACH.

❦

GERMAN-STYLE POTATO SALAD

2 pounds small new potatoes
3 thick slices Canadian-style bacon, diced
1 onion, chopped
½ cup diced red pepper or bottled pimiento, drained
¼ cup pickle relish
2 tablespoons cider vinegar
2 teaspoons each dry mustard and caraway or dill seeds
   Salt and black pepper to taste

1. Cover potatoes with boiling water; simmer for 20 minutes or until cooked. Peel and slice into a bowl.

2. Meanwhile, brown diced bacon in a nonstick skillet until crisp; transfer to paper towels. When cool, add to potatoes. Combine remaining ingredients with potato mixture and refrigerate. Serve chilled, or gently reheat in a nonstick skillet or in a microwave oven.

MAKES 6 SERVINGS, 155 CALORIES EACH.

❦

BASQUE-STYLE POTATO SALAD

3 potatoes
1 bay leaf
1 cup shelled cooked small shrimp
½ onion, thinly sliced
½ cup diced bottled pimiento or fresh red bell pepper
½ cup light mayonnaise
2 tablespoons lemon juice
1 teaspoon prepared mustard
   Salt and black pepper to taste
   Pinch each paprika and cayenne pepper

1. Boil potatoes and bay leaf in salted water to cover for 20 minutes or until potatoes are just tender. Discard bay leaf; peel potatoes and then slice them into a bowl.

2. Add shrimp, onion, and pimiento. Combine remaining ingredients and toss with potato mixture. Chill. Before serving, sprinkle with additional paprika, if desired.

MAKES 6 SERVINGS, 145 CALORIES EACH.

DALMATIAN-STYLE POTATO SALAD

1½ pounds new potatoes, scrubbed
3 tablespoons olive oil
3 tablespoons olive liquid from olive jar
3 tablespoons red wine vinegar
1 clove garlic, crushed
3 pounds large red, green, and yellow bell peppers
½ cup minced pitted black olives
½ cup minced red onions
4 ounces turkey salami, cut in ¼-inch-wide strips
   Freshly ground black pepper to taste
3 ounces feta cheese, crumbled
   Fresh chopped basil or oregano for garnish

1. Boil potatoes in salted water to cover for 20 minutes or until just tender; peel and slice into a bowl. While potatoes are still warm, gently stir in oil, olive liquid, vinegar and garlic. Cool to room temperature, then refrigerate.

2. Meanwhile, roast peppers under broiler, about 2 inches from heat, turning frequently, until skin is blistered on all sides. Peel under cold running water, seed, and cut into ½- to ¾-inch-wide strips.

3. Add peppers to chilled potato mixture along with olives, onions, turkey salami, and black pepper. Toss salad and sprinkle top with feta. Garnish with fresh chopped basil.

MAKES 6 SERVINGS, 275 CALORIES EACH.

COUNTRY CHEESE-STUFFED POTATOES

4   baking potatoes
1   cup pot-style low-fat cottage
     cheese
3   tablespoons chopped chives or
     scallions or onions
3   tablespoons minced fresh
     parsley
3   tablespoons plain low-fat
     yogurt
8   teaspoons diet margarine
     Paprika and lemon pepper to
     taste (optional)

1. Pierce potatoes and bake whole in a preheated 425-degree oven for 40 to 60 minutes or until tender, or in microwave oven according to manufacturer's directions. Let cool at room temperature.

2. When potatoes are cool enough to handle, slice each in half. Gently scoop out most, but not all, of potato and combine with cheese, chives, parsley, and yogurt. Mash or beat together in an electric mixer bowl or process with pulse setting of food processor until well combined. Spoon into potato shells and top mixture with margarine.

3. Arrange in a single layer on a nonstick shallow baking tray or cookie tin prepared with cooking spray. Bake in a preheated 425-degree oven until potatoes are heated through and tops are golden—about 20 minutes. Sprinkle with paprika and lemon pepper, if desired.

MAKES 8 SERVINGS, 110 CALORIES EACH.

BAKED TUNA-POTATO NIÇOISE CASSEROLE

2   cups thinly sliced potatoes
1   package (10 ounces) frozen
     kitchen-cut green beans,
     thawed or quickly cooked
½   cup chopped onions
1   tablespoon olive oil
2   tablespoons olive liquid from
     olive jar
¼   teaspoon each dried thyme,
     dried oregano, and dried
     tarragon
     Salt or garlic salt and pepper
     to taste
2   cans (6½ ounces each)
     water-packed tuna, with
     liquid
1   can (8 ounces) sliced
     tomatoes, with liquid
10   pimiento-stuffed green olives,
     thinly sliced
2   tablespoons lemon juice or
     vinegar

1. In a nonstick baking dish prepared with cooking spray, arrange a layer each of potatoes, green beans, and onions. Sprinkle each lightly with olive oil, olive liquid, some of the herbs, salt, and pepper.

2. Break tuna into chunks or flakes. Spoon into casserole. Spoon tomatoes on top and add olives. Squirt with lemon juice and sprinkle with herbs. Cover; bake 45 minutes in preheated 350-degree oven. Uncover; bake 15 to 20 minutes more.

MAKES 4 MEAL-SIZE SERVINGS, 280 CALORIES EACH.

RICE AND BEANS

RANGE-TOP RICE DRESSING

1   cup uncooked brown rice
1   cup chopped onions
1   cup chopped celery
1   cup chicken or turkey broth,
     skimmed of fat
1   cup boiling water
1   can (4 ounces) mushroom
     stems and pieces, with
     liquid
1   teaspoon poultry seasoning or
     ½ teaspoon each dried sage
     and dried thyme
     Salt or garlic salt and pepper
     to taste
¼   cup chopped fresh parsley

1. Combine all ingredients except parsley. Cover and simmer for 50 to 60 minutes in a nonstick pan. Fluff with a fork and stir in parsley just before serving. Serve with roast chicken or turkey.

MAKES 10 SERVINGS, 85 CALORIES EACH.

WINTER GARDEN RICE

1½   cups boiling water
1   cup tomato or mixed-vegetable
     juice
½   cup sliced onions
½   cup sliced celery
½   cup chopped green bell pepper
1   tablespoon diet margarine
1   tablespoon Worcestershire or
     soy sauce
½   teaspoon dried tarragon or
     dried rosemary or dried
     mixed herbs
1   cup uncooked long-grain
     rice
1   package (10 ounces) frozen
     mixed vegetables

1. Combine all ingredients except rice and frozen vegetables. Heat to boiling. Stir in rice; reheat to boiling.

Moroccan-Style Chicken Kebabs *(page 71)*

Quick Broccoli
Pasta *(page 107)*

Spicy Cajun Shrimp
(page 87)

Crab Imperial-Stuffed Shrimp *(page 88)*,
Crab Imperial-Stuffed Flounder
(page 86), Louisiana Hot Sauce *(page 99)*

Microwaved Spicy Beef
in Tortillas *(page 55)*

Lemon Chicken *(page 70)*

Microwaved Oriental Swordfish Steaks *(page 82)*,
Italian-Style Microwaved Halibut Steaks *(page 86)*

Warm Plum and Smoked Chicken Salad *(page 23)*

Indonesian Chicken and Pear Salad *(page 23)*

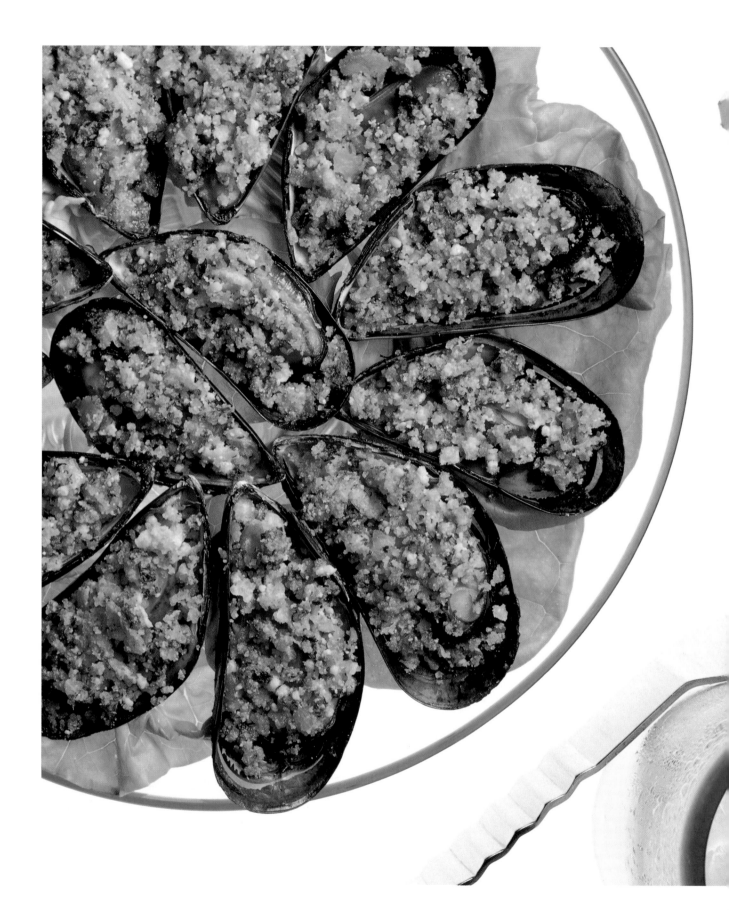

Petaluma Pepper
Pasta *(page 106)*

Mussels au Gratin
(page 87)

Provençal-Style
Tuna and Pear Salad *(page 25)*

Szechuan-Style
Snow Crab *(page 88)*

Nectarine Mousse
(page 152)

Turkey Lasagna Swirls
(page 108)

Strawberry Vanilla Bavarian *(page 155)*

2. Arrange block of frozen vegetables on top. Simmer for 25 to 30 minutes, until liquid is absorbed and rice is tender. Fluff with a fork to mix in vegetables.

MAKES 8 SERVINGS, 130 CALORIES EACH.

FRUITED BROWN RICE PILAF

1 cup uncooked brown rice
1 cup chopped celery
1 cup chopped onions
1 cup fat-skimmed broth or 1 cup water
1 cup orange juice
½ teaspoon curry powder
½ teaspoon ground cumin
½ teaspoon dried thyme
½ teaspoon pumpkin pie spice
1 cup diced fresh fruit (apples, oranges, pears, pineapples, etc.)
1 tablespoon light soy sauce
1 tablespoon toasted sesame seeds

1. Combine rice, celery, onions, broth, juice, curry, cumin, thyme, and pumpkin pie spice. Cover and simmer for 45 to 50 minutes.

2. Stir in diced fruit just before serving and sprinkle with soy sauce and sesame seeds. Good with roast lean pork.

MAKES 10 SERVINGS, APPROXIMATELY 110 CALORIES EACH.

APPLE PILAF

1 cup chicken or turkey broth, skimmed of fat
1 cup apple juice
¼ cup minced celery
¼ cup minced onion
4 eating apples (2 red or 2 yellow or 1 of each), cored
2 cups instant rice
¼ cup golden raisins
1 teaspoon each curry powder, cumin seeds, and lemon pepper
½ teaspoon apple pie spice

1. Combine broth and juice in a saucepan. Add celery and onion; heat to boiling. Cover and simmer for 5 minutes.

2. Meanwhile, shred or dice the unpeeled apples very fine, by hand or with the shredding disk of a food processor; set aside. Stir remaining ingredients (except apples) into simmering broth mixture. When mixture reboils, stir in shredded apples, and cook until heated through. Remove from the heat and cover tightly. Wait 5 minutes or more before serving, then fluff with a fork.

MAKES 10 SERVINGS, 115 CALORIES EACH.

SPANISH VEGETABLES AND RICE

2 cups uncooked long-grain white rice
2 cups water
1 can (10½ ounces) condensed chicken broth, skimmed of fat
1 tablespoon lemon juice
2 cups peeled chopped tomatoes
8 ounces frozen artichoke hearts or canned artichoke hearts, with liquid
1 can (2 ounces) sliced mushrooms, with liquid
1 onion, chopped
1 rib celery, minced
1 bay leaf
¼ teaspoon saffron
1 package (10 ounces) frozen French-cut green beans
1 package (10 ounces) frozen peas

1. Combine all ingredients except green beans and peas in a covered flameproof casserole. Simmer gently for 20 minutes.

2. Stir in green beans and peas. Continue to simmer, covered, stirring frequently, until rice is tender and liquid is absorbed. Remove bay leaf before serving.

MAKES 12 SERVINGS, 160 CALORIES EACH.

AMANDINE CURRY

3 tablespoons slivered almonds
½ onion, minced
1 cup water
1 cup plain skim-milk yogurt
3 tablespoons all-purpose flour
2 teaspoons curry powder, or to taste
Salt and pepper to taste (optional)
2 cups diced cooked lean meat or poultry
2 cups hot cooked brown rice
2 tablespoons minced fresh parsley
Light soy sauce to taste (optional)

1. Put almonds in a nonstick saucepan over moderate heat and toast gently until golden, shaking pan often; remove almonds and set aside. Combine onion with ½ cup water in same pan. Cover, bring to a simmer, and cook for 2 minutes.

2. Combine remaining water with yogurt, flour, curry, and salt and pepper, if desired; stir mixture into pan. Cook, stirring, until sauce simmers and thickens. Add meat or poultry to sauce; heat through. Serve over rice; garnish with almonds and parsley. Season with soy sauce, if desired.

MAKES 4 SERVINGS, 360 CALORIES EACH.

COCONUT SPICED RICE

2 teaspoons margarine or 4 teaspoons diet margarine
1 onion, chopped
1 clove garlic, minced (optional)
2½ cups water
1 cup uncooked long-grain rice
2 tablespoons lemon or lime juice
1 tablespoon fresh thyme or ½ teaspoon dried thyme
2 teaspoons grated orange, lime, or lemon peel
1 teaspoon coconut flavoring
¼ teaspoon ground allspice
Salt and coarse pepper to taste (optional)
1 package (10 ounces) frozen peas and carrots

1. Combine margarine, onion, and garlic, if desired, in a nonstick saucepan. Cook, stirring, until onion begins to brown. Stir in remaining ingredients except frozen peas and carrots, cover tightly, and simmer for 15 minutes.

2. Add frozen vegetables. Simmer, covered, 10 to 15 minutes more.

MAKES 8 SERVINGS, 125 CALORIES EACH.

QUICK CAJUN RICE

¾ cup plain or spicy tomato juice
3 tablespoons Worcestershire sauce
3 tablespoons lemon juice
2 cloves garlic, minced
2 teaspoons fresh thyme or ½ teaspoon dried thyme
1 to 2 teaspoons hot red pepper sauce
Water
1 rib celery, minced
1½ cups instant rice

1. In a saucepan, combine tomato juice, Worcestershire sauce, lemon juice, garlic, thyme, and hot red pepper sauce, if desired; add enough water to make 1½ cups liquid. Add celery, bring to a simmer, and then cook for 5 minutes.

2. Stir in rice. Cover tightly and let stand according to package directions. Fluff with a fork before serving.

Note: This dish can be made along with Spicy Cajun Kebabs (see page 90). Combine water with the reserved marinade from the kebabs and follow directions above, setting rice aside while meat cooks.

MAKES 6 SERVINGS, 105 CALORIES EACH.

CHICKEN TAJ MAHAL

½ cup uncooked long-grain rice
1 can (6 ounces) apple juice
2 tablespoons chopped onion
1 rib celery, minced
¼ cup diced dried fruit bits
2 teaspoons curry powder
2 frying chicken breasts, split
2 tablespoons plain low-fat yogurt
1 tablespoon light soy sauce

1. Combine rice, apple juice, onion, celery, fruit bits, and 1 teaspoon curry powder in an ovenproof casserole. Arrange chicken, skin side up, to cover rice mixture. Combine yogurt, soy sauce, and remaining teaspoon curry powder; spread over chicken.

2. Cover and bake for 45 minutes in a preheated 350-degree oven. Uncover and bake 20 to 30 minutes more.

MAKES 4 SERVINGS, 270 CALORIES EACH.

MIAMI RICE LIGHT PAELLA

12 chicken thighs
1 large Spanish onion, chopped
4 cloves garlic, minced
3 cups uncooked long-grain rice
3 cups chicken broth, skimmed of fat
3 cups water
1 cup chopped red and green bell peppers
6 tablespoons minced fresh cilantro or parsley
Salt and coarse black pepper to taste
2 teaspoons saffron threads or ground turmeric (optional)
3 pounds live mussels
1 cup peas, fresh or frozen
4 frozen stone crab claws, thawed, or 8 ounces cooked crabmeat
12 ounces small shelled cooked shrimp
1 cup tiny cherry tomatoes, halved
4 limes, in wedges, for garnish

1. Arrange chicken thighs, skin side up, in a large roasting pan. Bake in preheated 375-degree oven for about 30 minutes or until skin is crisp and brown. Drain and discard fat. Stir in

onion and garlic. Cover and bake for 10 minutes.

2. Stir in rice, broth, water, bell peppers, cilantro, salt, pepper, and saffron, if desired. Cover and bake for 10 minutes. Lower heat to 350 degrees, cover, and bake 15 minutes more.

3. Meanwhile, clean mussels under running tepid water; pull off and discard any clinging vegetation. Discard any mussels that don't close tightly when insides are tickled with tip of knife. Arrange mussels and peas on top of rice. Cover and bake for 10 minutes.

4. Crack thawed stone crabs, reserving colorful claw tips; extract meat. Add crab, reserved claw tips, shrimp, and tomatoes to oven mixture; bake 5 minutes more or until heated through. Discard any mussels that don't open. Serve with lime wedges.

MAKES 12 SERVINGS, 395 CALORIES EACH.

❧

RED SNAPPER, SHRIMP, AND RICE

1   cup chopped onion
2   cloves garlic, finely chopped (optional)
1   cup uncooked long-grain rice
2   generous pinches thyme
    Salt to taste
2   generous shakes hot red pepper flakes, or to taste
2   cups boiling water
¼   cup dry white wine
1   package (6 ounces) frozen tiny shelled shrimp
1   pound red snapper fillets
    Juice of 2 limes
1   teaspoon salad oil
    Minced fresh parsley for garnish

1. Spread onion and garlic, if desired, in a shallow layer on the bottom of a nonstick baking pan well prepared with cooking spray. Sprinkle on rice, 1 pinch of thyme, salt, and 1 shake of red

pepper flakes. Pour on water and wine. Cover and bake in a preheated 350-degree oven for 20 minutes.

2. Stir in shrimp. Arrange fish fillets on top in a single layer and sprinkle with mixture of lime juice, oil, additional thyme, salt, and additional red pepper flakes. Bake, uncovered, 5 minutes more. Serve sprinkled with parsley.

MAKES 4 SERVINGS, 350 CALORIES EACH.

❧

TURKISH TUNA AND RICE SALAD WITH PISTACHIOS

1   can (13 ounces) water-packed solid white tuna, with liquid
2   cups cold cooked rice
1   small red onion, minced
1   green bell pepper, seeded and diced
6   or 8 pitted black olives, sliced
2   tablespoons minced fresh parsley
1   clove garlic, minced
3   tablespoons liquid from olive container
3   tablespoons lemon juice
2   tablespoons olive oil
2   teaspoons minced fresh thyme or ¼ teaspoon dried thyme
    Salt and black pepper to taste
    Several bay leaves (optional)
    Lettuce leaves for garnish
1   large vine-ripe tomato, cut in wedges, for garnish
½   cup chopped pistachio nuts or slivered almonds for garnish

1. Toss together all ingredients, except lettuce, tomato, and nuts. Refrigerate for several hours. Before serving, remove bay leaves, if used. Arrange salad on lettuce leaves, garnish with tomato, and sprinkle with nuts.

MAKES 8 SERVINGS, 205 CALORIES EACH.

Variation

As a hot dish: Omit lettuce and tomato. Toss and refrigerate as

directed for salad. At serving time, heat mixture in a microwave oven at lowest setting, according to manufacturer's directions, only until it is warmed through. Remove bay leaves before serving and sprinkle with nuts for garnish.

EACH SERVING HAS 195 CALORIES.

❧

TUNA AND RICE SEVILLE

1   cup sliced onions
2   tablespoons liquid from olive jar
2   cups water
2   bell peppers (1 red, 1 green), seeded and diced
½   cup minced celery
2   teaspoons fresh thyme or ½ teaspoon dried thyme
1   teaspoon turmeric
1   bay leaf
8   pimiento-stuffed green olives, thinly sliced
1   can (6½ ounces) water-packed solid white albacore tuna
2   cups instant rice
    Paprika for garnish (optional)

1. In a large nonstick frying pan prepared with cooking spray, combine onion and olive liquid. Cook, stirring, until liquid evaporates and onion begins to brown. Add water, and heat to boiling. Stir in peppers, celery, thyme, turmeric, and bay leaf. Lower heat, cover pan tightly, and simmer for about 7 to 10 minutes.

2. Stir in olives and tuna. Cover and heat through. Remove bay leaf. Stir in rice; cover and let stand according to package directions. Fluff lightly; sprinkle with paprika, if desired.

MAKES 6 SERVINGS, 225 CALORIES EACH.

Variation

Yellow Rice and Shrimp: Substitute tiny peeled, cooked shrimp for the tuna.

SEAFOOD RISOTTO

- 2 teaspoons olive oil
- ½ cup finely chopped onion
- 1 clove garlic, minced
- 1 cup long-grain rice
- 2 cups chicken broth, skimmed of fat
- ½ cup diced zucchini
- ½ pound raw medium shrimp, peeled, deveined, and halved lengthwise
- ½ pound scallops (quartered, if large)
- ½ cup frozen peas, thawed
- ¼ cup minced parsley
- 3 tablespoons grated Parmesan cheese

1. Heat oil in a large nonstick skillet. Sauté onion and garlic over moderate heat until soft. Add rice and sauté until opaque—about 3 minutes.

2. Add 1 cup broth and bring to a boil. Cover and simmer for 10 minutes or until liquid is absorbed. Add remaining broth and zucchini; cover, return to a simmer, and then cook for 5 minutes.

3. Add shrimp, scallops, and peas. Simmer, covered, for 10 minutes, stirring once. Stir in parsley, and cook 5 minutes more or until liquid is absorbed, rice is tender, and seafood is opaque. Stir in Parmesan.

MAKES 4 SERVINGS, 345 CALORIES EACH.

SPICY RICE AND FISH

- 1 cup sliced onions
- 1 tablespoon olive oil
- 2½ cups water
- 1 cup uncooked long-grain rice
- 2 bell peppers (red or green), seeded and diced
- ½ cup minced celery
- 2 teaspoons minced fresh thyme or ½ teaspoon dried thyme
- ½ teaspoon turmeric or curry powder
- 1 bay leaf
- 8 pimiento-stuffed green olives, thinly sliced
- 2 tablespoons liquid from olive jar
- 1 cup flaked smoked whitefish or salmon or other smoked fish
- 2 tablespoons light mayonnaise
- ¼ cup plain low-fat yogurt
  Coarse black pepper to taste
  Paprika for garnish (optional)

1. In a large nonstick frying pan prepared with cooking spray, combine onions and oil. Cook, stirring, over moderate heat, until liquid evaporates and onion begins to brown. Add water, and heat to boiling. Stir in rice, peppers, celery, thyme, turmeric, and bay leaf. Lower heat, cover pan tightly, and simmer for 20 minutes or just until liquid is absorbed.

2. Stir in remaining ingredients; cover and heat through. Discard bay leaf. Sprinkle with paprika, if desired.

MAKES 6 SERVINGS, UNDER 250 CALORIES EACH.

BEEF AND RICE, MEXICAN STYLE

- 12 ounces diet-lean ground round steak
- 2 cups plain or spicy tomato juice
- 4 onions, minced
- 2 ribs celery, minced
- 2 green bell peppers, seeded and diced
- 1 teaspoon chili powder
- ½ teaspoon dried oregano
- ½ teaspoon ground cumin (optional)
- 1½ cups instant rice
- ¼ cup shredded sharp Cheddar cheese (optional)

1. Flatten meat in a large nonstick skillet. Brown over medium heat; turn and break into chunks, stirring occasionally to brown evenly. Drain and discard any fat.

2. Add tomato juice, onions, celery, peppers, and seasonings. Cover, bring to a simmer, and cook for 5 minutes. Stir in rice and reheat to boiling; cover and remove from heat. Let stand according to package directions until liquid is absorbed. Fluff with a fork and serve sprinkled with cheese, if desired.

MAKES 4 SERVINGS, 335 CALORIES EACH; CHEESE ADDS 30 CALORIES PER SERVING.

ITALIAN LENTIL AND RICE SALAD

¼   pound lentils, picked over and
      rinsed
1½ cups water
1   teaspoon salt
1   cup cooked rice
½   cup light Italian dressing
½   cup tomatoes, seeded and
      diced
¼   cup chopped green bell pepper
3   tablespoons chopped onion
2   tablespoons chopped celery
2   tablespoons sliced pimiento-
      stuffed green olives
      Chopped fresh parsley

1. Place lentils in a heavy saucepan with water and salt. Bring to a boil; reduce heat and simmer, covered, for about 20 minutes. Do not overcook; lentils should be tender with skins intact. Drain immediately.

2. Combine lentils with cooked rice; pour dressing over mixture and refrigerate until cool. Add remaining ingredients except parsley and mix everything well. Garnish with parsley before serving.

MAKES 5 SERVINGS, 185 CALORIES EACH.

BEEF AND THREE-BEAN CASSEROLE

8   ounces lean ground beef
2   cups cooked or canned
      drained chick-peas (ceci or
      garbanzo beans)
1   cup cooked or canned drained
      kidney beans
1   cup chopped onions
½   cup spicy tomato juice
2   tablespoons chili sauce
1   tablespoon prepared mustard
1   tablespoon wine vinegar
1   clove garlic, minced
½   teaspoon dried oregano
1   cup frozen kitchen-cut green
      beans

1. Brown the beef with no fat added in a nonstick skillet or

under the broiler. Drain and discard any fat.

2. In the skillet, combine browned beef with all remaining ingredients except green beans, and simmer, covered, over low heat for 1 hour. Or transfer to a casserole, cover, and bake for 1 hour in a preheated 325-degree oven.

3. Meanwhile, partially thaw green beans. Arrange green beans on top of mixture; cook, uncovered, just until green beans are heated through but still bright green and crunchy—6 to 8 minutes. Stir into mixture and serve immediately.

MAKES 4 SERVINGS, 295 CALORIES EACH.

LENTILS, TUSCANY STYLE

8   ounces low-calorie breakfast
      sausage
1   large sweet onion, chopped
2½ cups water or fat-skimmed
      broth
2   tablespoons chopped celery
2   tablespoons chopped parsley
2   bay leaves
1   cup dried lentils, picked over
      and rinsed
      Salt or lemon pepper to taste
      (optional)

1. In a large nonstick skillet or electric frying pan prepared with cooking spray, brown the sausage, turning to brown evenly. Drain and discard any fat. Remove sausage and set aside.

2. In the skillet, combine onion and 2 or 3 tablespoons of water. Cook over moderate heat just until onion begins to brown. Add remaining water, the sausage, celery, parsley, and bay leaves. Heat to boiling, then stir in lentils. Cover and cook over low heat, stirring occasionally, until lentils are tender—25 to 35 minutes. Season with salt or lemon pepper, if desired. Remove bay leaves before serving.

Note: Use either sausage links or bulk sausage shaped into small patties, or substitute Sicilian-Style Sausage Patties (see recipe on page 64).

MAKES 4 SERVINGS, 315 CALORIES EACH.

Variations

In the oven: Brown sausages under broiler; discard fat. Combine all ingredients in a covered dish and bake in a preheated 350-degree oven for 40 to 50 minutes or until lentils are tender but not mushy. Remove bay leaves before serving.

Lentil Soup: Double the amount of water, increasing it to 5 cups. Add 2 ribs celery and 2 carrots, thinly sliced.

MAKES 6 SERVINGS, 225 CALORIES EACH.

SMOKED TURKEY, BLACK-EYED PEAS, AND RICE

1   smoked turkey drumstick
1   pound black-eyed peas, fresh
      or frozen and thawed
1   cup uncooked brown rice
4   onions, chopped
4   ribs celery, sliced
1   green bell pepper, seeded and
      chopped
1   cup stewed tomatoes
1   cup tomato juice
1   cup dry red wine
1   cup water
4   cloves garlic, minced
1   teaspoon each dried rosemary,
      sage, and thyme
2   or 3 bay leaves
      Salt and black pepper to taste

1. Combine ingredients in a heavy Dutch oven. Cover and simmer on the range top or bake in a 350-degree oven for 2 hours.

2. Discard bone and skin from turkey leg; cut meat into bite-size chunks. Stir turkey meat back into rice mixture. Remove bay leaves before serving.

MAKES 8 SERVINGS, 270 CALORIES EACH.

VEGETARIAN CHUNKY CHILI

    1   teaspoon salad oil
    2   medium onions, chopped
    2   cloves garlic, minced
    2   cans (28 ounces each)
        tomatoes, with liquid
    2   cans (15½ ounces each) red
        kidney beans, with liquid
    1   can (15 ounces) chick-peas
        (ceci or garbanzo beans),
        drained
    2   cups chopped celery
    1   large green bell pepper, seeded
        and chopped
    1   can (4 ounces) chopped green
        chilies, drained
    3   tablespoons cider vinegar
    1   tablespoon chili powder
  1½   teaspoons each dried oregano
        and cumin seeds
    ¼   teaspoon ground cinnamon
   12   ounces light beer
    1   cup dry-roasted peanuts
    1   cup shredded sharp cheese
    3   tablespoons chopped fresh
        cilantro or parsley

    1. Preheat oil in a large cooking pot or Dutch oven over moderate heat. Add onions and garlic, and cook until onions are soft, stirring frequently. Add tomatoes, all beans, celery, bell peppers, chilies, vinegar, chili powder, oregano, cumin seeds, and cinnamon. Cover and simmer for 1½ hours.
    2. Add beer; simmer, uncovered, 30 minutes more. Stir in peanuts; sprinkle with cheese and cilantro before serving.

MAKES 10 SERVINGS, 315 CALORIES EACH.

YANKEE TURKEY CHILI WITH RICE

    1   pound ground turkey
    3   cups turkey or chicken broth,
        skimmed of fat
    1   can (16 ounces) chopped
        tomatoes
    1   can (6 ounces) tomato paste
    1   cup uncooked long-grain rice
    2   ribs celery, chopped
    1   onion, chopped
    1   green bell pepper, seeded and
        chopped
    1   clove garlic, minced
    3   teaspoons chili powder, or to
        taste

    1. In a nonstick pot prepared with cooking spray, arrange turkey in a shallow layer. Cook undisturbed until underside is brown. Break into chunks and turn to brown all sides. Drain and discard any fat.
    2. Add remaining ingredients. Cover and simmer, stirring occasionally, until rice is tender—about 25 minutes.

MAKES 6 SERVINGS, 335 CALORIES EACH.

CARIB CHILI WITH BROILED BANANAS

    2   pounds diet-lean ground beef
        round
    1   green bell pepper, seeded and
        chopped
    1   medium onion, chopped
    ½   cup chopped celery with leaves
    1   clove garlic, crushed
    1   can (28 ounces) tomatoes
    1   can (15 ounces) plain tomato
        sauce
    2   tablespoons chili powder
    2   teaspoons salt (optional)
    1   bay leaf
    ½   teaspoon each dried oregano
        and dried basil
    2   cans (16 ounces each) red
        kidney beans, drained
   10   firm bananas
    4   teaspoons diet margarine,
        melted

    1. Break up beef in Dutch oven or kettle and brown evenly. Pour off and discard any fat. Add bell pepper, onion, celery, and garlic. Cook, stirring frequently, until vegetables are tender.
    2. Add tomatoes, tomato sauce, chili powder, salt (if desired), bay leaf, oregano, and basil. Cook over moderate heat for 30 minutes. Add beans; cook 15 minutes more. Remove the bay leaf.
    3. Just before serving, peel bananas, cut in half lengthwise, and brush with melted margarine. Broil for 2 minutes or just until tender. Place 2 banana halves on each plate; top with chili mixture.

MAKES 10 SERVINGS, 375 CALORIES EACH.

TURKISH LENTILS

    1   pound dried lentils, picked
        over and rinsed
    3   cups fresh or canned turkey
        stock, skimmed of fat
    2   cups diced cooked turkey
        (optional)
    3   onions, chopped
    2   bell peppers (red, yellow, or
        green), seeded and diced,
        or 2 ribs celery, minced
    1   yellow squash, diced
    1   can (6 ounces) tomato paste
    3   tablespoons lemon juice
    2   cloves garlic, minced
    1   teaspoon each cumin seeds,
        dried mint, and dried
        oregano
    ¼   teaspoon each ground nutmeg
        and cinnamon
        Salt and coarsely ground black
        pepper to taste
    1   cup plain low-fat yogurt
        (optional)

    1. Put lentils in a pot and cover with cold tap water; soak them overnight. (Alternatively, boil lentils for 2 minutes, according to package directions, then drain well.)
    2. Combine them with all remaining ingredients except

yogurt. Cover and simmer for 40 minutes. If desired, put a dollop of yogurt on top of each serving.

MAKES 10 SERVINGS, 205 CALORIES EACH; OPTIONAL INGREDIENTS ADD 65 CALORIES PER SERVING.

✄

STIR-FRIED QUICK CHUNKY CHILI FRESCA

12 ounces diet-lean ground beef
½ cup light beer
1 can (8 ounces) sliced stewed tomatoes, with liquid
3 sweet bell peppers (1 red, 1 green, and 1 yellow), seeded and chopped
1 large Spanish onion, minced
1 clove garlic, minced
2 tablespoons chopped fresh cilantro
1 tablespoon chili powder, or to taste
2 teaspoons cumin seeds (optional)
Pinch dried oregano (optional)
Shredded iceberg lettuce (optional)
¼ cup shredded sharp Cheddar cheese (optional)

1. In a large nonstick skillet or electric frying pan prepared with cooking spray, spread meat in shallow layer. Brown over moderate heat. When underside of meat is brown, break into chunks and turn to brown all sides evenly. Drain and discard any fat.

2. Stir in beer, tomatoes, peppers, onion, garlic, and seasonings. Cover and cook for 3 to 4 minutes; uncover and cook over moderate heat 6 to 7 minutes more or until most liquid evaporates and peppers are crisp-tender. If desired, serve topped with shredded lettuce and cheese.

MAKES 4 SERVINGS, 245 CALORIES EACH; OPTIONAL INGREDIENTS ADD APPROXIMATELY 30 CALORIES PER SERVING.

MIDDLE EASTERN LENTIL CHILI

1 pound dried lentils, picked over and rinsed
Water to cover
3 cups fresh cold water or fat-skimmed broth
1 can (6 ounces) tomato paste
3 tablespoons lemon juice
3 onions, chopped
2 ribs celery, minced
1 yellow squash or 1 carrot, diced
1 green bell pepper, seeded and chopped
2 cloves garlic, minced
1 teaspoon each dried mint and dried marjoram or oregano
2 cups diced cooked lean lamb or chicken (optional)
Salt and coarsely ground black pepper to taste
1 cup plain low-fat yogurt (optional)

1. Soak lentils overnight in water to cover or boil 2 minutes according to package directions. Drain lentils and combine with remaining ingredients, except yogurt.

2. Cover and simmer for 40 minutes. Serve with a dollop of yogurt, if desired, on top of each serving.

MAKES 10 SERVINGS, 190 CALORIES EACH; OPTIONAL INGREDIENTS ADD 100 CALORIES PER SERVING.

ITALIAN CHICKEN AND CHICK-PEAS

3 tablespoons instant-blending flour
1 teaspoon seasoned salt or lemon pepper
6 frying chicken thighs, trimmed of fat
1 can (28 ounces) tomatoes, with liquid
1 can (16 ounces) chick-peas (ceci or garbanzo beans), drained
1 can (8 ounces) tomato sauce
½ cup chopped onions
½ cup long-grain white rice
1 clove garlic, minced
½ teaspoon each dried oregano, basil, thyme, and hot red pepper flakes

1. Combine flour and salt in a large, heavy brown grocery bag. Add chicken and shake until lightly coated. Arrange chicken, skin side up, in a shallow roasting pan. Bake in a preheated 425-degree oven for 25 to 30 minutes or until crisp. Drain and discard any fat.

2. Mix. remaining ingredients and place in pan with chicken on top. Lower heat to 350 degrees. Bake 20 to 30 minutes more until chicken and rice are tender and the liquid is absorbed.

MAKES 6 SERVINGS, 320 CALORIES EACH.

Fresh Appeal for Vegetables

LUCKY you if you grew up in a household that fostered a love of veggies! But even if you didn't, it's never too late to rethink a preschool prejudice against Mother Nature.

Lots of grown-ups who pride themselves on their open-mindedness on other matters are still operating on a 6-year-old level where vegetables are concerned. They still prefer meats and sweets over the stuff mom oversold as "good for you."

Forget veggies as vitamin prescriptions and think of them as an exotic new food to be savored and flavored in interesting ways, without butter!

HOW TO SEASON VEGGIES

Creative use of herbs, spices, and seasonings can heighten vegetables' fresh appeal. Hidden in those run-of-the-mill veggies are exciting adventures for the palate—all you need is a little ingenuity and a spice rack to turn the everyday into the extraordinary!

- *Broccoli:* Serve with a dollop of "light" mayonnaise spiked with oregano and parsley.
- *Brussels sprouts:* Season as you would cabbage. Or make a no-fat "cream sauce" with skim milk and flour. Omit fat or butter and add salt, marjoram, thyme, and pepper.
- *Cabbage:* Sauté shredded cabbage in oil, minced onion, white pepper, basil, and paprika. Or cook wedges in tomato sauce with onion, garlic, and basil.
- *Carrots:* Simmer in unsweetened pineapple juice and add a pinch of cinnamon.

- *Cauliflower:* Serve with a sauce made from thick yogurt and seasoned with curry and onion.
- *Celery:* Spice braised celery with minced onion, fennel seeds, and ground white pepper.
- *Corn:* Cook kernels with an equal amount of chopped red and green sweet pepper; add a pinch of chili powder or a dash of hot red pepper sauce.
- *Green beans:* Add dill seed, parsley, and coarse pepper. Basil, savory, and mixed Italian seasonings are also good choices.
- *Mushrooms:* Sauté in a small amount of butter or margarine and add either oregano or thyme for seasoning.
- *Peas:* Simmer with pearl onions and tarragon leaves.
- *Sauerkraut:* Cook with apple juice or unsweetened applesauce and caraway seeds.
- *Spinach:* Add a pinch of ground nutmeg or mace, or sprinkle with toasted sesame seeds.
- *Tomatoes:* Cooked or fresh, they're great with fresh basil or oregano, minced onion or garlic, or all of the above!
- *Winter squash:* Bake with apple juice and apple pie spice . . . or with orange juice and pumpkin pie spice.
- *Zucchini:* Make a sauce of plain unsweetened yogurt, minced onion, and sage. Pour over cooked zucchini and bake.

VEGETABLE VARIETY

There's nothing more flexible than vegetables—they go along with just about anything.

Here are a few ideas for updating old standbys and for making some new acquaintances, too.

- Try a vegetable raw if it is usually served cooked. Or cook a vegetable that is normally served in salad—braised celery is a good example.
- Try a new variety every week. When you shop, look for a vegetable you have never eaten before and give it a go.
- Combine vegetables. Put together a blend of old favorites with one you've never tasted or one you decided you disliked back when you were 10 years old.
- Try vegetables in season, preferably from a local farm. The deteriorated taste and texture of stored or processed produce may be what turns you off.
- Stir-fry vegetables the oriental way. One tablespoon of diet margarine (50 calories) is all you need to stir up a skilletful of crisp onions and green beans laced with soy sauce.
- Try cooking red or yellow vegetables in dry white wine. The alcohol calories evaporate. Simmer green vegetables in soup or stock from which you have skimmed the fat.
- For a fresh taste, add flavor favorites—chopped onions or sliced green peppers—especially when cooking canned or frozen vegetables.
- Cook red or yellow vegetables in unsweetened fruit juice. Apple, orange, and pineapple are some you might try.
- Turn the cooking water into a low-cal sauce. Combine a little flour with skim milk and stir it into the saucepan after the vegetables are cooked. It's a cream sauce without the cream—or cream calories.
- Spice and season your vegetables by adding fresh herbs from the garden.

LEMON AID

The zesty zing of lemon can more than make up for the lack of excess fat, salt, and calories. Lemon juice has another important contribution to the foods that fight fat: eye appeal. The ascorbic acid in lemon juice—vitamin C—is Mother Nature's color keeper. It works its spe-

cial magic on the very foods dear to the heart of dieters: fruits and veggies.

Here's some useful information you probably didn't catch in chemistry class:

- *To keep the red in:* The red compound in fruits and vegetables is anthocyanin. The rosy hue in red cabbage, beets, bing cherries, blueberries, black raspberries, and boysenberries is enhanced by lemon juice.
- *And the brown out:* Some fruits and vegetables quickly turn brown when peeled or cut: apples, pears, bananas, and potatoes, for example. The cause: oxygen in the air reaching the exposed surfaces. The ascorbic acid in lemon juice will prevent this from happening.
- *And the white light:* Lemon juice added to the cooking or poaching water can help certain white foods keep their whiteness by counteracting alkaline ingredients that promote yellowness. Add lemon juice to fish, cauliflower, rice, and potatoes.

Does lemon juice help the color of every fruit and veggie?

- *Can't touch orange:* Lemon juice doesn't change the color of carrots or other carotenoid-containing orange-colored veggies like sweet potatoes or rutabagas.
- *But it's mean to green!* The acid in lemon can destroy the fresh green color of cooked vegetables by displacing the magnesium in chlorophyll, causing it to form pheophytin, the murky olive-green pigment that's typical of canned or overcooked vegetables. So to keep the bright green color of veggies from turning yukky olive drab, don't add lemon juice (or any other acid ingredient: wine or vinegar, for example) to the cooking water. But there's one green food that lemon can help: lemon juice added to fresh raw avocado will help it keep its green color by protecting it from the browning caused by oxygen in the air.
- *But don't be foiled:* Here's one more point about lemon juice and food color: to prevent the discoloration of lemon-treated foods, avoid putting the food in contact with aluminum foil or uncoated aluminum cookware or storage containers.

ARTICHOKE HEARTS WITH BASIL

1   package (9 ounces) frozen
      artichoke hearts
3/4 cup canned or homemade
      chicken broth, skimmed of
      fat
2   or 3 fresh basil leaves
      Coarsely ground pepper to taste
      plus juice of 1 lemon, or
      lemon pepper to taste
      Salt to taste (optional)

1. In a saucepan, combine all ingredients except lemon juice, bring to a simmer, and cook for 6 to 7 minutes, until artichoke hearts are tender and cooking liquid is reduced.

2. Remove from heat and stir in lemon juice. Serve hot, with cooking liquid poured over artichoke hearts.

MAKES 3 SERVINGS, 45 CALORIES EACH.

YELLOW WAX BEANS AND TOMATOES WITH BASIL AND CHEESE

1   can (8 ounces) stewed
      tomatoes, well broken up
1/4 cup water
1/4 cup finely chopped onion
1   teaspoon minced fresh basil or
      oregano or 1/2 teaspoon
      dried basil or oregano
1½ cups sliced fresh yellow wax
      beans or 1 package (10
      ounces) frozen yellow wax
      beans, thawed
6   teaspoons grated Parmesan
      cheese

1. Combine all ingredients except beans and cheese in a saucepan. Bring to a simmer, covered, and cook for 8 minutes.

2. Add beans and simmer, uncovered, stirring often, just until beans are tender and liquid reduces to a thick sauce—about 5 minutes. Sprinkle with cheese.

MAKES 6 SERVINGS, 35 CALORIES EACH.

CREAMED GREEN BEANS

1¼ pounds fresh French-style green
      beans or 1 bag (20 ounces)
      frozen French-style green
      beans, partially defrosted
1   onion, minced
1   red bell pepper, seeded and
      diced
1   cup condensed chicken broth,
      skimmed of fat
1   cup skim milk
2   tablespoons flour
8   teaspoons American-style
      grated cheese

1. Combine vegetables and broth in a nonstick saucepan. Bring to a simmer, covered, and cook for 5 minutes.

2. In a bowl, combine milk and flour thoroughly. Stir mixture into saucepan; cook, stirring, until sauce is thick. Sprinkle with cheese.

MAKES 8 SERVINGS, 65 CALORIES EACH.

GREEN BEANS, SERBIAN STYLE

1   pound fresh green beans or
      frozen green beans, thawed
2   teaspoons olive or safflower oil
1   small onion, minced
1   clove garlic, finely minced
1   teaspoon all-purpose flour
1/2 cup beef or chicken broth,
      skimmed of fat
1   tablespoon chopped fresh dill or
      parsley
1   tablespoon plain low-fat yogurt
1   tablespoon paprika

1. Cut green beans lengthwise and set aside. Add oil to a nonstick pan and sauté onion and garlic lightly. Sprinkle with flour, stirring to combine it thoroughly.

2. Add beans to pan. Stir in broth and dill. Bring to a simmer and cook for 12 minutes, until beans are crisp-tender and most liquid has evaporated. Add a dol-

lop of yogurt on top and a generous sprinkle of paprika.

MAKES 4 SERVINGS, 75 CALORIES EACH.

CREOLE GREEN BEANS

1   can (16 ounces) sliced stewed
      tomatoes
1/2 cup chopped green bell pepper
1/2 cup chopped onions
1/2 cup chopped celery
3   tablespoons minced fresh
      parsley
1   clove garlic, minced
1/4 teaspoon each dried thyme,
      dried marjoram, ground
      cloves, ground allspice, and
      cayenne pepper
1¼ pounds fresh or frozen green
      beans or 3 cans (8 ounces
      each) green beans, drained,
      with liquid reserved

1. Combine all ingredients except green beans. (If using canned green beans, add reserved liquid to the mixture.) Simmer for 20 minutes.

2. Add green beans and cook until crisp-tender if fresh or frozen, or just until heated through if canned.

MAKES 10 SERVINGS, 35 CALORIES EACH.

Variation

Cajun Sausage and Green Beans: Brown 1 pound low-calorie breakfast sausage links in a nonstick skillet with no fat added or under the broiler. Turn to brown evenly. Add all ingredients except green beans from preceding recipe. Proceed as above.

MAKES 8 SERVINGS, 185 CALORIES EACH.

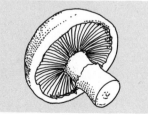

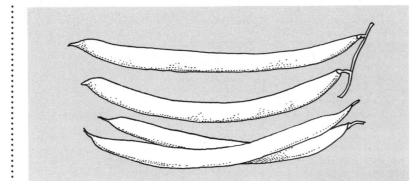

GREEN BEANS ROMANOFF

2 teaspoons cornstarch
1 cup plain low-fat yogurt
2 cans (1 pound each) cut green beans, well drained
½ cup chopped onion
1 envelope beef bouillon granules
1 teaspoon prepared mustard
1 teaspoon Worcestershire sauce
6 tablespoons grated Romano cheese
6 tablespoons herb-seasoned bread crumbs

1. Stir cornstarch into yogurt. Mix in all remaining ingredients except cheese and bread crumbs. Prepare a nonstick baking dish or casserole with cooking spray. Spoon in green bean mixture and sprinkle evenly with cheese and bread crumbs.

2. Bake in preheated 350-degree oven for 25 minutes or until topping is browned.

MAKES 8 SERVINGS, 85 CALORIES EACH.

QUICK GREEN BEANS AND MUSHROOMS

1 can (4 ounces) mushroom stems and pieces
1 can (16 ounces) sliced green beans, drained
2 tablespoons chopped onion or 2 teaspoons dried onion flakes
1 teaspoon diet margarine

1. Drain mushroom liquid into beans. (Add dried onion, if using.) Set beans aside.

2. Prepare a nonstick skillet with cooking spray; add margarine and mushrooms. Cook over high heat until mushrooms begin to brown. Add remaining ingredients, and cook, stirring often, over high heat until green beans are heated through and most of mushroom liquid has evaporated.

MAKES 4 SERVINGS, 35 CALORIES EACH.

CUT ASPARAGUS WITH DILLED MOCK-HOLLANDAISE SAUCE

Light mayonnaise stirred into the cooking liquid for vegetables makes the ideal healthy alternative to heavy-hearted hollandaise!

1 pound fresh asparagus spears, diagonally cut in 1-inch lengths
¼ cup water or fat-skimmed chicken broth
2 tablespoons light mayonnaise
2 tablespoons chopped fresh dill
Lemon pepper to taste

1. In a saucepan, bring the asparagus and water to a simmer, and cook just until crisp-tender—3 to 5 minutes, depending on thickness and age of spears.

2. Remove asparagus from pan; stir mayonnaise and dill into pan juices until well blended. Season to taste. Serve mayonnaise sauce over asparagus.

MAKES 4 SERVINGS, 55 CALORIES EACH.

CABBAGE WEDGES IN SPICY SWEET 'N' SOUR SAUCE

1 small head cabbage
2 cups spicy tomato juice
1 cup apple juice or cider
2 teaspoons lemon juice
Low-calorie sweetener to taste (optional)

1. Cut cabbage into 4 even wedges, with leaves attached to base. In a saucepan, combine juices, add cabbage wedges, and bring to a simmer, covered tightly. Cook just until cabbage wedges are crisp-tender—about 8 minutes.

2. Remove from heat, transfer cabbage to a serving bowl, and sweeten sauce to taste, if desired. Pour sauce from pan over wedges.

MAKES 4 SERVINGS, 80 CALORIES EACH.

LEMON-DILLY BRUSSELS SPROUTS

1 container (10 or 12) fresh brussels sprouts
½ cup condensed chicken broth, skimmed of fat
1 tablespoon chopped fresh dill leaves
Juice of 1 lemon

1. Combine all ingredients except lemon juice in saucepan. Bring to a simmer, covered, and cook for 5 minutes. Uncover and continue to simmer, stirring frequently, until nearly all liquid evaporates. (If sprouts require more cooking, add a little water.) Remove from heat and stir in lemon juice.

MAKES 2 SERVINGS, 60 CALORIES EACH.

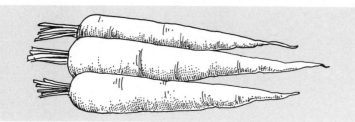

5-MINUTE SAUCY BROCCOLI

¼ cup boiling water
2 tablespoons light mayonnaise
1 tablespoon minced onion or 1 teaspoon dried onion flakes (optional)
  Salt and pepper to taste
1 package (10 ounces) chopped frozen broccoli, thawed

1. In a saucepan, combine all ingredients except broccoli; mix well. Stir in broccoli. Cover, bring to a simmer, and cook for 3 minutes. Uncover and continue to simmer until nearly all liquid evaporates.

MAKES 3 SERVINGS, 45 CALORIES EACH.

❦

SPICED SHREDDED CARROTS AND RAISINS

1 pound fresh carrots, thoroughly scrubbed
¼ cup water
3 tablespoons frozen pineapple juice concentrate
3 tablespoons raisins
  Pinch apple pie spice or pumpkin pie spice
  Salt and pepper to taste (optional)

1. Shred carrots in a food processor or by hand. Combine with remaining ingredients in a saucepan. Cover, bring to a simmer, and cook for 2 minutes. Uncover and simmer until most of the liquid evaporates.

MAKES 4 SERVINGS, 85 CALORIES EACH.

APPLE-GLAZED CARROTS

2¼ pounds fresh small whole carrots or 2 packages (10 ounces each) frozen carrots, thawed
1 cup apple juice or cider
3 tablespoons raisins
1 teaspoon salad oil
¼ teaspoon ground cinnamon
  Salt and pepper to taste

1. Combine ingredients in a saucepan. Cover, bring to a simmer, and cook for 10 minutes. Uncover and simmer 8 to 10 minutes more or until carrots are tender and glazed.

MAKES 6 SERVINGS, 110 CALORIES EACH.

❦

QUICK-PICKLED CARROTS

1 bag (20 ounces) frozen sliced carrots
1 can (6 ounces) apple juice or cider concentrate, thawed
¾ cup water
¾ cup cider vinegar
1 tablespoon mixed pickling spices
1 teaspoon apple pie spice
  Salt and pepper to taste

1. Combine ingredients in a nonstick saucepan, bring to a simmer, and cook for 5 minutes. Cool, then chill for several hours in refrigerator.

2. Remove carrots with a slotted spoon. Strain liquid to remove whole spices; pour strained liquid over carrots. Serve chilled.

MAKES 6 SERVINGS, 100 CALORIES EACH.

NIPPY CAULIFLOWER AU GRATIN

1 package (10 ounces) frozen cauliflower, thawed
½ cup skim milk
¼ cup water
1 teaspoon cornstarch
½ teaspoon dry mustard
  Salt or seasoned salt and black pepper to taste
  Pinch cayenne pepper
2 tablespoons shredded extra-sharp Cheddar cheese
2 teaspoons seasoned bread crumbs

1. Arrange cauliflower in a shallow ovenproof casserole; set aside. In a small nonstick saucepan, combine milk, water, and cornstarch; stir over low heat until simmering. Season to taste with mustard, salt, black pepper, and cayenne pepper.

2. Pour sauce over cauliflower and sprinkle with cheese and bread crumbs. Bake in a preheated 350-degree oven for 15 to 30 minutes.

MAKES 4 SERVINGS, 55 CALORIES EACH.

❦

SAUCY CAULIFLOWER

1 head fresh cauliflower, broken in florets
1 cup skim milk
½ cup water
1 teaspoon butter or margarine
2 tablespoons instant-blending flour
½ teaspoon curry powder, or to taste
  Salt or butter-flavored salt and pepper to taste

1. In a nonstick saucepan, combine cauliflower with ½ cup milk, the water, and butter. Cover, bring to a simmer over low heat, and cook until cauliflower is just tender—about 5 minutes. Remove cauliflower with a slotted spoon to a serving dish; reserve the cooking liquid.

2. Combine remaining milk with flour and curry powder; stir until smooth. Heat cooking liquid over low heat; stir in flour mixture and continue to stir over low heat until sauce is thick. Season to taste and pour over cauliflower.

MAKES 6 SERVINGS, 50 CALORIES EACH.

❦

BEETS IN ORANGE SAUCE

- 1 can (16 ounces) sliced beets, with liquid
- 1 tablespoon orange juice concentrate
  Pinch each ground ginger and cinnamon

1. Combine ingredients in a saucepan and heat through.

MAKES 4 SERVINGS, 45 CALORIES EACH.

❦

CIDER-PICKLED BEETS

- 1 can (16 ounces) sliced beets
- ¼ cup cider vinegar
- 1 tablespoon apple juice concentrate
- 1 tablespoon whole pickling spices

1. Drain beet juice into a saucepan and add vinegar and concentrate. Bring to a simmer and cook for 5 minutes; add beets and heat through.

2. Pour into a nonmetallic dish, cover, and refrigerate for several hours for flavors to blend. Drain before serving.

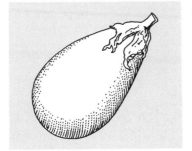

Serve beets cold or reheat and serve hot.

MAKES 4 SERVINGS, 50 CALORIES EACH.

❦

CARROT AND ZUCCHINI MEDLEY

- 1 pound carrots, scrubbed and cut in ⅛-inch slices
- 1 cup water
- 1 pound zucchini, cut in ¼-inch slices
- ¼ teaspoon ground cinnamon
  Pinch ground ginger
  Salt and coarsely ground pepper to taste

1. Bring carrots to a simmer in water, and cook, covered, for 10 minutes. Add zucchini, return to a simmer, and cook 5 minutes more. Season and serve.

MAKES 6 SERVINGS, 45 CALORIES EACH.

❦

QUICK AND CRUNCHY SUMMER RATATOUILLE

- 2 cups sliced zucchini
- 2 cups peeled cubed eggplant
- 1 can (8 ounces) sliced stewed tomatoes
- 1 green bell pepper, diced
- ½ cup sliced onion
- 2 or 3 fresh basil leaves, chopped, or ½ teaspoon dried basil
- 3 tablespoons light French-style salad dressing

1. Combine ingredients, cover, and bring to a simmer. Cook for 10 minutes. Serve hot or cold.

MAKES 6 SERVINGS, 60 CALORIES EACH.

Variation

Hot Caponata: Add ½ cup thinly sliced celery and 12 pimiento-stuffed green olives, thinly sliced, to Quick and Crunchy Summer Ratatouille ingredients. Proceed as above.

MAKES 7 SERVINGS, 65 CALORIES EACH.

NO-EGGPLANT RATATOUILLE

- 2 teaspoons olive oil
- 1 small onion, chopped
- 1 clove garlic, minced (optional)
- 4 ribs celery, trimmed and cut in 1-inch lengths
- 4 cups cubed zucchini
- 2 green bell peppers, seeded and diced
- 2 vine-ripe tomatoes, diced
- 1 tablespoon chopped fresh basil or 1 teaspoon dried basil
  Pinch dried thyme
  Salt and black pepper to taste

1. Heat oil in a large saucepan or skillet. Add onion and garlic, if desired, and sauté for 5 minutes. Add remaining ingredients; cover and simmer for 15 minutes.

2. Uncover and simmer 30 minutes longer, stirring occasionally. Serve hot or cold.

MAKES 8 SERVINGS, 45 CALORIES EACH.

❦

SLIM RATATOUILLE

- 1 eggplant, peeled and diced
- 2 green bell peppers, seeded and diced
- 1 medium zucchini, cubed
- 1 onion, thinly sliced
- 1 can (16 ounces) stewed tomatoes
- ¾ cup tomato juice
- 4 pitted black or green olives, sliced
- 2 tablespoons liquid from olive jar
- 1 or 2 cloves garlic, minced
- ½ teaspoon each dried thyme, oregano, and basil
  Salt and freshly ground black pepper to taste

1. Combine all ingredients. Cover and simmer for 25 to 30 minutes.

2. Uncover and continue to simmer until most of the liquid evaporates. Season to taste. Serve hot or cold.

MAKES 8 SERVINGS, 50 CALORIES EACH.

ISRAELI-STYLE MOUSSAKA
(Layered eggplant or zucchini)

1   large sweet onion, thinly
     sliced
1   large eggplant or 3 zucchini,
     sliced ½ inch thick
1   pound lean ground lamb or
     lean ground beef
3   cups tomato juice
¼   cup chopped fresh parsley
1   teaspoon ground cumin
     (optional)
½   teaspoon dried oregano
     (optional)
    Pinch grated nutmeg
     (optional)
    Salt and pepper to taste

1. Layer ingredients in a shallow roasting pan in the order listed: first onion, then eggplant slices. Crumble meat on top, pour on tomato juice, and sprinkle with parsley and seasonings, if desired. Bake in a preheated 350-degree oven for 30 to 35 minutes.

MAKES 4 SERVINGS, 220 CALORIES EACH.

CURRIED GREEN PEAS

1   cup dried chick-peas (ceci or
     garbanzo beans)
1   tablespoon diet margarine
1   cup chopped onions
1   clove garlic, minced
2   teaspoons whole cumin seeds
1½ cups water
1½ cups chicken broth, skimmed of
     fat, or 1½ cups water
½   cup diced red or green bell
     pepper
1   to 2 teaspoons curry powder
    Salt or lemon pepper to taste
1   package (10 ounces) frozen
     green peas

1. Cover chick-peas with water and soak overnight, or boil for 2 minutes and let soak for 1 hour. Drain, discarding water.

2. Combine margarine, onions, garlic, and cumin seeds in a large nonstick skillet or electric frying pan. Cook, stirring, until moisture evaporates and onions begin to brown. Stir in chick-peas, water, broth, bell pepper, curry powder, and salt. Cover and simmer until beans are tender—about 2 hours.

3. Add peas and cook, uncovered, just until peas are thawed and heated through—6 to 8 minutes.

MAKES 4 SERVINGS, 285 CALORIES EACH.

PEPPERS AND PINEAPPLE

3   bell peppers (1 red, 1 green, 1
     yellow), seeded and cut in
     bite-size pieces
1   onion, sliced
1   teaspoon toasted sesame oil or
     salad oil
¼   teaspoon 5-spice powder or ¼
     teaspoon pumpkin pie spice
     and pinch anise or fennel
     seeds
1   can (8 ounces) pineapple
     tidbits, drained, with liquid
     reserved
    Light soy sauce to taste
     (optional)

1. Combine peppers with onion, oil, seasonings, and pineapple liquid. Bring to a simmer and cook for 10 minutes; stir in pineapple tidbits and heat through. Add a dash of soy sauce, if desired. Good with broiled chicken or fish.

MAKES 6 SERVINGS, 50 CALORIES EACH.

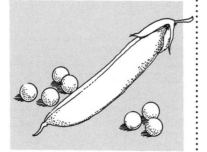

WINE-SPIKED SAUTÉED MUSHROOMS

8   ounces fresh mushrooms, sliced
¼   cup dry white wine
2   teaspoons butter or margarine
    Salt and pepper to taste

1. Combine ingredients in nonstick skillet. Cook, stirring, over high heat until all liquid evaporates.

MAKES 4 SERVINGS, 45 CALORIES EACH.

GOLDEN VEGETABLE PIROSHKI

1   cup chopped golden delicious
     apple
1   medium onion, chopped
1   tablespoon butter or
     margarine
1½ cups chopped cabbage
2   hard-cooked eggs, chopped
1   teaspoon caraway seeds
1   tablespoon fresh minced
     parsley
    Salt and pepper to taste
    Pastry for 2-crust 9-inch pie
    Skim milk for glaze

1. Sauté apple and onion in butter until tender. Add cabbage, and cook over low heat for 15 minutes; do not brown. Add eggs, caraway, parsley, salt, and pepper. Cool.

2. Roll pastry ⅛-inch thick. Cut into 6 rounds, about 5 inches in diameter. Mound filling in center of each piece. Moisten edges, bring together, seal, and flute. Place on nonstick baking sheet; brush lightly with milk.

3. Bake in preheated 375-degree oven for 30 minutes or until golden brown. Serve with meat broth or borscht.

MAKES 6 SERVINGS, 360 CALORIES EACH.

Note: Piroshki can be wrapped tightly in foil and frozen. To reheat: Bake in foil for 20 minutes at 375 degrees. Then uncover and bake 5 minutes longer or until thoroughly heated. Or remove from foil and wrap individually in paper towels; microwave each on high power (100%) for 1 minute or until thoroughly heated. Turn once during cooking period.

ITALIAN "FRIED" PEPPERS AND TOMATOES

2   teaspoons olive oil
1   can (16 ounces) stewed
      tomatoes
4   Italian frying peppers, seeded
      and diced
½   cup water
1   tablespoon chopped fresh onion
      or 1 teaspoon dried onion
      flakes
1   tablespoon each chopped fresh
      oregano and basil or 1
      teaspoon each dried oregano
      and basil

1. In a nonstick saucepan, combine all ingredients. Cover, bring to a simmer, and cook over low heat until peppers are tender—12 to 15 minutes. Uncover and simmer 3 minutes more or until thick.

MAKES 6 SERVINGS, 50 CALORIES EACH.

SPICED RUTABAGA

3   cups peeled diced rutabaga
      (yellow turnip), fresh or
      frozen
¾   cup apple cider
¼   teaspoon ground cinnamon
      Pinch ground ginger
      Salt and coarsely ground
      pepper to taste

1. In covered saucepan, cook rutabaga with cider until very tender—about 15 minutes. Remove rutabaga and mash in a bowl with a potato masher or process until smooth in an elec-

tric blender, food processor, or with an electric mixer. Season with cinnamon, ginger, salt, and pepper.

MAKES 6 SERVINGS, 35 CALORIES EACH.

GOLDEN APPLE SAUERKRAUT

1   yellow (golden delicious) apple
1   onion, chopped
1   can (28 ounces) sauerkraut
2   tablespoons caraway seeds
½   cup white wine or cider

1. Shred the apple by hand or in a food processor. Combine with remaining ingredients. Cover and simmer for 1 hour.

MAKES 8 SERVINGS, 40 CALORIES EACH.

SPINACH PUFF

2   packages (10 ounces each)
      frozen chopped spinach
4   ounces light cream cheese
3   eggs, beaten
¾   cup skim milk
¼   teaspoon ground nutmeg
      Salt to taste
      Dash white pepper
1½ cups crushed wheat crackers
¼   cup shredded Cheddar cheese

1. Cook spinach according to package directions. Drain thoroughly; while spinach is still hot, add cream cheese. Stir over low heat until cheese melts and looks like cream sauce. Beat in all other ingredients except cracker crumbs and Cheddar.

2. Prepare a square baking pan with cooking spray. Place ½ of spinach mixture in it. Top with ½ of the crumbs. Layer the remaining spinach mixture, then Cheddar, and finally the remaining crumbs.

3. Bake in preheated 350-degree oven for 30 minutes or until puffed and golden.

MAKES 6 SERVINGS; 215 CALORIES EACH.

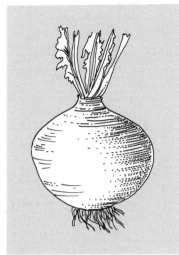

THREE-VEGGIE "CONFETTI"

The shredding disk of your food processor can make short work of cooked vegetables as well as raw salad veggies. Whole or sliced carrots that take 20 or 30 minutes to cook are ready in 5 minutes or less if you shred them into confetti in the food processor before you cook them. No need to peel them, either! Valuable nutrients go down the drain when you toss away the skin of fresh carrots.

8   ounces carrots, shredded
1   small onion, halved and thinly
      sliced
3   tablespoons water or fat-
      skimmed chicken broth
8   ounces zucchini, shredded
8   ounces yellow squash, shredded
1   tablespoon butter or
      margarine
¼   teaspoon ground cinnamon
      Salt and coarsely ground
      pepper to taste

1. Combine carrots, onion, and water in a nonstick skillet prepared with cooking spray. Cover and cook for 4 to 5 minutes over moderate heat.

2. Stir in remaining ingredients. Uncover and cook, stirring for 1 to 2 minutes.

MAKES 6 SERVINGS, 50 CALORIES EACH.

GREEK-STYLE PUFFY PANCAKE

1   Puffy Pancake (recipe follows)
8   ounces fresh mushrooms, sliced
1   large onion, sliced
1   cup shredded carrots
3/4 cup tomato-vegetable juice
1   teaspoon cornstarch
1/2 teaspoon dried basil, crushed
4   ounces feta cheese, crumbled
2   tablespoons sliced pitted ripe
    olives
2   tablespoons chopped fresh
    parsley

1. Prepare Puffy Pancake.
2. Meanwhile, prepare a 10-inch nonstick skillet with cooking spray. Over moderately high heat, cook mushrooms, onion, and carrots for 5 minutes or until vegetables are tender, stirring often.
3. In small bowl, stir together juice, cornstarch, and basil. Stir mixture into skillet, and cook for 4 minutes or until slightly thickened, stirring often.
4. Sprinkle half of the feta onto the pancake. Spoon vegetable mixture over feta. Sprinkle with the remaining feta, the olives, and parsley. Cut into wedges.

MAKES 4 SERVINGS, 270 CALORIES EACH.

PUFFY PANCAKE

1/2 cup all-purpose flour
1/2 cup skim milk
2   eggs
    Pinch salt (optional)
1   tablespoon vegetable oil

1. Place 10-inch ovenproof skillet on middle rack in preheated 450-degree oven for 5 minutes.
2. Meanwhile, in medium bowl with an electric mixer at medium speed, beat flour, milk, eggs, and salt, if desired, until well blended. Carefully remove skillet from oven and add oil, tilt-

ing to coat bottom and sides. Pour batter into pan. Bake for 10 minutes; then reduce heat to 350 degrees and bake 10 minutes more, until puffed and browned.

MAKES 1 PANCAKE, 550 CALORIES TOTAL.

BROCCOLI BREAD QUICHE

6   slices whole-grain light bread
1   cup raw broccoli florets
1   cup plain low-fat yogurt
2   beaten eggs or equivalent egg
    substitute
    Pinch grated nutmeg
    Salt and lemon pepper to taste

1. Toast bread lightly; cut each slice in half. Arrange bread slices in a shallow nonstick baking pan and layer broccoli florets on top. Stir yogurt into eggs until blended, then spoon over broccoli. Sprinkle with nutmeg, salt, and lemon pepper.
2. Bake in a preheated 350-degree oven for 50 to 60 minutes or until a knife inserted in center comes out clean.

MAKES 4 SERVINGS, 180 CALORIES EACH WITH EGG; 150 CALORIES EACH WITH EGG SUBSTITUTE.

CRUSTLESS SPINACH QUICHE

4   cups low-fat ricotta cheese
1/3 cup all-purpose flour
2   eggs or equivalent egg
    substitute
1/2 teaspoon salt
1/8 teaspoon grated nutmeg
    Pinch pepper
1   package (10 ounces) chopped
    spinach, thawed and
    drained
3/4 cup shredded part-skim
    mozzarella cheese

1. Drain ricotta through a strainer, colander, or filter paper

set over a bowl. Cover and refrigerate for several hours or leave overnight.
2. In an electric blender or a food processor process ricotta until smooth. Blend in flour, eggs, and seasonings. Fold in drained spinach and mozzarella. Pour mixture into a 9-inch springform pan prepared with cooking spray.
3. Bake in a preheated 325-degree oven for 1 hour and 10 minutes or until set and lightly browned. Let rest at room temperature for 5 to 10 minutes before loosening edges with a knife and removing the sides of pan to serve.

MAKES 10 SERVINGS, 195 CALORIES EACH.

SPAGHETTI SQUASH AND RED WINE MEAT SAUCE

1   medium spaghetti squash
12 ounces lean ground beef
1   onion, minced
1   clove garlic, minced
1   can (8 ounces) stewed
    tomatoes, with liquid
1   can (6 ounces) tomato paste
1   cup water
1/2 cup dry red wine
3   tablespoons chopped fresh
    parsley
1/2 teaspoon each dried basil and
    dried oregano
1/4 teaspoon dried thyme
    Grated Parmesan or Romano
    cheese to taste

1. Puncture the spaghetti squash in several places. Bake in a preheated 350-degree oven for about 30 minutes or cook in a microwave oven on high setting for about 20 minutes or longer, until squash yields to pressure.
2. Spread meat in a nonstick stockpot or large skillet; brown over moderate flame with no added fat. Break into bite-size chunks and turn to brown evenly. Drain and discard any fat.

3. Add onion and garlic; cook, stirring, until onion just starts to brown. Stir in remaining ingredients. Cover and simmer for about 20 minutes, until flavors are well blended. Uncover and simmer until the meat sauce is thick.

4. Slice spaghetti squash in half; scoop out and discard seeds with a spoon. Scoop spaghetti squash strands into a bowl. Separate the strands and fluff with a fork. Spoon the vegetable "spaghetti" into plates and top with meat sauce. Sprinkle with some grated Parmesan or Romano cheese, if desired.

MAKES 4 MEAL-SIZE SERVINGS, 215 CALORIES EACH; CHEESE ADDS APPROXIMATELY 25 CALORIES PER TABLESPOON.

ORANGE CURRIED SQUASH

2   *yellow squash, sliced*
¾   *cup orange juice*
1   *teaspoon butter or margarine*
¼   *teaspoon curry powder*
    Pinch each ground cinnamon and ginger

1. Combine ingredients. Bring to a simmer and cook for 5 minutes.

MAKES 4 SERVINGS, 45 CALORIES EACH.

ORANGE-GLAZED YELLOW SQUASH

1½ *cups orange juice*
½   *teaspoon ground cinnamon*
1½ *cups thinly sliced carrots*
2   *yellow squash, sliced*
2   *tablespoons minced onion*
    Salt and pepper to taste
1   *teaspoon cornstarch*
¼   *cup cold water*
1   *tablespoon minced fresh parsley*

1. In a saucepan, heat orange juice to boiling. Add cinnamon and carrots, bring to a simmer, and cook, covered, for 10 minutes. Add squash, onion, salt, and pepper. Cover and simmer until vegetables are just tender 4 to 5 minutes.

2. Combine cornstarch and cold water, add to sauce, and stir over low heat until mixture thickens. Sprinkle with parsley.

MAKES 6 SERVINGS, 60 CALORIES EACH.

CHINESE 5-SPICE STIR-FRIED SQUASH

2   *teaspoons toasted sesame oil*
2   *tablespoons water*
1   *pound summer squash or zucchini, quartered lengthwise and cut into 2-inch-long strips*
1   *onion, halved and thinly sliced*
½   *teaspoon 5-spice powder or ½ teaspoon pumpkin pie spice plus pinch anise or fennel seeds*
2   *tablespoons light soy sauce*

1. In a large nonstick skillet prepared with cooking spray, combine oil, water, squash, onion, and 5-spice powder in a shallow layer. Cook mixture over high heat for 5 minutes, stirring occasionally, until water evaporates. Sprinkle with soy sauce.

MAKES 4 SERVINGS, 55 CALORIES EACH.

ZESTY SHREDDED ZUCCHINI

1   *pound fresh zucchini*
1   *clove garlic, minced*
1   *tablespoon butter or margarine*
    Dash hot red pepper sauce or pinch cayenne pepper, to taste
    Salt and coarsely ground black pepper to taste

1. Trim the ends of the zucchini; shred it coarsely using a hand shredder or put it through the shredding disk of a food processor. In a nonstick skillet prepared with cooking spray, combine shredded zucchini, minced garlic, and butter in the skillet. Cover tightly and cook over moderate heat for 1 minute. Uncover the skillet; cook, stirring, 1 minute more. Season to taste.

MAKES 4 SERVINGS, 45 CALORIES EACH.

ACORN SQUASH WITH PINEAPPLE

3   *small acorn squash, halved and seeded*
6   *teaspoons diet margarine*
12 *tablespoons pineapple juice*
    Pumpkin pie spice to taste

1. Arrange squash halves, cut side up, in a shallow baking pan. Put 1 teaspoon margarine and 2 tablespoons pineapple juice in each squash cup. Sprinkle lightly with pumpkin pie spice (or ground cinnamon, clove, ginger, and nutmeg). Cover loosely with foil and bake in a preheated 350-degree oven for 45 to 50 minutes, until tender.

MAKES 6 SERVINGS, 110 CALORIES EACH.

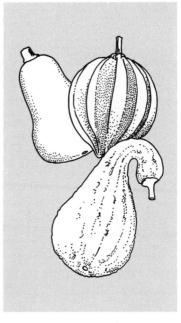

Spicy Quickbreads, Snacks, and Sweets

DID you know that spice can save you from your sweet tooth? A sugar-shy dessert or snack seems sweeter if it's fragrant with cinnamon or spiked with clove. Intensifying the perception of sweetness makes it possible to reduce the amount of empty-caloried sugar.

USE HEALTHY INGREDIENTS

Fruit and fruit juices can be combined with other healthy, tasty ingredients to make calorie-light desserts and snacks that can take the place of heavy cakes and pies. Yogurt and fresh cheeses can make creamy pies and cheesecakes with fresh fruit toppings. Whole grains can be used for cookies and spicy muffins.

SPICY MUFFINS AND QUICKBREADS

Conventional yeast-raised breads are time-consuming, but there's one category of bread that's extra quick and easy to make. That's why they're called "quickbreads"!

Muffins, biscuits, and quickbreads are leavened with baking powder instead of yeast. They're easy to make and versatile . . . ideal for flavor enriching with spices and herbs. Whole grains, cereals, dried fruit, and garden veggies are healthy additions quickbreads invite.

The category runs the gamut from simple drop biscuits to nippy cornbreads and earthy whole-grain loaves; from spice-scented bran muffins with fruit, to fragrant tea loaves that can take the place of cake . . . without its calories! Compared with cakes, pies, and cookies, quickbreads offer a healthier alternative for people who like to bake but can't spare the time or the calories.

NATURALLY SWEET FRUIT

Luckily for waistline watchers, the best and healthiest "sweets" are Mother Nature's bounty: fresh fruit. Fruit contains sugar as nature intended it to be enjoyed, as part of a balanced packaged of vitamins, minerals, and roughage. The sugar in fruit is combined with so much natural appetite-appeasing fiber that it's difficult to overdo on either calories or sugar in the form of fruit.

If fruit doesn't seem "special" enough to qualify as dessert, spices can add a new dimension. Try:

- apples with cinnamon
- peaches with ginger
- pears with clove
- strawberries with coarsely ground pepper
- oranges with cinnamon or clove
- grapes with allspice or nutmeg

The tropics offer an exotic harvest of fruit: finger-size sweet bananas, marvelously ripe pineapples, buttery-smooth mangoes and papayas, funny grapefruitlike ugli fruit, custard apples, star fruit, sapodilla, and soursop. Many are increasingly available in the U.S. Combinations of the exotic and the everyday make quick and easy desserts—not to mention tasty!

BASIC CALORIE-LIGHT MUFFINS

2   cups all-purpose wheat flour
1   tablespoon granulated fruit sugar (fructose) (optional)
3   teaspoons baking powder
½   teaspoon salt
1   egg or 2 egg whites or ¼ cup egg substitute
1   cup nonfat fresh milk, or ⅓ cup nonfat dry milk and ¾ cup cold water
¼   cup diet margarine
½   to 1 teaspoon mixed ground spices (optional)

1. Stir together flour, sugar, if desired, baking powder, and salt. Combine remaining ingredients and beat with an electric mixer until fluffy. Sprinkle flour mixture over egg mixture; stir just until batter is blended but still lumpy. Don't overmix.

2. Prepare 16 nonstick muffin cups lightly with cooking spray, then spoon in batter. (Cups will be less than ½ full.) Bake in a preheated 375-degree oven for 15 to 20 minutes or until golden on top and a toothpick inserted in the center of a muffin comes out clean.

Note: Do not use sugar substitute in batter and do not omit the salt.

MAKES 16 MUFFINS, 80 CALORIES EACH WITH EGG; 77 CALORIES WITH EGG WHITES OR EGG SUBSTITUTE. SUGAR ADDS 3 CALORIES PER MUFFIN.

Variation

Whole Wheat Muffins: Replace 1 cup of white flour with 1 cup of whole wheat flour. Increase baking powder to 4 teaspoons.

❦

REALLY CORNY CORN MUFFINS

1   cup cut corn, defrosted
1   cup cold water
2   large eggs
2   cups self-rising flour

1. Combine corn, water, and eggs in a food processor and process until corn kernels are completely puréed. Add flour; process briefly with quick on-off pulses until blended, occasionally scraping down the sides of the container.

2. With a rubber scraper, transfer batter to nonstick muffin tins prepared with cooking spray. Bake in a preheated 425-degree oven for about 15 minutes or until a toothpick inserted in the center of a muffin comes out clean. Caution: Top will not brown; don't overbake. Serve warm.

MAKES 16 MUFFINS, 75 CALORIES EACH.

Variations

Really Corny Cornbread: Follow preceding recipe but transfer batter to a 9-inch nonstick square or round cake pan prepared with baking spray. Bake 20 to 25 minutes or until bread tests done. To serve, cut into 16 squares or wedges. When cool, wrap leftovers in plastic or foil. To reheat, slice and lightly toast.

Mexicali Muffins: To the ingredients listed, add 2 teaspoons cumin seeds and ¼ teaspoon dried oregano. For chili-flavored muffins, add 1 fresh jalapeño pepper, seeded and chopped, or substitute ¼ cup finely chopped green bell pepper. Stir all these ingredients into the batter last, just before baking. Proceed as already described.

❦

INDIAN BLACKBERRY CORN MUFFINS

Blackberries are exceedingly high in fiber; look for them in your supermarket's frozen food case. If unavailable, substitute blueberries.

1¼   cups all-purpose flour
¾   cup corn meal
1   tablespoon brown sugar (optional)
2   teaspoons baking powder
½   teaspoon salt
¼   teaspoon baking soda
¾   cup skim milk
¼   cup diet margarine, melted
1   egg, beaten, or equivalent egg substitute
1   cup frozen blackberries or blueberries, partially thawed

1. Thoroughly combine flour, corn meal, sugar, if desired, baking powder, salt, and baking soda. Stir in milk, margarine, and egg just until mixture is evenly moistened. Fold in berries.

2. Prepare bottoms only of 12 medium muffin cups with cooking spray or line with paper baking cups. Fill cups ¾ full of batter. Bake for 15 to 20 minutes in a preheated 425-degree oven or until tops are golden brown. Serve warm.

MAKES 12 MUFFINS, 110 CALORIES EACH WITH EGG; 105 CALORIES EACH WITH EGG SUBSTITUTE. BROWN SUGAR ADDS 5 CALORIES PER MUFFIN.

APPLE RAISIN MUFFINS

1¼ cups all-purpose flour
1 cup regular or quick oats
2 teaspoons baking powder
½ teaspoon baking soda
½ teaspoon ground cinnamon
½ teaspoon salt
¾ cup skim milk
¼ cup diet margarine
1 egg or ¼ cup egg substitute
½ teaspoon vanilla extract
1 apple, finely chopped
3 tablespoons raisins

1. Thoroughly combine flour, oats, baking powder, baking soda, cinnamon, and salt. Add milk, margarine, egg, and vanilla; mix just until moistened. Stir in apple and raisins.

2. Prepare bottoms only of 12 medium muffin cups with baking spray or line with paper baking cups. Fill cups ¾ full with batter. Bake in a preheated 400-degree oven for 20 to 25 minutes—until a toothpick inserted in the center of a muffin comes out clean.

MAKES 12 MUFFINS, 115 CALORIES EACH WITH EGG; 110 CALORIES EACH WITH EGG SUBSTITUTE.

HEALTHIER GARLIC BREAD WITH OLIVE OIL

1 loaf (1 pound) Italian bread (preferably whole grain or sesame seeded)
3 tablespoons extra-virgin olive oil
2 cloves garlic, very finely minced
Dash salt (optional)

1. Split loaf in half lengthwise and spread both sides lightly with olive oil and minced garlic. Add a dash of salt, if desired. Put halves back together again and wrap tightly in foil. Arrange on shallow pan and bake in a preheated 350-degree oven for 20 minutes.

EACH 1-OUNCE SERVING, 100 CALORIES.

KASHA CORN MUFFINS

Kasha is the Russian name for toasted whole-grain buckwheat, a nutty good-tasting grain, low in calories and ultrahigh in fiber. Buckwheat contains nearly three times as much fiber as bran breakfast cereal, and it has a calorie count that's below rice and other grains. Roasting gives the grain a healthy color, grainy texture, and a rich nutty taste. Use it as a muffin ingredient.

½ cup kasha (roasted buckwheat)
2 tablespoons diet margarine
⅔ cup boiling water
½ cup skim milk
1¼ cups all-purpose flour
⅓ cup cornmeal
4 teaspoons baking powder
½ teaspoon salt
1 egg, lightly beaten, or equivalent egg substitute

1. Combine kasha and margarine in a mixing bowl; stir in boiling water. Stir in milk and set aside for 10 to 15 minutes.

2. Combine dry ingredients and mix well. Stir into the kasha mixture. Mix in the lightly beaten egg.

3. Prepare nonstick muffin pans with cooking spray and spoon in the batter. Bake in a preheated 425-degree oven for 18 to 20 minutes or until a toothpick inserted in the center of a muffin comes out clean.

MAKES 12 MUFFINS, 105 CALORIES EACH WITH EGG; UNDER 100 CALORIES EACH WITH EGG SUBSTITUTE.

CARAWAY-SPICED IRISH SODA BREAD

4 cups bread flour or all-purpose flour
3 teaspoons baking powder
1 teaspoon salt
¾ teaspoon baking soda
1 cup raisins or currants
2 tablespoons caraway seeds
2 eggs
1½ cups buttermilk

1. Stir dry ingredients, raisins, and caraway seeds together. Fork-blend eggs and buttermilk, then add to dry ingredients. Stir until a sticky batter is formed. Scrape batter onto a well-floured surface and knead lightly.

2. Shape batter into a ball and place in a round nonstick casserole prepared with cooking spray. Mark a cross in the center, using a sharp knife. Bake in a preheated 350-degree oven for about 1¼ hours or until golden. Wait 10 to 15 minutes before attempting to remove bread from casserole; then allow bread to cool on a wire rack. To serve, slice thin. (If desired, cut loaf in quarters; wrap and freeze the extras for later use.)

MAKES 40 SLICES, 70 CALORIES EACH WITH BREAD FLOUR; 65 CALORIES EACH WITH ALL-PURPOSE FLOUR.

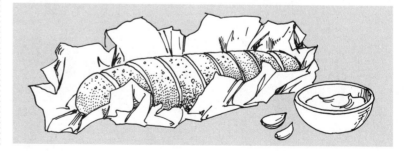

ALMOND QUICKBREAD

1 cup all-purpose flour
1 teaspoon baking powder
Pinch salt (optional)
1 egg
2 tablespoons oil
2 tablespoons water
½ teaspoon each vanilla extract and almond flavoring
1 ounce chopped almonds
Ground cinnamon to taste
2 packets low-calorie sweetener

1. Stir together flour, baking powder, and salt, if desired. Beat together egg, oil, water, vanilla extract, and almond flavoring; beat into flour mixture. Stir in almonds.

2. On a lightly floured surface, shape dough into a cylinder approximately 9 inches long. With a sharp knife cut several diagonal slashes along top surface. Sprinkle with cinnamon.

3. Place on nonstick baking sheet prepared with cooking spray. Bake in a preheated 375-degree oven for approximately 30 minutes or until golden. Remove from oven and sprinkle with sweetener. Serve warm or cooled.

MAKES 8 SERVINGS, 120 CALORIES EACH.

❧❧❧

GOLDEN SUMMER SQUASH BREAD

1 cup all-purpose flour
3 packets (3 grams each) granulated fruit sugar (fructose)
1 teaspoon ground cinnamon
1 teaspoon baking soda
¼ teaspoon baking powder
Pinch salt (optional)
2 eggs or equivalent egg substitute
¼ cup orange juice
1 tablespoon oil
1 teaspoon vanilla extract
1 summer squash, grated
5 tablespoons golden raisins

1. Thoroughly mix flour, sugar, cinnamon, baking soda, baking powder, and salt, if desired; set aside. Beat together eggs, juice, oil, and vanilla extract; beat into flour mixture. Stir in squash and raisins.

2. Spoon batter into a nonstick 9- by 5-inch loaf pan prepared with baking spray. Bake in a preheated 350-degree oven for 55 to 60 minutes or until golden.

MAKES 12 SLICES, 90 CALORIES EACH WITH EGG; 80 CALORIES EACH WITH EGG SUBSTITUTE.

❧❧❧

WINTER SQUASH QUICKBREAD

This delightful bread is equally delicious when pumpkin is substituted for the winter squash.

1½ cups all-purpose flour
1 tablespoon sugar
1 teaspoon baking soda
¾ teaspoon ground cinnamon
½ teaspoon grated nutmeg
1 cup mashed cooked fresh winter squash or pumpkin or 1 cup mashed canned plain pumpkin
2 eggs or equivalent egg substitute
1 tablespoon salad oil
½ cup dried fruit bits

1. Thoroughly mix together flour, sugar, baking soda, and spices; set aside. Beat together squash, eggs, and oil. Beat liquid mixture into dry mixture. Stir in fruit.

2. Spoon batter into a 9- by 5-inch nonstick loaf pan prepared with cooking spray. Bake in a preheated 350-degree oven for 1 hour or until golden.

MAKES 12 SLICES, 110 CALORIES EACH WITH SQUASH; 105 CALORIES EACH WITH PUMPKIN; 10 CALORIES LESS PER SLICE WITH EGG SUBSTITUTE.

❧❧❧

RAISIN BISCUITBREAD

1 cup self-rising flour
1 egg or equivalent egg substitute
3 tablespoons water
1 tablespoon diet margarine
3 tablespoons raisins
2 tablespoons chopped nuts (optional)

1. Fork-blend flour, egg, water, and margarine. Knead lightly. Roll out dough on a lightly floured surface to form a rectangle approximately 8 by 10 inches. Sprinkle with raisins and nuts, if desired. Roll up lengthwise, pinching ends together slightly.

2. Place on a nonstick baking sheet prepared with cooking spray. Bake in a preheated 375-degree oven for 25 to 30 minutes or until golden. Serve warm.

MAKES 10 SERVINGS, 65 CALORIES EACH WITH EGG; 60 CALORIES EACH WITH EGG SUBSTITUTE. NUTS ADD 10 CALORIES PER SERVING.

SPAGHETTI SQUASH BREAD

1¼   cups all-purpose flour
¼   cup sugar
1   teaspoon baking soda
¼   teaspoon each ground cinnamon, nutmeg, and allspice
   Dash salt (optional)
2   eggs or equivalent egg substitute
2   tablespoons oil
¼   cup orange juice
⅔   cup cooked spaghetti squash strands
2   tablespoons raisins

1. Thoroughly stir together flour, sugar, baking soda, spices, and salt, if desired; set aside. Beat together eggs, oil, and juice. Gradually beat the dry mixture into the egg mixture. Stir in squash and raisins.

2. Pour batter into a 9- by 5-inch nonstick loaf pan prepared with cooking spray. Bake in a preheated 350-degree oven for 40 minutes or until golden.

MAKES 20 SLICES, 65 CALORIES EACH.

LIGHT AND SPICY GINGERBREAD

3   very ripe bananas
2   eggs
¼   cup skim milk
⅓   cup molasses
2   cups self-rising flour or 2 cups all-purpose flour plus 2 teaspoons baking powder plus 1 teaspoon salt
2   teaspoons ground ginger
1   teaspoon baking soda
1   teaspoon ground cinnamon
½   teaspoon ground cloves
½   teaspoon ground nutmeg

1. Combine bananas, eggs, milk, and molasses in an electric mixing bowl; beat until creamy. Stir remaining ingredients together and add to batter. Beat on

low speed for 15 seconds. Scrape bowl with spatula. Beat on high speed for 30 seconds more.

2. Spoon mixture into a 9-inch square nonstick cake pan prepared with cooking spray. Bake in a preheated 350-degree oven for 30 minutes or until set. Serve warm or cold.

MAKES 9 SERVINGS, 195 CALORIES EACH.

GERMAN PFEFFERNUSSE

The name *pfeffernusse* means peppernuts in German (they're called *pepparnotter* in Sweden). These spicy little cookies have only 12 calories each. Because of their intense flavor, they don't invite a cookie pig-out. They're very popular in northern Europe at Christmas.

¼   cup lightly salted butter or margarine, at room temperature
1   cup granulated sugar
1   cup light molasses
1   large egg
½   cup ground almonds
1   teaspoon finely crushed anise seed
½   teaspoon ground cinnamon
¼   teaspoon salt
¼   teaspoon ground pepper
   Pinch ground cloves
   Pinch ground nutmeg
1   teaspoon baking soda
3¼   to 3½ cups all-purpose flour

1. Cream butter and ½ cup of the sugar together. Beat in molasses and then egg. Mix in almonds, anise, cinnamon, salt, pepper, cloves, nutmeg, and baking soda. Stir in flour a little at a time to make a very stiff dough. Cover dough and chill.

2. Spread remaining sugar on a jelly-roll pan or tray. Take 2 tablespoons of dough at a time and roll out strips ½ inch wide. Coat strips with sugar and cut into ½-inch pieces.

3. Arrange ½ inch apart on nonstick baking trays. Bake for 10 minutes in a preheated 375-degree oven, until cookies are firm and lightly browned. Remove from oven and cool.

MAKES 350 TINY COOKIES, 12 CALORIES EACH. (Recipe can be halved.)

APRICOT PINWHEEL COOKIES

1   cup finely chopped dried apricots
½   cup boiling water
1   container (8 ounces) diet margarine
6   tablespoons sugar
1   teaspoon vanilla extract
2½   cups sifted flour
¼   teaspoon baking powder
4   packets low-calorie sweetener (optional)

1. Put apricots in a small bowl and pour on boiling water; set aside. Combine margarine, sugar, and vanilla extract in a bowl and beat with an electric mixer; set aside.

2. Mix flour and baking powder; add to margarine mixture. Stir in with a fork, then knead lightly until mixture forms a ball. Flatten dough and quick-chill in freezer.

3. Roll dough out on a lightly floured surface to a rectangle 24 inches long. Spread apricot mixture over surface. Roll lengthwise to form a 24-inch cylinder. Wrap in waxed paper; chill thoroughly.

4. When firm enough to slice, cut off ⅛-inch slices. Place slices 1 inch apart on a nonstick cookie tin. (Make only as many as you need and freeze remaining roll.) Bake in a preheated 375-degree oven for 12 minutes. If desired, sprinkle lightly with low-calorie sweetener *after* baked cookies have cooled.

MAKES 72 (6 DOZEN) COOKIES, 35 CALORIES EACH.

JAMOCHA CHOCOLATE CHIP MERINGUE COOKIES

    2   egg whites, at room
         temperature
    ¼   teaspoon cream of tartar
         Pinch salt
    9   tablespoons granulated sugar
    ¼   cup plain cocoa powder
    1   teaspoon powdered instant
         coffee
    ¾   teaspoon rum flavoring
    7   teaspoons miniature chocolate
         chips

1. Combine egg whites, cream of tartar, and salt in an electric mixer bowl; beat until peaks form. Beat in sugar a little at a time until egg whites are stiff. Add cocoa, coffee, and rum flavoring; beat until stiff and glossy.

2. Line cookie sheets with aluminum foil, shiny side up. Drop meringue mixture onto the foil by the tablespoon, 1 inch apart. Sprinkle a few miniature chocolate chips on each cookie. Bake in a preheated 200-degree oven for 1 hour and 15 minutes. Cool completely before removing from foil.

MAKES 36 (3 DOZEN) COOKIES, UNDER 20 CALORIES EACH.

FRENCH BREAD PUDDING WITH APPLES AND RAISINS

    12   to 15 very thin slices from a
         skinny loaf of French bread
         (preferably whole grain)
    2   apples, thinly sliced
    ½   cup golden raisins
    3   cups skim milk
    4   eggs or equivalent egg
         substitute
    ½   cup rum
    1   tablespoon vanilla extract
    2   teaspoons apple pie spice
    2   tablespoons honey or
         granulated fruit sugar
         (fructose) (optional)
         Salt to taste (optional)

1. In a nonstick pie pan well prepared with cooking spray, arrange bread and apple slices together in overlapping circles. Sprinkle with raisins. Beat together remaining ingredients and then pour over bread and fruit.

2. Cover pan with foil; bake in a preheated 300-degree oven for 1¼ hours. Uncover pan and raise temperature to 400 degrees. Bake for 15 to 20 minutes more or until top is crisp. Serve warm or chilled.

MAKES 8 SERVINGS, 185 CALORIES EACH; 160 CALORIES EACH WITH EGG SUBSTITUTE. HONEY OR FRUCTOSE ADDS APPROXIMATELY 15 CALORIES PER SERVING.

FRENCH APPLE CHARLOTTE

    4   cups peeled, thinly sliced apples
    ¼   cup sugar
    1   teaspoon ground cinnamon
    ½   teaspoon ground cloves
    ¼   teaspoon grated lemon peel
         Salt to taste
    ½   cup water
    3   tablespoons apple brandy
    1½   cups soft whole-wheat bread
         crumbs
    3   tablespoons melted butter or
         margarine
         Low-calorie sweetener to taste
         (optional)

1. Combine 3¾ cups of the apples with the sugar, spices, lemon peel, salt, water, and brandy. Set aside. Toss the bread crumbs with 2 tablespoons of the butter.

2. Prepare a 1-quart casserole with cooking spray. Layer ⅓ of the bread crumbs and ½ the apple mixture (including the liquid). Repeat layering, ending with bread crumbs. Arrange remaining apple slices on top; drizzle with remaining tablespoon of butter.

3. Cover and bake in preheated 350-degree oven until apples are almost tender—about 30 minutes. Uncover and bake until apples become soft and crumbs turn golden—about 15 minutes more.

MAKES 8 SERVINGS, 175 CALORIES EACH.

LIGHT AND SPICY HOMEMADE MINCEMEAT

Less than half the calories of the commercial kind!

    2   cups peeled cubed cooking
         apples
    1½   cups raisins
    ¼   cup orange juice
    2   tablespoons brandy
    1   tablespoon cracker crumbs
    1   teaspoon cider vinegar
    1   teaspoon grated orange rind
    ½   teaspoon salt
    ½   teaspoon ground cloves
    ½   teaspoon ground cinnamon or
         apple pie spice
    ½   cup sugar or equivalent low-
         calorie sweetener

1. Combine all ingredients except low-calorie sweetener, if using instead of sugar, in a covered casserole. Bake at 350 degrees until tender—about 30 minutes. After baking, stir in low-calorie sweetener, if desired. Serve warm or chilled.

MAKES 6 SERVINGS, 150 CALORIES EACH.

PUMPKIN RICE PUDDING

1 can (16 ounces) plain pumpkin purée
1 can (14 ounces) evaporated skim milk
2 eggs
⅔ cup instant rice
½ cup golden raisins
¼ cup loosely packed brown sugar
¼ cup white sugar
2 teaspoons pumpkin pie spice
Pinch salt

1. Beat ingredients together and spoon into a nonstick baking dish. Put dish in a larger pan, containing 1 inch hot water. Place pan on middle shelf of a preheated 350-degree oven. Bake for 20 minutes, then stir.

2. Bake for an additional 40 or 50 minutes, until set. Remove and let cool. Serve warm or chilled.

MAKES 10 SERVINGS, 150 CALORIES EACH.

♥♥♥

SPICED RUM EGGNOG MOUSSE

1 envelope plain gelatin
¼ cup dark rum
¾ cup boiling water
1 cup low-fat vanilla ice milk
2 eggs, separated
1 teaspoon rum flavoring
Pinch each ground cinnamon and nutmeg
1 cup low-fat vanilla yogurt
½ cup diced mixed dried fruit or fruit bits
Pinch salt

1. Sprinkle gelatin on rum and set aside for 1 minute for gelatin to soften. Scrape softened gelatin-rum mixture into boiling water; heat, stirring, until dissolved. Remove from heat.

2. Cut ice milk into chunks and stir into pan a little at a time, until ice milk completely melts. Beat in egg yolks, rum flavoring,

cinnamon, and nutmeg. Fold in yogurt and fruit. Chill until partially set.

3. Beat egg whites with salt until stiff; then gently but thoroughly fold into mousse mixture. Chill until set.

MAKES 8 SERVINGS, 105 CALORIES EACH.

CINNAMON-SPICED CHOCOLATE SWIRL MOUSSE

1 envelope plain gelatin
½ cup plus 2 tablespoons skim milk (approximate)
1 cup boiling water
1 cup ice cubes
5 single-serving envelopes sugar-free vanilla milkshake mix
1 ounce milk chocolate, broken up
½ teaspoon ground cinnamon

1. Put gelatin in an electric blender or a food processor; add 2 tablespoons cold skim milk. Wait 1 minute until gelatin is soft, then add ¾ cup of the boiling water. Process until gelatin granules are completely dissolved.

2. Fill a 1-cup measure with ice cubes, then add fresh skim milk to the top. Add to gelatin mixture; process until ice is completely melted. Add milkshake mix; process until thoroughly blended. Divide ¾ of the mixture among 4 dessert cups, and reserve the remaining mixture.

3. Weigh the chocolate on a food or postage scale; chop fine. Combine in the blender (or processor) with cinnamon, the remaining ¼ cup boiling water, and the reserved milk mixture. Cover; process smooth. Pour chocolate mixture into the 4 vanilla desserts; swirl lightly. Chill until set.

MAKES 4 SERVINGS, 140 CALORIES EACH.

♥♥♥

NECTARINE MOUSSE

4 medium-ripe fresh nectarines, pitted and quartered
¼ cup sugar or equivalent low-calorie sweetener
1 teaspoon vanilla extract
¼ teaspoon ground ginger
¼ teaspoon salt (optional)
1 envelope unflavored gelatin
¼ cup cold water
1 cup plain low-fat yogurt
2 egg whites

1. Purée nectarines, sugar, vanilla extract, ginger, and salt, if desired, in an electric blender or food processor. Set aside.

2. Sprinkle gelatin over water in saucepan; let soften for 1 minute, then heat and stir until gelatin dissolves. Stir into purée. Stir yogurt into mixture.

3. Beat egg whites until stiff. Gently fold into mixture. Pour into individual glasses. Chill for 4 hours.

MAKES 4 SERVINGS, 170 CALORIES EACH WITH SUGAR; 135 CALORIES EACH WITH LOW-CALORIE SWEETENER.

♥♥♥

STRAWBERRIES CURAÇAO

3 tablespoons Curaçao or other orange liqueur
1 pint small fresh ripe strawberries, hulled
½ cup light pressurized whipped cream

1. Stir liqueur into berries several hours before serving; refrigerate to marinate. Spoon into stemmed wineglasses and top with whipped cream.

MAKES 3 SERVINGS, 115 CALORIES EACH.

❦

QUICKIE LIGHT AND SPICY CARROT CAKE

No need to shred carrots!

1   can (8 ounces) sliced carrots, drained
4   eggs, separated
1   teaspoon orange liqueur
½   cup sugar
1   teaspoon grated orange peel
    Pinch salt
½   cup all-purpose flour
1   teaspoon baking powder
¼   teaspoon ground cinnamon
¼   teaspoon ground nutmeg
    Pinch ground cloves
    Pinch ground allspice

1. Put carrots in an electric blender with egg yolks, orange liqueur, ¼ cup of the sugar, and the grated peel. Blend until smooth.

2. Combine egg whites and salt in an electric mixer bowl and beat until stiff. Gradually beat in remaining ¼ cup sugar. Fold carrot mixture into beaten egg whites gently but thoroughly.

3. Sift flour, baking powder, and spices together. Sprinkle over liquid mixture in several additions, very gently cutting and folding in each addition. Spoon into an ungreased 8- or 9-inch tube pan. Bake in a preheated 325-degree oven for about 1¼ hours or until an inserted cake tester comes out clean. Invert pan to cool; cool completely before removing from pan.

MAKES 10 SERVINGS, 100 CALORIES EACH.

❦

LIGHT CINNAMON STREUSEL

BATTER:

1   whole egg
5   tablespoons cold water
3   tablespoons butter or margarine
1   teaspoon vanilla extract
1½   cups biscuit mix

TOPPING:

3   tablespoons biscuit mix
2   tablespoons brown sugar
1   tablespoon butter or margarine
2   teaspoons ground cinnamon
    Low-calorie sweetener to taste (optional)

1. Combine all batter ingredients except biscuit mix in an electric mixer bowl. Beat on high speed until smooth. Add biscuit mix. Beat on low speed until blended. Scrape bowl, then beat on high speed for 3 minutes. Spread batter evenly in a 9-inch square nonstick cake pan prepared with cooking spray.

2. For the topping, combine biscuit mix, sugar, butter, and cinnamon in a small mixing bowl and fork-blend just until crumbly. Sprinkle crumb mixture on top of cake. Bake in a preheated 400-degree oven until cake is done and topping is browned—18 to 20 minutes.

3. Let cool before serving. For a sweeter cake, with few additional calories, sprinkle the baked dessert lightly with low-calorie sweetener *after* it cools. Cut into squares to serve.

MAKES 9 SERVINGS, 145 CALORIES EACH.

❦

PLUM RUM COBBLER WITH LATTICE PASTRY

4   cups sliced fresh apples
4   purple plums, pitted and thinly sliced
1   cup juice-packed crushed pineapple, with liquid
6   tablespoons golden raisins
¼   cup 80-proof rum
3   tablespoons cornstarch
1½   teaspoons ground cinnamon or apple pie spice
¼   cup granulated fruit sugar (fructose) (optional)
    Pinch salt (optional)
1   ready-to-fill 8-inch pie shell
    Low-calorie sweetener to taste (optional)

1. Combine all ingredients except pie shell and low-calorie sweetener; spoon into a 9-inch pie pan. Flatten pastry and cut into strips ½ inch wide. (If using a frozen pie shell, let it thaw first at room temperature.) Put longest strip across middle of pan. Then alternate additional strips, ½ inch apart, in crisscross lattice-work pattern. Trim away excess pastry and discard.

2. Bake in a preheated 425-degree oven for 30 minutes or until crust is golden. (After removal from oven, cobbler can be sprinkled lightly with low-calorie sweetener if a sugar-free pie is desired.) Cool 30 minutes or more before slicing.

MAKES 9 SERVINGS, 170 CALORIES EACH; 190 CALORIES EACH WITH FRUIT SUGAR.

SUGARLESS SPICY PEAR TART

1 homemade or frozen ready-to-fill 8-inch pie shell
2 cans (16 ounces each) juice-packed pear halves, drained, with juice reserved
¼ teaspoon ground cinnamon
Pinch ground allspice
Low-calorie sweetener to taste (optional)

1. Prepare a 9- or 10-inch glass pie pan with cooking spray and line it with the pastry. (If using a frozen pie shell, allow it to thaw first at room temperature.) With your fingertips, gently stretch the pastry until it fits the larger glass pan.

2. Arrange pear halves in the pie shell. Place the pie on the bottom shelf of a preheated 425-degree oven. Bake until crust is lightly browned—20 to 25 minutes.

3. Meanwhile, simmer the reserved juice in a saucepan until reduced by half. Remove pie from oven and spoon on the juice. Sprinkle lightly with cinnamon, allspice, and sweetener, if desired. Serve warm or chilled.

MAKES 10 SERVINGS, 115 CALORIES EACH.

❦

SPICED IRISH CREAM CHOCOLATE PIE

1 envelope plain gelatin
¼ cup Irish whiskey cream-style liqueur
1 cup boiling water
1 cup part-skim ricotta cheese
½ cup cold fresh skim milk
1 box (4 servings) sugar-free chocolate pudding mix
½ teaspoon ground cinnamon
Pinch salt (optional)
1 ready-to-fill chocolate or graham cracker pie shell

1. Sprinkle gelatin on liqueur in an electric blender or a food processor. Wait 1 minute for gelatin to soften, then add boiling water. Cover and process until gelatin is dissolved. Scrape sides of container with rubber scraper.

2. Add ricotta and milk, and process until completely smooth. Add chocolate pudding mix, cinnamon, and salt, if desired; process smooth. Spoon into pie shell and chill until firm.

MAKES 8 SERVINGS, 170 CALORIES EACH.

❦

BANANA-RUM ICE CREME PINEAPPLE SUNDAE

2 bananas, thinly sliced and frozen
1 or 2 tablespoons ice-cold rum
1 or 2 tablespoons water or pineapple juice
¼ cup drained juice-packed crushed pineapple

1. Combine bananas with rum and water in a food processor and process until the mixture has the texture of a soft-serve ice cream. Serve immediately in parfait glasses with crushed pineapple on top.

MAKES 3 SERVINGS, 100 CALORIES EACH WITH WATER; 105 CALORIES EACH WITH PINEAPPLE JUICE.

Variation

Without rum: Substitute pineapple juice for rum and add a few drops rum flavoring.

EACH SERVING HAS APPROXIMATELY 90 CALORIES.

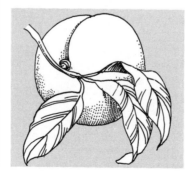

GINGER-PEACHY ÉCLAIRS

SHELLS:
⅓ cup water
¼ cup diet margarine
½ cup sifted all-purpose flour
2 eggs

FILLING:
1 envelope plain gelatin
1 can (16 ounces) juice-packed peaches, drained, with juice reserved
2 eggs
¾ cup part-skim ricotta cheese
1 teaspoon lemon juice
¼ teaspoon ground ginger
Low-calorie sweetener to taste (optional)
Pinch salt (optional)

1. To make the shells: Combine water and margarine in a saucepan. Heat gently until margarine melts. Beat in flour over low heat until batter leaves sides of pan and holds together. Remove pan from heat and beat in 1 egg at a time.

2. Put batter in a pastry tube and make 16 éclairs or cream puffs arranged 2 inches apart on a large nonstick cookie tin prepared with cooking spray. Or use a tablespoon, with a teaspoon as a "pusher" to shape the batter into éclairs or cream puffs. Bake in a preheated 425-degree oven for 20 to 25 minutes until golden and crisp. Cool thoroughly before filling.

3. To make the filling: In a saucepan, sprinkle gelatin on ½ cup of the reserved juice. Wait 1 minute, then heat gently to melt gelatin. Meanwhile, combine peaches with remaining ingredients in an electric blender or a food processor; purée. Add gelatin mixture and process until smooth. Refrigerate until thick.

4. Split éclairs open with the tines of a fork. Spoon the filling into éclairs.

MAKES 16 ÉCLAIRS, UNDER 100 CALORIES EACH.

STRAWBERRY VANILLA BAVARIAN

½ cup fresh or thawed
    unsweetened strawberries
½ teaspoon lemon juice
1 cup skim milk
2 eggs, separated
1 envelope plain gelatin
2 envelopes (¾ ounce each)
    vanilla reduced-calorie
    dairy drink mix

1. In an electric blender or food processor, purée strawberries with lemon juice; set aside.

2. In medium saucepan, combine milk with egg yolks. Sprinkle gelatin over top; leave for 1 minute to soften, then slowly stir in drink mix. Heat and stir until gelatin dissolves. Remove from heat; chill until mixture starts to set.

3. Beat egg whites until they form peaks that are stiff but not dry; fold into gelatin mixture. Spoon vanilla mixture alternately with strawberry purée in glass dessert cups or serving bowl to create layered effect. Chill and serve within 2 to 3 hours. Garnish with whole strawberries, if desired.

MAKES 6 SERVINGS, 75 CALORIES EACH.

❖

HEALTHY FRESH PEACH ICE CREAM

6 or 7 medium-size fresh peaches
    or nectarines, pitted
1 envelope plain gelatin
2 cups low-fat milk
1 cup plain low-fat yogurt
½ cup sugar or equivalent low-
    calorie sweetener
1 tablespoon vanilla extract
¼ teaspoon ground cinnamon

1. Chop enough peaches to measure 1 cup. Purée remaining peaches to yield 2½ cups purée.

2. Sprinkle gelatin over milk in medium saucepan. Heat,

stirring, until gelatin dissolves; remove from heat. Add chopped peaches, purée, yogurt, sugar, vanilla extract, and cinnamon to gelatin mixture; mix well. Freeze in ice cream maker according to manufacturer's directions.

MAKES 7 CUPS, 80 CALORIES PER ½-CUP SERVING WITH SUGAR; 60 CALORIES EACH WITH LOW-CALORIE SWEETENER.

❖

CINNAMON PEAR SHERBET

You don't need an ice cream machine to make this dessert; it's made with fresh-frozen diced ripe pears in a food processor or an electric blender. It's the best-tasting pure essence of pear "ice cream" you'll ever eat. No sugar needed.

This dessert tastes best when it's made with freshly frozen, fully ripe pears.

2 large fresh ripe pears
    Pinch ground cinnamon
    Low-calorie sweetener to taste
    (optional)
⅓ to ½ cup low-fat milk

1. Dice pears into ½-inch cubes and spread in a single layer on a foil tray or a baking sheet. Quick-freeze, uncovered, in the coldest part of the freezer.

2. Put the frozen pear cubes in an electric blender or a food processor with cinnamon and sweetener, if desired. Adding milk a little at a time, process quickly, just until mixture resembles soft-serve frozen custard.

MAKES 4 SERVINGS, 70 CALORIES EACH.

PEACH-RASPBERRY ICE CREAM

3 medium-size fresh peaches or
    nectarines, pitted and
    quartered (about 3½ cups)
8 ounces fresh raspberries (about
    2 cups)
2 tablespoons fresh lemon juice
1 envelope plain gelatin
2 cups low-fat milk
½ cup sugar or equivalent low-
    calorie sweetener
1 teaspoon almond extract
¼ teaspoon ground cinnamon

1. Purée peaches, raspberries, and lemon juice in an electric blender until smooth. Set purée aside.

2. Combine gelatin, milk, sugar, almond extract, and cinnamon in medium saucepan. Stir over low heat until gelatin dissolves. (If using low-calorie sweetener, stir in after cooking.)

3. Pour fruit purée and milk mixture into ice cream maker. Freeze according to manufacturer's directions.

MAKES 8 CUPS, 55 CALORIES PER ½-CUP SERVING WITH SUGAR; 40 CALORIES EACH WITH LOW-CALORIE SWEETENER.

❖

PINEAPPLE YOGURT COOLER

½ cup juice-packed crushed
    pineapple, chilled
½ cup plain low-fat yogurt
    Dash vanilla extract
½ cup ice cubes

1. Blend all ingredients in a covered electric blender until smooth.

MAKES 1 SERVING, 140 CALORIES.

INDEX